The History of

Leyland

and district

by David Hunt

Carnegie Press, 1990

In memory of Eric Blakeman

The History of Leyland and District
by David Hunt

First edition, paperback, April 1990

Published by Carnegie Press, 18 Maynard Street, Preston PR2 2AL. Tel (0772) 881246.
Designed and typeset in Times Roman and Caslon by Carnegie Press.
Printed by Leyland Printing Co., Leyland Lane, Leyland PR5 3BT.

ISBN 0 948789 48 4

Contents

About the author

DAVID HUNT is a part-time tutor for the WEA and the University of Liverpool, and since 1982 has been Custodian of South Ribble Museum and Exhibition Centre in Church Road, Leyland. Dr Hunt has written and lectured extensively on the development of the Lancashire cotton industry and the history of Preston and the townships of South Ribble. He has travelled widely in the North and West and his two-volume study of the early archaeology of Scotland was published in 1986.

Introduction

Next, I shall declare what may concerne
The Wapentak of Leylandshire or Hundred
And then proceed to the Village: the Parish
with the general Townships with the same contained
How described obtained and possessed by
the several Lords and owners of the same

R.K.

Richard Jackson (alias Dr. Kuerden), Scholar of the Leyland Free Grammar School, and of the Universities of Oxford and Cambridge, Doctor of Medicine, father of the history of Lancashire. (1623-1690/5.)

HE story of Leyland, like that of its neighbouring towns, is the history of the making of our Lancashire landscape, of life in medieval England, of Reformation and Civil War, of the rise to pre-eminence of an ancient handicraft, and the first industrial revolution in the history of the world. Yet it is also much more. Industrial developments from the middle of the last century onwards were to ensure that the name of Leyland came to be known all over the world. Throughout its history, a number of prominent locals have left their marks, as subsequent pages will endeavour to show - the Bussels, Sir Henry Farington, the William Faringtons, Anthony Browne, Edward Robinson, Thomas Moon and the Masters of the Free Grammar School, the vicars of Leyland - Vicar Rothwell and the Baldwins, James Quin, Richard Sumner and the three Henry Spurriers.

Since the past is merely the prologue to the present, what of the future? The 'new town' plans of the 1960s envisaged a new Greater Leyland, doubling its population by the present day. Its subsequent curtailment in the 1970s ensured that Leyland will remain familiar for a while longer: the pleasant rural hamlet of Ulnes Walton with about 1,000 inhabitants was intended to have had a population of over 20,000 by the 1990s.

Each local history study has its own peculiarities, and newcomers to the history of Leyland are often confused by the various spellings of the surname of the lords of the manor - the Faringtons, and by the existence of two Worden Halls. The first point was clarified by Susan Maria Farington, the family historian,

> As to the spelling of the name, that was various enough, of course, as it would follow the custom of the period, and the custom of the period seems to have been to vary the spelling of a name as much as possible. It was a

capital before the block letter came in, and then the usual two small ffs when they became universal. We keep the two small ffs yet, because no one has had the courage to abandon them as the written signature of Worden. Sir Henry de ff (whose is the first sign manual we have) spelt it so, and every generation since has done the same, but it is now an affectation.

Ph occurs occasionally in Henry the Third's and Edward the First's time, but be it a capital F, little f, two little ffs, a capital F and a little one, or a Ph, we have by no means got over our difficulties, for the 'a' is sometimes (though rarely) an 'e', the 'r' is often double, the 'i' till Queen Elizabeth's time is usually 'y', the 'n' is unopposed but not always followed by a 'g', the 't' is sometimes 'd', the 'o' in the older documents is 'u', and the final 'n' has sometimes an 'a' put to it so as to make us Farintona.

The Leyland crest, executed in stained glass in the parish church.

Except with regard to references, I have consistently spelled the name Farington, the same as that of the adjacent township from which the family take their name.

There are two Worden Halls: modern Worden Hall - of park and maze fame - was known as Shaw Hall up to the 1840s. The original Worden Hall (now referred to as 'Old Worden') is located in the grounds of the former Euxton Royal Ordnance Factory in the extreme east of the township beyond the Wigan Road. Property of the Knights of St. John of Jerusalem in pre-Reformation days, and long the home of the Anderton family, it remains one of the oldest and architecturally most important buildings in the district.

All histories should be published with a 'sell-by' date and this is no exception. As a guide to future students I have provided references to the main historical sources and to relevant current research - much of it by fellow members of the Leyland Historical Society and published in its journal *The Lailand Chronicle.* Many thanks are due to the large number of people who have assisted me in many ways, to Mr R. Rushton and the staff of the Leyland library and local history centre, the friends of Leyland Museum, members of the Leyland Historical Society and the staff of the Lancashire Record Office. I am most grateful to South Ribble Museum and Exhibition Centre, Leyland Library and the Lancashire Record Office for allowing items from their collections to be reproduced, and to acknowledge the assistance of my wife, Anne, and the encouragement and support of my local history evening classes at Leyland Library since 1983. The British Commercial Vehicle Museum here in Leyland was also very helpful in providing many of the photographs of the early history of Leyland Motors, while Mr Peter Barrow kindly allowed us to reproduce his plan of the Grammar School building. Thanks also to everyone at Leyland parish church for allowing us to take some interesting photographs in the church.

Particular thanks are due to Mr W. E. Waring, editor of the *Lailand Chronicle*, who has advised me on all aspects of the work, and has contributed very materially to it. Quite simply his knowledge and understanding of the history of the town is not surpassed. The work is dedicated to the late E. T. Blakeman (1920 - 1987), educationalist and chairman of the Leyland WEA, who first proposed and later encouraged my work in adult education.

Chapter One

Early Leyland

OR over a century, the Domesday Book has been the favourite starting point for local historians since, for most places, it provides the first written reference. Though similar surveys may well have been compiled for earlier Saxon kings, they have not survived and Saxon deeds and charters, which often survive for towns in the south of England, are very rare in the North.

Hence the significance of the Domesday survey. William the Conqueror spent the Christmas of 1085 at his Court in Gloucester. To settle his lingering doubts about the extent, the wealth and the people of his realm, he ordered his agents to be sent to survey all parts of his kingdom. Their labours were bound together in what became known as the Domesday Book, (the name is a reference to the Day of Judgement, the final court from which there can be no appeal). It is important to realise, however, that the England of the Domesday Book consisted of a landscape which had already been extensively settled for well over five thousand years, and that many of the settlements described in it were already many centuries old.

Prior to 1086, therefore, any attempt to reconstruct the early landscape or history of Leyland must rely on the science of archaeology and the considerable art of historical inference.

Archaeology

RELICS of the bands of hunters and gatherers who settled the North West at the close of the most recent phase of the Ice Age, the so-called Mesolithic or Middle Stone Age peoples, have frequently been found in Lancashire. Their stone arrowheads are still recovered in large numbers on the fells above Chorley, and the remains of their hapless victim, the Poulton-le-Fylde elk, can still be seen in the Harris Museum, Preston.

During the Mesolithic period the level of the sea fluctuated considerably, causing marked changes to the coastline and disrupting the flow of the lower courses of the rivers Wyre, Ribble and Douglas. During the periods of low sea level, extensive forests developed on the coastal flats, which subsequently became waterlogged and died when sea levels rose, thus forming the basis of the great peat mosses of West Lancashire. Even today huge trees, or 'bog oaks', dragged from the depths by ploughing operations, can often be seen along the sides of mossland roads. They used to be a valuable source of fuel and even building material for local people.

Already, over four thousand years before the arrival of the Normans, farming communities had occupied most if not all of the naturally fertile parts of the country, and the study of plant pollens preserved in ancient peat deposits clearly shows both the range of their crops and the start of the clearance of the primeval deciduous forests. This process gathered pace during the Bronze and Iron Ages, and large numbers of burial sites and the findspots of implements are known in Lancashire, dispelling or at least qualifying the traditional notion that Lancashire was more or less devoid of human occupation in prehistory.

It was perhaps during the early part of this period that the first woodland clearances occurred in the vicinity of Leyland. Intense agricultural and later industrial and urban activity in the area mitigates against the survival of archaeological evidence, though an extensive range of remains was discovered along the Ribble during the construction of Preston Dock at the end of the nineteenth century, and a Bronze Age burial has been excavated at Astley, near Chorley.

The Romans and after

EVIDENCE of the Roman occupation of Lancashire is much more extensive. The classical writers referred to the people living in the region as the Setantii – or the dwellers by the water – a description which fits well with what we know of the geography of the area, with its heavily indented coastline, frequently flooding rivers, and boundless mosses.

Close by Leyland was the extensive and important station at Walton-le-Dale; to the north of the Ribble the outpost at Kirkham; and a short distance up the Ribble valley, the colony and fort of Bremetennacum – modern-day Ribchester. Exactly where the line of the coastal north-south road connecting Walton and Wigan cuts through the parish of Leyland remains uncertain, but it was probably not a great distance from the present-day A49 road. Traces of it have occasionally been found, notably during the building of the North Union Railway in the 1830s, and it may yet be possible to locate and excavate a portion of it.

Given the proximity of so many known Roman settlements, and easy access from at least one known road, it seems unlikely that the great agricultural potential of the soils of the district was not known and exploited in some way, particularly in a part of the country where

A very early gravestone next to the chancel wall. One of the earliest pieces of Leyland's history.

such well-drained arable land is not very common. That this substantially was the case is indicated by the range of Roman finds which have been made - and continue to be made.

In May 1819 a box containing eleven silver and seventeen brass coins was found during turf-cutting operations on the moss; the dateable specimens indicated a date of between 96AD and 160AD, with the hoard thus probably having been deposited in the second half of the second century AD.

Then, in 1850, workmen employed somewhere in the old medieval townfields close to the town centre discovered a hoard of over 120 coins buried about eighteen inches below the ground surface. Since it was found on Farington property it was taken to the Museum at Worden Hall and has subsequently been known as the Worden Hoard; it is now preserved in the Harris Museum. These coins appear to have been later in date than the moss-hoard, with dates ranging between 258 - 282 AD, indicating concealment at the end of the third century or early in the fourth.

A noted Victorian antiquarian, W. T. Watkin, recorded the discovery of a ring: 'There is preserved at Worden Hall, by Miss Farington, a ring of much alloyed gold, found at or near Leyland, many years since . . . it resembles, in form, Roman rings, but, from inspection, I am doubtful if it is of Roman origin. The letters S.P.Q.R. are chased upon it in very low relief. From its lightness it must be hollow . . . Mr. Hardwick calls it a "massive gold ring" but this description is erroneous'.[1]

Hoards pose many problems for the archaeologist - most notable is the enormous stock of Norse and Saxon silver found at Cuerdale in 1840, the Cuerdale Hoard - who buried them? when? why? and exactly where? Most of these questions can never be answered, but in the case of the Worden Hoard one point is critical - its discovery close by the ancient and natural centre of the township, a locality ideally suited for the exploitation of the surrounding farmland. Indeed, the find might more properly be known as the Leyland Hoard.

In the centuries following the withdrawal of the Roman legions, the peoples of the North West came into contact with quite different groups. From the sixth century onwards, Anglo-Saxon peoples began to enter from the east coast along the Ribble Valley, whilst from the ninth century the lowlands to the west fell prey to Scandinavian incomers. The Welsh-speaking natives thus found themselves with English-speaking Saxon and Norse-speaking Nordic neighbours.

On a wider level the region remained marginal to the rest of England, lying between and contested by, the kingdoms of Northumberland and Mercia. Something of this patchwork of settlements and peoples with their different languages and customs, is revealed by the place-names of the district. The great authority on these remains Eilert Ekwall, whose *Place-Names of Lancashire* was first published as long ago as 1922. A great linguistic scholar, he paid close attention to geography and topography in the understanding of the evolution of place-names.

From this Saxon period - the centuries just prior to the Norman Conquest and the Domesday Survey - the settlement pattern of the region becomes clearer. In the west, with its generally very flat, poorly-drained peaty soils, settlement was restricted to the areas of slightly higher glacial deposits, as at Rufford, Longton and Tarleton. Much more favourable for settlement were the light, gently sloping and well-drained deposits of the Lancashire plain, at heights of between fifty and three hundred feet above sea level.

Following the onset of the present damp climatic phase in the thousand years before the Roman conquest, peat was already extensive on the high moorland to the east of Chorley. Away from the extremes of lowland marsh and high moorland, dense oak-alder woodland still extended over large areas, and if the settlements to the west were to some extent 'islands' amid the wetlands, those of the plain - such as Leyland - were still essentially clearances in a woodland environment.

From an agricultural point of view, therefore, the Leyland district was well endowed. The sandy soils which comprise much of the township were both well-drained and inherently fertile, well suited for either arable or pastoral use. It has also been suggested that, in contrast to the boulder clay based soils to the south of Preston in the vicinity of Bamber Bridge, woodland cover might have been relatively less dense and therefore easier to clear.[2]

The general distribution pattern of place-names coincides closely with this broad geographical pattern. In mid-Lancashire native British and Anglo-Saxon place-names indicative of long-established settlement are confined to the higher ground of the Ribble Valley and the Lancashire plain. Following the work of Ekwall, we know that the native settlements included Penwortham, Eccleston, Charnock Richard, Ulnes Walton and Walton-le-Dale. With the exception of Anglezarke and Brinscall in the hilly country to the east, the Norse settlements lie to the west of the river Douglas and include Hesketh, Becconsall and Tarleton. The Norse settlement of this region therefore does not appear to have replaced an earlier pattern but rather to have complemented it, suggesting perhaps fairly peaceful immigration into what was a sparsely populated area, rather than the conquest of existing settlements.The popular old notion of freebooting Vikings might, therefore, be misplaced, at least for this area.

In the absence of documentation or archaeological evidence, this approach to writing history is fraught with speculation, particularly since only a tiny proportion of the total of possible place-name elements has yet been studied. A comprehensive analysis of the place-names occurring in the early-thirteenth-century land deeds would be particularly interesting.

Spellings also vary, as generations of erstwhile scribes endeavoured to spell out on paper the sounds of names for which no standard form of spelling existed. Hence 'Leyland' appears as Lailond in Domesday (1086), as Leiland in 1212, Leyland in 1243, but Laylond in 1284. Ekwall states, 'I take the name to be simply Middle English Ley-land - fallow land, laid down to grass: first element Lea, Ley, Lay, fallow, unploughed'.[3] If this interpretation is taken literally it might support the hypothesis suggested: that by Saxon times a significant part of the township had been cleared of extensive woodland.

It was thus a very distant and a rather confused assortment of peoples and places that awaited King William's men in 1086, and it is their efforts which provide the earliest written evidence for the existence of Leyland and the Leyland Hundred.

The Leyland Domesday

AT the time of the Norman Conquest the administrative division that became the county of Lancashire had not yet been formed and the Domesday entries form only brief postscripts to the longer and more complete accounts of Cheshire and Yorkshire, reflecting the region's marginal location to the centres of power in the east and south.

The 'land between the Ribble and Mersey' is described at the end of the entry for Cheshire, and it seems unlikely that the surveyors ever set foot in the region itself. Then, as now, an important function of the Saxon system of local government was the collection of taxes, for the king ('Firma'), and to bribe the Danes to stay away ('Geld'). To this end the region had long been divided into large units called 'hundreds'. Each hundred comprised a main or 'capital' manor and a number of subsidiary ones. They usually took their name from that of the most important settlement. Thus Domesday tells us that Leyland was of sufficient importance in Saxon times to have given its name to the hundred. Leyland Hundred measured fifteen miles south from Preston, to the outskirts of Wigan, and roughly the same from the Snoter stone at Hundred End to Rivington, and Leyland manor occupied a position roughly central to it. From early times into the last century the hundred was often referred to as 'Leyland-shire'.[4]

The role of Domesday was simply to discover the value of land and its owners, before and after the Conquest. Unlike the BBC 'Domesday Project' of 1986 it did not seek to provide a systematic description of the district for future local historians. To complicate matters further much of the terminology used is very specialised and does not necessarily have the meaning which the terms have today. Money, for instance, was largely an abstract accounting medium, since pounds and shillings were not in circulation, whilst a 'manor' was a unit used as the basis of the taxation system and did not always have the overtones of feudal land, manor house, village and church which are now associated with the term. The Domesday Book is basically an enormous tax return, and the remoteness and social and linguistic complexity of the region obviously gave the locals plenty of scope to avoid paying it. There is thus a strong inbuilt tendency to underestimate the extent of local resources.

The entry for Leyland and the Leyland Hundred is perhaps best considered section by section:

> In Lailand Hundred
>
> King Edward held Lailand [Leyland (Manor)]. There [are] one hide and two carucates of land. Wood[land] two leagues long and one [league] broad and an eyrie of hawks.

Following wars with the Scandinavians in the tenth century, large tracts of the region had been held directly in the royal estates. It is unlikely that King Edward the Confessor had ever heard of, let alone visited, his lands at Leyland. The Norse influence is strongly indicated by the use of both Saxon ('hide') and Norse ('carucate') units of land measure, here roughly equivalent to 120 acres:

> To this manor belonged twelve carucates of land [twelve berewicks] which twelve freemen held for as many manors. In these [are] six hides and eight

carucates of land. [There is] wood[land] there six leagues long and three leagues and one furlong broad [in Leyland Hundred].

This passage is usually considered to contain a slip of the pen by the scribe, who wrote twelve carucates instead of twelve berewicks. A berewick was an outlying settlement, and although they are not listed they may have included such places as Standish, Chorley, Eccleston and Croston. As with the previous section specific reference is made to woodland. Ekwall has suggested that place-names ending in -ley are indicative of such districts, and that this remaining woodland formed a belt between Leyland and the moors to the east, by way of such places as Clayton-le-Woods, Whittle-le-Woods, Astley, Baggonley, Knowley, Roughlee, Heapey and Chorley.

The men of this manor and of Salford used not to work by custom at the King's hall nor to reap in August; they only made one enclosure [*haia*] in the wood and had the forfeiture of bloodshed and of an outraged woman. In the other customs they went with [*erant consortes*] the other above [mentioned] manors.

Forfeiture was the fine levied for various misdemeanours. The other customs referred to may have included those which are listed for the Hundred of West Derby:

All these thegns had by custom to render two ores of pence for each carucate of land, and by custom used to make the king's houses and [the things] which appertained thereto [*ibi pertinebant*] as the villeins [did], and the fisheries [*piscarias*] deer hays [*stabilituras*]; and [he] who went not to these [tasks] when he ought paid a fine of [*emendabat*] two shillings and afterwards came to the work and laboured until it was completed.

Each one of them sent his reapers one day in August to cut the King's crops. If not he paid a fine of two shillings.

If any free man committed theft, or 'forsteal' [*forestel*], or 'hámfare' [*heinfara*], or broke the king's peace, he paid a fine of forty shillings.

If any committed bloodshed [*faciebat sanguinem*], or rape [*raptum de femina*], or if he [*qui*] remained away from the 'shiremote' [*siremot*] without reasonable excuse, he paid a fine of ten shillings. If he remained away from the hundred [court] or went not to a pleas when the reeve [*prepositus*] ordered, he paid a fine of five shillings.

If [the reeve] ordered anyone [*cui*] to go upon his service and he went not, he paid a fine of four shillings.

If anyone wished to withdraw from the king's land, he gave forty shillings and went wither he wished.

If anyone wished to have the land of his deceased father, he paid a relief [*relevabat*] of forty shillings; [he] who would not, the king had both the land and all the goods [*pecuniam*] of the deceased father.

The Leyland entry continues:

The whole manor of Lailand with the hundred used to pay in farm [*firma*] to the king nineteen pounds and eighteen shillings and two pence.

Of this land of this manor Gerard holds 1½ hide, Robert three curacates of land, Ralph two curacates of land, Roger two curacates of land, Walter one curacate of land. There are there four radmans, a priest, and fourteen villeins and six bordars and two oxherds. Between [them] all they have eight ploughs. [There is] wood[land] three leagues long and two leagues in width and there [are] four eyries of hawks. The whole is worth fifty shillings. In part it is waste [*ex parte est wasta*].

After the Conquest, as the Saxon aristocracy was swept away, lands in the North West had been given to Roger of Poitou, one of William's henchmen, and he in turn shared the spoils with the men listed in the Domesday Book. In the absence of a general money economy dues were paid from inferior to superior by military service, and at the lowest local level by working in the lord's fields. A radman was a mounted escort or messenger, a villein was a farmer, and a border was an occupier of a smallholding. These individuals were clearly only a tiny part of the total population. The estate now paid only fifty shillings to the king, but 'waste' need not necessarily mean that the area had undergone wholesale destruction during the Conquest.

> King Edward held Peneuerdant [Penwortham]. There [are] two carucates of land and they used to render ten pence.
>
> Now there is a castle there, and there are two ploughs in the demesne and six burgesses and three radmans and eight villeins and four oxherds. Between [them] all they have four ploughs. There [is] half a fishery, wood[land], and eyries of hawks as in the time of King Edward. It is worth three pounds.

The entry for Penwortham is very interesting, referring to a castle at Penwortham, but its chief importance in the context of Leyland is that it indicates that the township was of rising importance relevant to Leyland - worth sixty shillings compared with fifty shillings for Leyland. The subsequent Barony of Penwortham co-existed with the hundred and they remained for centuries the two feudal forces in the district.

The precise extent of the Manor of Leyland only really becomes clear after around 1200 when lands in the township were granted by Roger de Lacy to Robert Bussel, who is listed as the tenant in 1212 and 1242, and many of his land grants and related papers have survived. On his death the manor was split up into portions (called moieties by scholars), and the whole was not united (through inheritance and purchase) until the sixteenth century. In 1617 a large proportion of the whole manor was purchased by William Farington, whose family remain lords of the manor to the present day.

The Leyland Hundred: Speed's Map of Lancashire, 1610: this map reveals the importance of the mosses to the north of the River Yarrow. Notice the different spellings of 'Lailand' Hundred and the township of 'Laland'.

Leyland Parish and Church

IF the Domesday survey provides only sketchy details of the manor and hundred, it reveals nothing of the parish of Leyland. By the seventeenth century, the hundred had six parishes, Leyland, Eccleston, Penwortham, Brindle, Standish and Croston, whilst Leyland parish itself comprised nine townships, Clayton-le-Woods, Cuerden, Euxton, Heapey, Hoghton, Wheelton, Whittle, Withnell and Leyland.

David Grant's sketch of Leyland Parish Church (1881).
This view illustrates the scale of the rebuilding in 1819. The wide nave completely overwhelms the higher and more graceful scale of the original church. Ornamental stonework from the ancient structure demolished at the time of this rebuilding was recovered in 1986 and is now displayed in the adjacent museum. (Leyland Museum).

By modern standards this was a very large parish and in early times it may have been even larger, so that for administrative purposes it was divided into four parts, Leyland, Euxton, Whittle-Clayton-Cuerden, and the Moor Quarter - Heapey, Wheelton, Hoghton and Withnell. Although Domesday mentions a priest, there is no indication as to where he lived, nor of a church in Leyland. Throughout the country this is a fairly common state of affairs since the survey was not intended to delve directly into ecclesiastical affairs, and Leyland may well have had both church and priest.

Thus the Domesday Book provides only a vague picture of the hundred, manor and parish of Leyland. Its lasting importance lies in the fact that no such information exists before it, and it is well over a century before adequate documentary evidence begins to piece together people and places again.

In most villages in England the parish church in the oldest and most interesting building, providing both a strong sense of continuity through the ages and an introduction to the lives and times of the local people, who have been its parishioners. Happily, the church of St. Andrew in Leyland is no exception. In common with the ancient churches of St. Leonard at Walton-le-Dale, and St. Mary the Virgin at Penwortham, it occupies a prominent position within its township, and from the top of the tower much of Lancashire can be surveyed on a clear day.

No one can be certain exactly when the first churches were built on these sites, since the earliest documentary references to them are only passing notes of churches that may already have been centuries old. As

Above: *Leyland Parish Church c1910.*

This photograph clearly shows the ancient chancel, and the private entry to the Farington Chapel in the corner of the nave. The impressive size of this building, particularly apparent in the tower, points to the church's importance in pre-Reformation times. (Leyland Museum).

Below: *Interior of the church c1900.*

The site of the Farington Chapel may be seen to the right of the chancel screen, above the family crypt. The church's three-decker pulpit seems to have been removed last century after a visiting Bishop had become wedged and had to be extricated from its narrow stairway! During alterations in 1987 it was possible to see the outline of the original nave preserved beneath the present wooden floor.

we have seen, the Domesday Survey does not assist matters.

Shortly after 1100 the church appears with other lands in grants to Evesham Abbey made by members of the Bussel family, Barons of Penwortham, as part of the endowment of Penwortham Priory. These grants were added to in the following centuries, so that by the Reformation the Priory was a very important local landowner. About 1190 'Sweyn' is referred to as chaplain at Leyland, and from 1300, when the income of the church was estimated at £10 yearly, the list of priests and vicars is fairly complete to the present day.[5]

Given the frequent lack of convincing early documentation, historians turn to the architectural features of churches as a guide to their age and history. This is a very inexact science, because styles of building, like fashions, can overlap in time, and the churches have usually been rebuilt on a number of occasions. Once again we are left with only the surviving evidence, though occasionally archaeology can be of assistance. Our local parish churches basically consist of three elements, the chancel (or altar end of the building), the nave (or body of the church), and the tower. Because the nave usually has to support the highest and widest roof, requiring frequent and expensive repair, it is usually the latest part of the surviving church, and that at Leyland was rebuilt as recently as 1817.

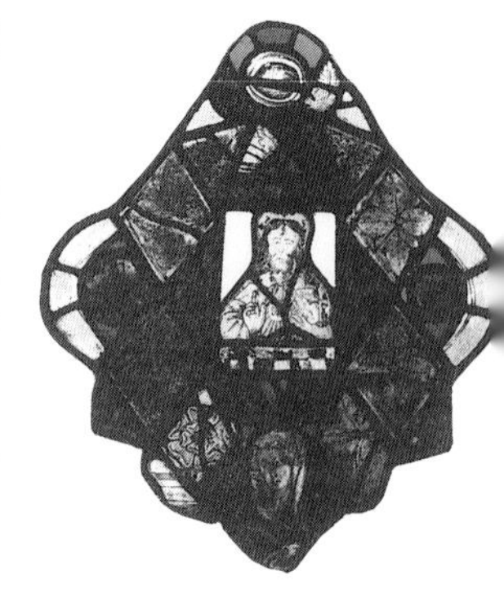

A fragment of pre-Reformation glass, preserved at Leyland Parish Church.

The towers by contrast, being four square and massive, have survived well, albeit with occasional modifications to repair or extend the range of bells. A simple carving of a bird on the front of the Leyland tower just below its castellated top, and clearly visible from below in oblique sunlight, is usually taken to be a woodcock and indicative of the rebuilding of the tower during the incumbency of Seth Woodcock (1494-1516). The stonework in the tower is very massive and parts of it may be much older, whilst the timber-work supporting the roof has the appearance of being very ancient and may be among the oldest surviving woodwork in the parish.

By contrast to the nave, the chancel is very old, and clearly belongs to a pre-Reformation building. It contains a sealed-up priest's door, a stone inset for holy water with two bowls (piscina), three similarly inset stone priests' seats (sedilia) (see page 20), and the unlikely remains of a leper's squint hole (more probably the remains of a small window through which the altar could be seen from an earlier structure on the site of the vestry). Fragments of pre-Reformation stained glass are preserved in a modern window towards the rear of the nave. At the south-east corner of the nave a modern screen marks the site of the Farington Chapel, given to the church in 1956 by Sir Henry Farrington. Here, a chantry dedicated to Saint Nicholas, the patron saint of pawnbrokers, was established by the family in about 1360, and a second chantry was founded by Sir Henry Farington in 1524. The latter clearly illustrates the function of chantries, for Sir Henry's successors were 'To levy and pay at two times of the year by equal portions to an able and well-disposed priest daily to say and do masses at the altar of St. Nicholas chapel within Leyland church and every divine service daily to say and do there forever. To pray especially for his soul and certain persons departed and for the prosperity and welfare of Dame Alice, my mother, and of me, the said Henry Farington, and my heirs, during all our lives, and all other benefactors and maintainers of the said service and chantry hereafter.'[6] This endowment is also important because it established the Leyland Free Grammar School.

In addition to St. Nicholas, the pre-Reformation church also had altars dedicated to Jesus, the Great Rood, and the Blessed Virgin Mary. In 1591 William Farington had his family's rights to the chapel confirmed, 'To sit, stand, and otherwise repose themselves therein', and to a burial crypt beneath the chapel. 'Two several vaults or toumbes, in the upper of the same lying eastward, to bury the dead bodies of the men, and in the lower standing westward, to bury the dead bodies of the women'.[7] This crypt was finally sealed in 1894 on the death of the final member of the direct line of the Faringtons of Worden, Susan Maria Farington.

The Farington Chapel, like other fittings in the church, has been re-arranged from time to time during the various rebuildings. The most extensive reconstruction came in 1816/19. The nave was demolished - the old walls having to be blown up by gunpowder - and the old Norman building was widened and the roof was raised. During alterations in 1987 it was possible to see the bases of the old walls nine feet in from the present 'gothicised Georgian structure' which replaced them, whilst the roof lines of the old building can still be seen on the tower wall.

Sir William Farington in a 'wretched squabble' complained bitterly that the changes obstructed the view from his box and that of his servants, and subsequent opinion of the changes has been similarly critical. A later vicar, Leyland Baldwin, complained of 'the destruction of our old parish church,' and Susan Maria Farington was scathing, 'Oh, these church restorers (as they mis-call themselves) of the nineteenth century: what mischief have they done in the way of destroying antiques and obliterating family records! Talk of the reformers and the Puritans! What havoc did they make under the sway of conscience, compared with the complacent self-righteous mischief wrought by semi-wise architects and over-zealous incumbents in the present day in the name of good taste? They turn our places of worship into something they never were before, and then flatter themselves they have gone back to antiquity!' [8]

The much maligned efforts of Mr Longworth 'some inferior architect, more celebrated as a combatant at Waterloo than as a skilled and competent architect',[9] did at least have the effect of considerably increasing the seating capacity of the church, and the result is both light and airy.

These changes swept away much potential dating evidence, but changes in 1852 removed part of the foundations below the Farington chapel revealing the fabric of a much older Norman church which still awaits discovery. In addition to the very fine stained glass, the various memorial tablets and brasses (most notably in the Farington chapel), the church possesses a fine range of old chained books, including a volume of Fox's *Book of Martyrs.*

The ancient graveyard along Church Road, the burial place of Leylanders for a thousand years, has been systematically extended since the nineteenth century. Canon Jacques, who was curate from 1861 to 1868, has left a vivid and colourful description of services in the church during his curacy.

> The organ, played by a talented blind man, and the chair were located in the west gallery, and a hymn board with the number of the portions to be sung was hung out. There was also a brass rod with red curtains in front of the singers. The church had a three-decker pulpit, and the clerk occupied the lower portion. Prayers were said and lessons read from the middle part, and the pulpit, approached by a winding staircase, had a carved

sounding board on four oaken pillars, and on the desk was a velvet cushion with silken tassles. The Beadle, who had a wand, escorted the clergy and, after prayers, the preacher retired to the vestry to change his surplice for a black gown, and he also wore bands . . . at the time the University dress. The erection I have described was situated in front of the chancel, and the top of the canopy nearly touched the centre of the arch.[10]

Leyland Cross before and after restoration in 1887.
Left: *In the background can be seen a number of the very old buildings which formerly lined the west side of Towngate, including the very fine three-storey building which occupied the corner of Cow Lane. The Osbaldeston Charity building on the left of the picture was removed in 1989, but the inscription stone is preserved in Leyland Museum.*
Right: *Restoration was achieved only after a long struggle between Miss Farington and Vicar Baldwin and a recalcitrant town council. Like the structure at Croston, there were four steps, whilst the ancient town well is still intact beneath the present monumental pump. (Leyland Museum).*

A short distance west from the church in an open space in the middle of the village stands Leyland cross. Its origins are uncertain, but it may date from the rebuilding of the church in early medieval times. Stuart White, another former curate, made the following notes around 1900.

This stands very nearly in the centre of the hundred of Leyland. Hence, it appears to me, more than likely that it indicates a very ancient place of common concourse. There the hundred mote, the folk mote, the military and civil assemblies of later times most likely were held. The Wapentake, the gathering of the sheriff's bands, or the meeting of armed men, would naturally take place here. The presence of an ancient well in immediate proximity to it is according to precedent (There is now an ornamental fountain supplied by the Waterworks Company, but there was before 1887 a very old pump on the site, hence I conjecture a spring or well). The cross was a broken shaft until 1887, when it was restored . . . probably broken in Puritan times . . . very probably an old preaching station before the building of the first Leyland church.[11]

Although much of this is clearly colourful speculation, there may be a grain of truth in it. The cross does not stand on a cross roads, as is often the case, since both Fox Lane and Church Road were formerly little more than footpaths across the townfields, but it may have been central to the town's market place. Other local crosses stood in Sandy Lane, Bow Lane, Golden Hill and Dawson Lane. The cross has certainly fared badly. It is broken in the earliest drawing of it, dated 1769, while at the end of last century the local council planned to replace it with public lavatories, and in this century it has been demolished by cars, World War Two tanks and vandals.

At the turn of the century the cross appeared to have a flight of three steps, but examination of the structure during repairs in 1986 revealed that it originally had four, two of which are now buried by the road surface. Clearly it dominated the central space of the old town as an obvious public meeting place and landmark. The well, which still survives below the adjacent Victorian monument, must have been an important supplier of water, whilst the town's stocks and 'whipping post' were only removed at the end of the last century.[12]

A reconstruction of Leyland township in around 1250, showing what we know about land use and the location of the townfields at that time.

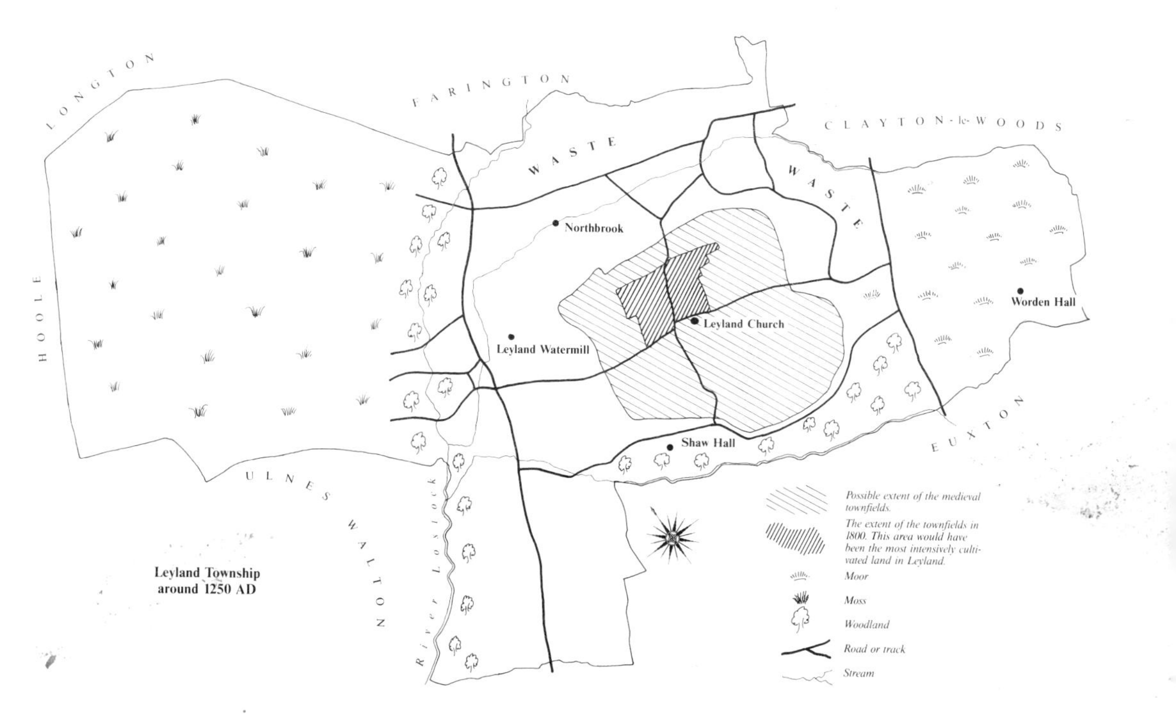

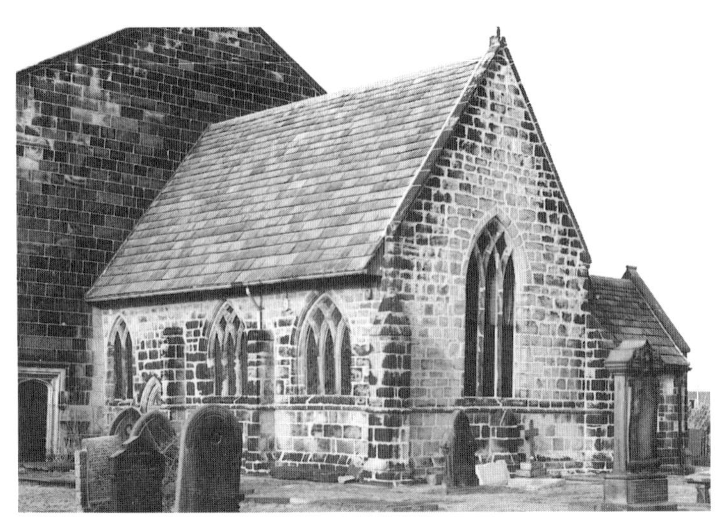

Top left: *Fragments of the earlier parish church were built into this monument which can still be seen today in the graveyard of the church.*

Top right: *The chancel of the parish church today.*

Centre: *Just visible in certain light is this relief sculpture of what is thought to be a woodcock, which leads some people to suppose that the tower on which it is carved was built during the incumbency of Seth Woodcock. The sculpture is just under under the parapet of the tower, above the clock.*

Left: *One of the oldest parts of the parish church is the south wall of the chancel, seen here complete with sedilia and, on the left, a piscina.*

Chapter Two

The making of the Leyland landscape

IN the centuries following the Norman Conquest the range of surviving documents becomes gradually more comprehensive, and from around 1200 - 1250 onwards it is possible to provide a fairly clear picture of people and places. The geography of Leyland at this time is broadly recognisable today: a rectangle of tracks surrounding Leyland town, comprising Golden Hill Lane (the way from Clayton to the moss) east to the A49 Wigan Road, then south to Back Lane (in pre-motorway days roughly along the line of Langdale Road and the path through Worden Park) to Leyland Lane, and north along Leyland Lane to the end of Golden Hill Lane at Earnshaw Bridge.

References to rivers and streams frequently appear in early deeds, and the River Lostock forms a natural barrier in the west, with the streams of the Northbrook and Shawbrook lying either side of the town - which is thus centrally placed to exploit the most fertile soils of the district. Beyond this loose framework of roads and watercourses, the township also came to have lands to the east beyond the Wigan road forming the Worden Old Hall estate, and to the west beyond Leyland Lane and the river Lostock in the mosslands of present-day Moss-side. Significant areas of woodland remained and the great lowland mosses of Lancashire lay as an almost impenetrable barrier from Lostock Hall to Ormskirk and beyond. With this amount of space any land shortage could thus be met for many generations to come by extended woodland clearance and by land reclamation.

The Wigan to Preston road (A49) c1900.

The Wigan road, one of the great arteries of English history, patronised by marauding Scots and Parliamentarian and Royalist armies, formed the eastern edge of the township, with only the Worden Old Hall estate beyond it.

On a rise overlooking the surrounding fields near the centre of the township lay Leyland church, and beside it a few timber-framed and thatch-roofed houses, each with their small plot or croft. To the north and

New Inn, Wigan Road c1925.
The crossroads at the ends of Dawber Lane, Heald House Lane and the Wigan road.

Turpin Green Lane c1905.
Another ancient trackway, Turpin Green Lane was an integral part of the early plan of the township, providing access to local deposits of turf (peat) for fuel.

Church Road, Leyland c1900.
Church Road still retains traces of its origins as an ancient sunken trackway. Although Church Road and Fox Lane are important routes through the town today, in earlier times they formed only a part of the web of tracks which radiated out from the church across the townfields, and which included Sandy Lane and Cow Lane.

south of the 'main street' – or Towngate – and extending outwards from the town lay the two great open fields or perhaps groups of open fields, the Upper Townfield on the church side and the Lower Townfield on the Fox Lane side. In these fields lay the individual strips of land worked by the townspeople which even by 1250 must have been cultivated for centuries, and which by the present century must have been farmed continuously for over a thousand years.

Originally these would have comprised all of the town's arable land, but with time clearance (called 'assarting' in deeds) would tend to bring ever more land into cultivation, so that their relative importance would decrease. By about 1250, quite large areas beyond the townfields had been brought into use, and many of these fields may also have been subdivided into strips. Here lay the larger landholdings or early estates – Worden Hall, Northbrook and Shawe Hall – although the latter may equally have been the manor farm in the days of Domesday. Around these outer fields lay the 'waste' which was beginning to be taken in, along Golden Hill Lane, Turpin Green (turf-pit), and Leyland Moor (along the Wigan Road),

In this gradual process of development several quite distinct hamlets became absorbed into the main township. Worden may be a case in point, but the most notable example is the hamlet of Honkington. A deed of around 1230 records 'Land which Thomas of Honkynton held in Honkynton',[1] and one of 1316 talks about, 'The annual rent of 6d from land in the hamlet of Honkynton in Leyland'.[2] Fifty years later its existence is still recorded, but after 1404 silence. The hamlet perhaps lay along the river Lostock near Seven Stars.

Many of the field-names of the time here survived from the early-thirteenth century (c.1200-1250):

> Grant: Robert Busel to Thomas, son of Richard Busel by Margery his wife – three acres in Leyland, beginning at Halresnapebrook, following by the eastern bounds as far as the way in the north towards the oak marked with a cross, so following the way in the north to the Alresnapebrok, ascending which in the south as far as the first mentioned bound – rendering yearly a pair of white gloves.[3]

The Vicarsfields c.1890. The Church had extensive lands in Leyland from early Norman times. During the nineteenth century the Vicarsfields became a popular if unofficial leisure ground, a venue for early cricket matches and visitors to the 'garden of Lancashire'. They were largely built over in the 1960s and 1970s.

Grant and confirmation: Geoffrey Bussel son of Robert Bussel of Laylond to John Farington, son of William of Mel – all the woods and woodlands and soil of the woods, with the agistment of the herbage and pannage and right of assarting, from Norbroc as far as Sanpsanpbroc, and ascending Sanpsanpbroc as far as Rondeshaebroc and ascending Rondeshaebroc as far as Lostoc, ascending Lostoc as far as Norbroc, with all the waste within or without the hedges, reserving only the field of Waltunlee and the homage and service of Henry of Qualay with 1lb. of pepper, or Nicholas Bussel with a pair of white gloves, of Benet the Clerk with 12d., of Thomas of Hakeslee with 12d., of Hugh Kay with 9d., of Thomas the Tailor with 6d., and of Avice with 8d., as in the charter of Robert Bussel.[4]

Society in medieval Leyland

ALTHOUGH these deeds reveal land transactions between members of the Bussel family who at that time were lords of the manor, it is clear that all such relationships were carefully regulated in terms of rents and services:

Thomas, son of Geoffrey, son of Umfray of Layland, to his lord, John of Layland – half an acre of land in Lamforlong, as contained in the charter of Robert Bussel paying yearly for his other lands as in the said charter. If he has ten pigs he will give the second best to his lord and if more 2d. for each old pig and 1d. for each young one.[5]

Yet the most onerous burden of all fell upon the peasants who comprised nearly all of the medieval population. The range of rents, taxes and services a peasant had to supply would confound even the Inland Revenue: if his daughter wished to marry, or he wished to sell a beast, he had to make a payment to his lord; when he died, his lord could take his best animal and the local priest the second best. Alternatively he had some rights to items he could obtain 'by hook or

Leyland Watermill (Crawshaw Mill) c1850.

Located on Hall Lane at Seven Stars, it was the site of the ancient manor corn mill. This very old and interesting structure was in use into the present century but was removed in the 1970s. A brief 'rescue dig', directed by Mr Peter Barrow, was able to explore its archaeological trace prior to housebuilding on the site in 1989.

by crook,' such as hay-bote (wood used to repair fences), hous-bote (wood to repair a house), fire-bote (fuel), and the right to graze his animals on the common fields and mosses. Of particular importance in Leyland was the right to dig turf for fuel.

The lord could thus exact a payment of some kind for virtually everything his tenants did. Particularly resented was his monopoly of the grinding of corn, for tenants were forced to use his mill. The mill of Leyland Manor was in Mill Lane (off Leyland Lane), and remained in use into the present century. It is mentioned in a deed as early as around 1250:

> Grant for 12d. rent: Adam, son of Roger of Ulbas, to Adam, son of Adam of Rideleys, and Alice of Ulbas – properties in Leyland, within these bounds: beginning at the lands of John, his brother, following Nort Valle to the great mill dam of Adam of Waleton, following the dam to Cressevallebroc thence to Chaynstalledhock in the new assart and so following to the middle of Blakelache, thence to the oak tree marked with a cross, thence to Schinerhaker, thence to the bank of Northbroc, and then to the land of John, son of Roger.[6]

A small stream was usually fed into a mill-pond banked up with clay and turves, and the water to the wheel arch and mill stones was regulated by sluices. Once the pond had emptied, milling had to stop. Millers were especially disliked, as the medieval riddle ran, 'What is the boldest thing in the world? – A miller's shirt, for it clasps a thief by the throat daily!'[7]

Yet this was a changing world, and the passing of the Bussels as lords of the manor around 1250 must have brought many changes in its train. The havoc wrought by the bubonic plague or 'Black Death' in 1348-50 accelerated these national trends. Society became less obviously feudal in nature and money rather than service became the most important medium of exchange. The great revolt in the south east of England against the Poll Tax of 1381 marks a further significant stage in the political development of the English people, for whereas half the population were serfs in 1350, by 1600 there was hardly any.

The Townfields

CENTRAL to this social system and the economy of Leyland well into the seventeenth century were the great townfields extending along either side of Worden Lane and Towngate. However, the open fields beloved of school history books – of two or three fields each heavily cropped, each with its year of fallow, and annually re-distributed in strips among the community – do not seem to have been typical of Lancashire.

In Leyland, the system used was one much better equipped for local conditions, different in several respects to that of the Midlands.[8] The large fields were indeed divided into strips, but crops of oats, barley, beans and peas were sown in spring and harvested in autumn, whereupon pasture animals were allowed onto the land as it lay fallow

Towngate c1910.

Towngate preserves the line of the way between the town's main open fields, the Upper and Lower Townfields. All buildings on the left of this photograph have now been removed, revealing for perhaps the first and last time in centuries the top of the ancient lower Townfield.

through the winter. The fields thus had two phases of use, six months in crop, six months in fallow; accordingly they were known as half-year lands.

All this was very carefully regulated by the reeve, and pinders were appointed to round up stray animals in the pinfold on Towngate and to fine their owners. A copy of the rules has survived:

> Agreed upon and set down ye second day of Aprill in the year 1612. By and with agreement and full consent of the freeholders and tenants to the ladie Dorothie Huddleston and others which have any lande lyinge in the towne ffeildes of Leyland . . . for the good quiet and peacable occupation of the said fields.[9]

In Longton the pattern of field strips can still be seen, particularly along Hall Lane and Back Lane and, although much of central Leyland is now built up, a clear picture of the distribution of these lands can be gained from surviving estate papers. The fields were sub-divided at three levels, firstly into groups of ridges called furlongs; the furlongs in turn were divided into holdings called butts or doles, which in turn were ploughed into strips or ridges known as lands or selions. To complicate matters these individual strips and smallest units of landholding were sometimes also known as butts or doles. A small part of the townfield has survived along the Worden Lane front of Worden Park, between the main entrance and the car park, and here the remains of the patchwork pattern of strips can be seen in oblique sunlight as low ridges that are clearly visible from the air.

A great deal of attention was obviously given to the marking out of these strips, for a farmer would often have strips spread over a wide area: clearly he had to get on well and co-operate with his neighbours.

To facilitate this fairly strong community institutions - either at the manorial or, more usually in Lancashire, at the township level - were needed to settle disputes and ease friction; in addition, stones were often set up as landmarks. In Leyland the 'hill stone' stood in the Upper Townfield, and the 'Meer stone' was set in the road dividing the township and Ulnes Walton. Disputes did occur, however, and in 1691 the jury of the manor court found that 'Henry Waterworth or his servant hath in the Lower Towne field lately ploughed to near the division balk betwixt the lands of Henry Farington esq. and Richard Monck in so much that the sayd division balke is quite covered with the furrows ploughed up'.[10] Clearly such boundaries were jealously guarded.

The early deeds (c1200-1250) contain many references to these strips and the larger fields:

> Grant: Hugh Freman, to John, son of William of Melis, that part of his lands in Leylande, being a selion of Quitulfurlong, three selions in Staynfurlong, and a selion next to the cemetery between church land of the said William and land of Robert Bussel - rendering yearly an arrow.[11]

> Grant: Robert, son of Adam, son of John of Leyland, to William, son of William of Farington, 3 selions in Leyland in the place called Quithacres, extending eastwards from a path leading from the house of William of Farington to the church of Leyland, as far as the highway through the centre of Leyland.[12]

The consolidating of these strips by mutual agreement through sale, inheritence or exchange appears to have begun early in Lancashire, without the social unrest which resulted from enclosure in other parts of the country. As more land was cleared and brought into cultivation, particularly from mosses, the importance of the townfields as the main area of arable land in the township, must have been reduced.

The many references to the fields, however, point to their continued importance. The lands bequeathed 'Upon trust to the use of the poor of Leyland' by John Osbaldeston in 1665 to form the charity which still bears his name, included 'two doles in the Townfields of Leyland,'[13] and there are many seventeenth-century references to 'the butt lying in the lower Townefielde' or to 'the close in the Upper Townefielde of Leyland'. A deed of sale dated 1618 lists 'A close called the three roode lands in the manor of Leyland in the lower townefielde, a close called the halffe acre in Leyland, in the lower townefielde, a close called the roodland in the lower townefielde, a moiety of the slacke meadow in Leyland'.[14]

This point is well illustrated by the early surveys of the Farington estate in Leyland, particularly that produced for William Farington. 'A booke of rents, bones, acreage and service ap[er]teyning to William Ffarington esquire which lands and tenements where surveyed by mesure Anno Domini 1569'.[15] This describes the largest Farington holdings such as 'The capitall mansion house called Worden with the gardens, courts and folds', with its estate of 97 'acres', providing a 'yearlie rente' of £13-6-8d, whilst 'One windemilne standing upon the same lande is of the yearlie rente of 13/-6d'.

Many of the tenants' holdings included numbers of the individual strips, and the survey defines their size and precise location in some detail. The 'Parcels of lande in the holdinge of Thomas Rigbye' contained 4 strips or 'dowlles', one of which for example

> lyinge in the little Towne Fielde nere unto the brexe and which dowlle lieth east and west in the same field and the same in the west cont[ains] in bredthe too rodes and abbutteth at the said west ende and north side uppon a hedge which divideth the same from a close in the tenure of Henrie Yonge, at the east ende the same dowlle abutteth uppon a hedge which divideth the said Townefielde frome a close in the holding of John Clayton otherwaies called Jenkyn Clayton at which end hit conteyneth also too rodes in bredth at the south side hit abbutteth uppon the north end of too sevrall dowles lyinge in the said towne fielde whereof the one is in the holdinge of the said John Clayton and the other in the holdinge of the said Rigbye and this said dowlle conteyneth in lengthe eight rodes and a halfe which amounteth unto 0a, 0r, 16f.

The townfields of Leyland, probably pre-Norman in origin and intensively worked in medieval times, thus continued to be an important element of the local landscape well into the seventeenth century, and as will be seen later, they were to shape profoundly the layout of nineteenth-century Leyland.

Reclamation of the mosses

THE townfields, worked on a half-yearly basis, thus proved to be an efficient adaptation of the Midlands common field system to Lancashire conditions, whilst the consolidation into larger holdings was a gradual process from early times. The reclamation of the wetlands, a much greater process of environmental change, also had early, if piecemeal origins. Thus, the outstanding features usually associated with the golden age of British agriculture of the eighteenth century - the enclosure of the common fields and the 'improvement' of wasteland - can both be traced to a much earlier period in Leylandshire.

Prior to the industrial and urban revolutions, environmental impact in Lancashire was felt in two main directions - the reduction of the forests and the draining of the lowland mosses. Such areas provided for a readily accessible expansion of agriculture provoked by a steadily rising population and demand for rents and food in the early-modern period.

Woodland clearance or 'assarting' is referred to in the early documents in the context of the reduction of the woods referred to in the Domesday Book. To the north and west the township lay on the verge of the great mosslands of west Lancashire. Their original extent is difficult to comprehend today, but after many centuries of enclosure and draining they were still vast when William Yates drew his famous map of the county published in 1786.

Between the Liverpool road (the A59) and Leyland Lane (the B5253), and to the north between Golden Hill Lane and the Brownedge at Bamber Bridge, they formed a belt which was to be scarcely penetrated until the nineteenth century. If these districts are removed from the *'ates' Map of Lancashire 1786. Notwithstanding steady ncroachment from Norman imes, the great mosslands still osed formidable problems of ommunication between the nid-Lancashire towns and the vestern parishes. Evidence of ncient trackways across the noss found at Pilling and in he Somerset levels have not een found in this part of ancashire, but such tracks nay well have existed.*

modern map, and since we can in assume that only a part of the remainder was woodland, it is clear that, historically, Leyland township was quite a small, compact unit surrounded by forests and wetlands, and that the townfields must have formed a very large proportion of the available farmland. Conversely much of modern Leyland is reclaimed land, the result of considerable pressure on the moss margins from an early date.

Use of these resources, like everything else in the manor, was carefully regulated. A deed of Robert Bussel of around 1230 refers to the wastes in Leyland and the right of common pasture, whilst enclosure from Leyland Moor near Northbrook is recorded in 1350. The importance of peat or turf as a fuel source (the right of turbary) is illustrated in a deed of 1423; for 20d. a year Edmund of Anderton was

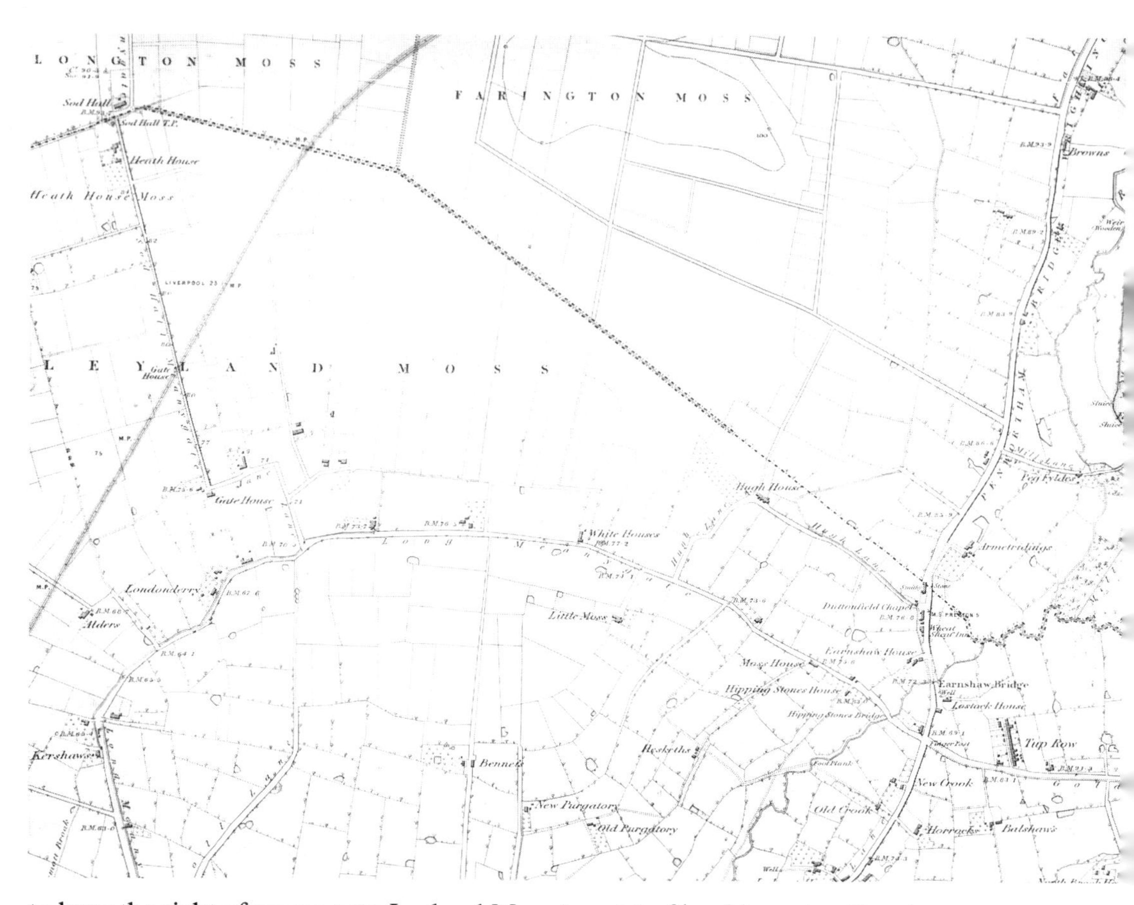

First edition 6" Map c1840, Leyland Moss-side.

For centuries Leyland Lane effectively formed the western margin of the township, but a series of enclosures from medieval times onwards culminated in the great sweep of the Longmeanygate and the construction of the two major roads across the moss via Sod Hall and Midge Hall. The lines of earlier enclosures are preserved in the curvilinear field pattern to the west of the River Lostock. The more regular pattern of the trackways on Farington Moss was the product of an Act of Parliament in 1819. This map also reveals the ancient situation of both Farington Hall and Northbrook.

to have the right of access onto Leyland Moss to cut turf 'and leave to spread and dry it' during his lifetime.[16]

These early 'intakes' were very small, if significant for the tenants, and seem to have been concentrated along Golden Hill (c1620, the road from Clayton to the mosses in Leyland), Turpin Green (1607, 'Turpett Moore enclosure'), Leyland Moor (slightly higher land to the west of the A49 road, perhaps heathland), and along the river Lostock. The process intensified in the sixteenth century, and a deed of August 1545 describes land lately improved on 'The commons of Faryntune' between 'Curedyne More' and 'Leylounde More', where there was an estimated 1,000 acres of moss and heath.[17]

All this was, of course, marked by disputes. In 1580 William Farington was ordered to repair the sixty acres of enclosures belonging to Edmund Huddleston which he had wrecked, and the latter was to be allowed to take in a further twenty-four acres, but none from Leyland Moor or the 'Goldynhill' and only four acres east of the Lostock.[18] Potential threats also had to be guarded against, 'A rememberance of sundrye matters . . . to bee objected against the pretended challendge claymes and tytle of Richard Fleetwoode of Penwortham esquire, and Mr William Blackleeche of Padington to have anye parte of the comons, moses and wastes in Leyland' (dated 1603).[19] With the loss of the manor of Farington by the Farington family, and the reduction of

The enigmatic and now vanished Farington Roundhouse.
In fact the last building in Leyland, at the centre of the moss on the boundary with Longton. A delightful wooden framed building with a thatched roof, it may have originated as a collecting point for tolls on the Sod Hall Meanygate, the first road across the moss and a direct route between Leyland and Longton and Penwortham. A unique relic of its formerly wetland environment, this unique building was in a fair state of repair in 1980 but had virtually vanished from the landscape ten years later.

the 'waste' in the central areas of the township, attention in the subsequent centuries shifted to Leyland Moss – the district west of the Lostock and the final area for agricultural expansion in Leyland.

Leyland Moss and Moss-side formed only the local portion of the great arc of mossland which encompassed Charnock Moss in Penwortham, Farington Moss, Longton Moss, Little and Much Hoole Mosses and Bretherton Moss. The pattern of long rectangular fields produced by enclosure is very clear from the Leyland tithe map. A short distance west of the River Lostock, between Seven Stars and Earnshaw Bridge, soils change abruptly from types based on sands and gravels to those formed on basal peat about three feet deep, composed of reeds and sedges with occasional tree stumps in the lowest layer. In the centre of these mosslands fragments of the original peats remain, perhaps fifteen feet deep, although reclamation, shrinkage through drainage and digging for fuel have greatly reduced them. They now form some of the most fertile soils in the country.[20]

That the move onto lands west of the Lostock was well underway by the seventeenth century is indicated by the many old houses that still survive in the district. Penetration seems to have been along the lines of Slater Lane and Dunkirk Lane, extending north by a series of fairly straight roads or Meanygates onto the moss, culminating in the Longmeanygate. Only in the nineteenth century was a road put through to Longton via Midge Hall, shortly after the Sod Hall Meanygate by the Farington Roundhouse. Prior to this the Longmeanygate was simply the access road to the moss strips.

The gradual extension outwards is suggested by the sequence of named tracks, the 'Oulde Mennygate' is mentioned in 1616, the 'Newe Meaniegate' in 1620, and the 'Long Meaniegate' in 1726.[21] Exactly which of the surviving tracks formed the earlier meanygates is uncertain but Paradise Lane and Jane Lane are clearly strong candidates. Thus in the Moss-side area the edge of the former peatlands is readily apparent, and historically the extension onto the moss in a series of overlapping roads is fairly clear.

Further lands are taken into cultivation

BY about 1750 the Parliamentary Enclosure Act became a common means of effecting large-scale enclosure, and of allotting the new land through legally binding awards. Prior to this formally recognised local customs governed the reclamation process. When land was enclosed it was allotted in relation to the proportion of land an individual owned in the parish, and people with such rights were known as charterers. Since the Faringtons by the seventeenth century owned a large proportion of the township, the other charterers' share was small, so that Leyland Moss was enclosed without recourse to an Act of Parliament.

Many of these enclosures were very small, 'A note of New Inclosures made by the lord since the last by the consent of the lord and not of the Charterers' dated 1674, describes fifty-nine lots, but in just sixty-nine and a half acres. Only one piece was over three acres ('Mr Faringtons thirteen acres . . . a brewhouse and garden'), and many of them were intended for buildings – thirteen houses, eighteen barns, a brewhouse, smithy and two shops, including 'a nayle shop'.[22]

At each of the main rounds of enclosure the charterers were allotted their share, for example in 1620, 1697, 1724, 1748 and 1785.[23] Articles of agreement for the enclosing of fifty-four acres in 1724 provide a clear picture of what this entailed. The area of moss not yet enclosed amounted to 961 acres, and since for each acre the charterers owned in Leyland they were awarded nine 'falls or perches' 897 acres of it

St. James' Church, Moss-side, c1900.

The growing importance of this district was recognised at the middle of the nineteenth century by the construction of St. James' Church, as a memorial to James Nowell Farington. The cottage, long since removed, is fairly typical of much housing in Leyland prior to the coming of the railway, utilising locally available building materials. Such houses can still be recognised today by the broad collars around their chimneys, built originally to accommodat the great thickness of thatch, but now standing proud of much thinner slate roofs.

'belonged' to George Farington. Twelve charterers are named, of whom seven are yeomen of Leyland, Edward Atherton, William Woodcock, William Burscow, Robert Farington, William Green, Hugh Charnock and Robert Walsh. However, 'whereas Nicholas Rigby and Richard Crooks . . . are named as charterers but upon examination [of] both their deeds it planely appears they have no right to any, but it belongs to the lord of the manor.'[24]

Many of the Farington tenants had their 'moss-piece', and with the rapid expansion of villages and towns and their increased demand for agricultural produce, together with the stimulus of the railway at Midge Hall, these must have been well worth having. In addition even smallholders had their 'Mossroom', a small area of moss in which turf could be dug for fuel. A list of 1735 records 140 of these, each generally three to four rods broad and laid out along the Great Moss and Little Moss between Bretherton and Farington. In addition to the tenantry, local gentry and the vicar had 'rooms', with the 'Poor house', the 'Almes house', Northbrook, and the Worden and Shaw Hall mossroom – the largest being of seventeen rods.

The historical origin of these is very confused, and seems to have been based on ancient custom. In 1869 Susan Maria Farington recorded,

> from time to time parties have applied to my brother and me to give them a fresh 'moss-room' . . . as theirs 'was now worn out'. We have anxiously endeavoured to find out on what ground the claim was made. Whether they had any papers to show or any clear story to tell. From want of these our attorneys have been able to give no help in the matter . . . under the circumstances, we have declined to give new mossrooms . . . while the turf lasted it lasted, and when it was done there was an end of the claim to it.[25]

Seven Stars c1900.

The district along Leyland Lane, well away from the town centre, seems to have developed quite rapidly from Tudor times and is frequently referred to as the 'lower parte of Leyland' in documents. An important sector of the town's textile industry the inhabitants duly derided the 'superior ways of the 'upper' Leylanders'.

The late William Rigby recalled the following story. Passing by an inebriated and unconscious 'lower portioner', thoughtfully incarcerated by his drinking companions in the stocks at the rear of the old Grammar School, an 'upper' Leylander stopped and leaned forward, kindly pushed the individual's tongue back into his mouth with his walking cane. Thus restoring a symmetry of neatness, gentility and taste, he passed on.

On the Longton and Farington portions of the moss, recourse was ultimately had to Enclosure Acts, but prior to these, intakes must also have been made on a piecemeal basis. The 'Awards' (of the Enclosure Commissioners) provide very detailed descriptions of the enclosures to which they refer. For Longton an Act was obtained in 1760; the award is dated 1761, and enclosures were made in 1761 (750 acres of moss) and 1821 (281 acres of sea marsh). Many of the roads along the north side of the moss were laid out at this time.[26] The Farington Act 'An Act for inclosing Farington Moss, and other commons and waste grounds within the Manor and township of Farington, in the parish of Penwortham, in the county of Lancaster', received the Royal Assent in May 1819. The extent of the moss was estimated at 470 acres, and the award and plan is dated 1833.[27] Other local Acts include Croston (1724), Chorley (1768) and Horwich (1821), whilst wastes in Cuerden (1804), Penwortham, Ulnes Walton, Hutton and Ribbleton were reclaimed without Acts.[28]

Thus by the eighteenth century, under pressure from increased population and the beginnings of industrial development in Preston, Liverpool and Leyland itself, the landscape around the village was very different to that which would have greeted a traveller in the Middle Ages. Gone was the wide belt of woodland around the townfields; the mosses were being enclosed and reclaimed; and the fields and pastures of Leyland were more extensive than they had ever been.

Chapter Three

Building a great estate: The earlier Faringtons of Worden

Although the Farington Family have been seen to enter the story of Leyland as early as the thirteenth century, when Robert Bussel granted half of the manor to his son-in-law, John de Farington, they were not to acquire the remaining portion (although they did rent it) or to reside in the township until after the Reformation over three hundred years later.

Throughout the Middle Ages the Faringtons of Farington were among the principal landowners in the district, along with the Andertons, Waltons, Charnocks and Leylands; their relations with the church and priory of Penwortham and their land dealings and marriage settlements are well recorded, and the family history reveals that its members played their full part in the various wars of the Norman kings with the Welsh, Scottish, Irish and French.

One of the family crests preserved in the stained glass windows of the parish church. This one shows the Farington family crest.

These were troubled times indeed. In 1322 Robert the Bruce led a band of Scottish marauders as far south as Samlesbury, stealing from the church there and sacking Preston, whilst disputes among the local gentry themselves were rife, frequently resulting in tumult and murder.[1]

This was a good time in which to make some impression and it seems that the Faringtons were good soldiers, so that they managed to forward their interests in much the same way as other prominent Lancashire families like the Stanleys and Cliftons. By 1500 through purchase, clever marriages and inheritance, Leyland formed only one part of a great Farington estate which extended over parts of Ulnes Walton, Leyland, Farington, Coppull, Worthington, Cuerden, Salesbury, Preston and Howick, all controlled from the moated manor house off Golden Hill Lane in Farington.

The Leyland aspect always loomed large in family affairs and did so increasingly as time went on. The nearest church to the family home was at Leyland and from an early date members of the family seem to have been buried close by the Farington Chapel. Yet it was to be events in the sixteenth century which, bringing in their train something of a family revolution, were to ensure that the family home would

Worden Old Hall c1930.
This photograph, taken after heavy rain, indicates the extent of the contraction of the building from a manor house to a farmhouse. The apparent front of the building is in fact a later addition, with the original ornate timber-framed structure preserved some feet within it. Much of the fine oak panelling which was a feature of the house in its heyday was subsequently removed to the new Worden Hall (Shaw Hall) when the family headquarters moved there: fragments of it still survive in the Derby Wing. (Leyland Museum).

thereafter be Worden, and that their influence on Leyland would be prominent for a further 250 years.

Henry Farington

IN 1501 Henry Farington (1471-1551), then aged about thirty, inherited the estates on the death of his father. He was very much a man of business, as well as a courtier to two kings. In 1498 he had been appointed 'Squire of the King's Body' - a sort of royal bedroom doorman - and a patent of Henry VIII dated 1539 describes him as 'Knight of Our Body'. Perhaps through this position he was aware of the coming difficulties with Rome, which began from 1527 onwards with the quarrel over Catherine of Aragon and developed year by year culminating in the Act of Supremacy (1534) which made the king head of the English Church, the seizure of church assets, and the dissolution of the great monasteries in 1539. Henry Farington's affairs reveal that he had a clear grasp of the significance of these events.

When he founded his chantry at the parish church in 1524 he took great pains to ensure that various valuable items which were included in the chantry would remain family property and could not be taken over by the Crown.[2] Similarly his son Robert, Rector of North Meols 1530-7, conveniently left the priesthood just prior to the dissolution of the monasteries.

The breaking up of the great ecclesiastical estates obviously presented opportunities for such a man. He was appointed one of the Crown Commissioners for the suppression of the monasteries, and on November 17th 1539 Evesham Abbey, together with its priory at

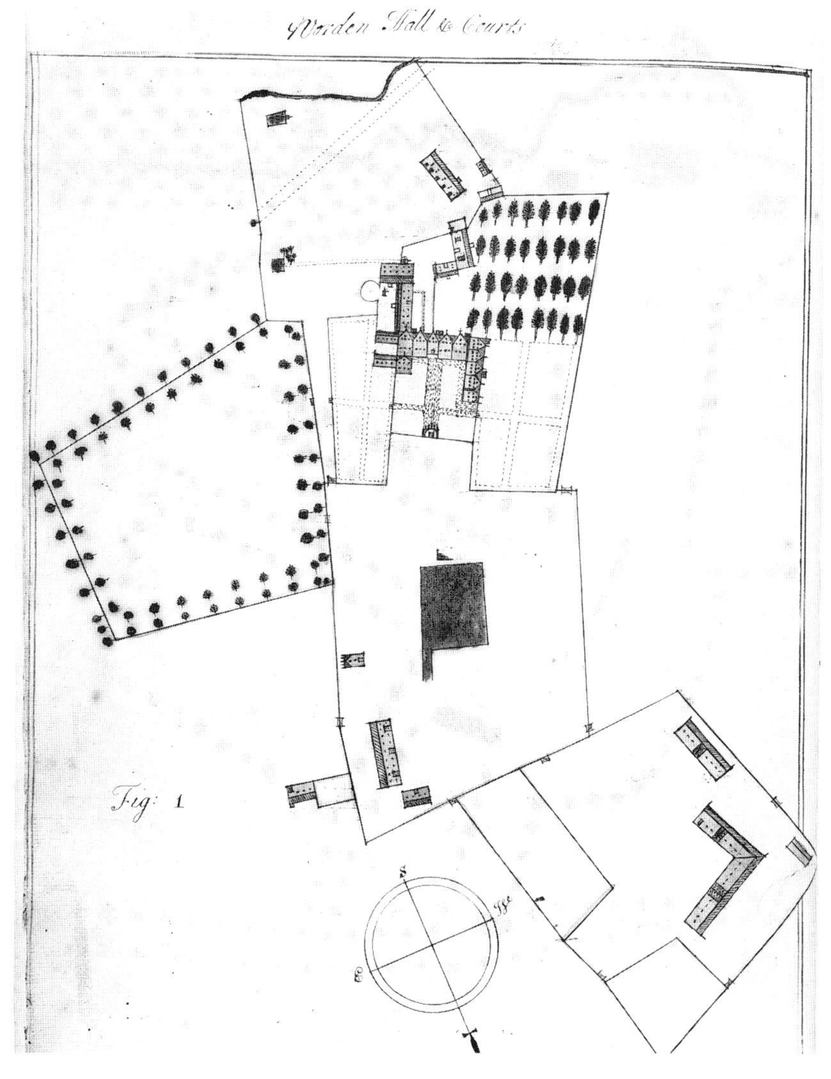

Estate Plan 1725. Old Worden Hall.
Now inaccessible to the general public in the 'Euxton' Ordnance Works, this comparitively well preserved building is perhaps the most interesting, both historically and architecturally, in Leyland. The home of the Farington family from shortly after the Reformation to the early-eighteenth century, the 1725 plan indicates a building of considerable size. (Lancashire Record Office).

Penwortham, was duly suppressed. Canon Raines described him as 'A zealous promoter of the views of Henry VIII, and affected to be a favourer of the Reformation' yet 'sufficiently mindful of his own interests, having cautiously enlarged his estate and influence out of the wreck by which he was surrounded'.[3] How far this is a fair assessment is open to conjecture, but the first half of the sixteenth century was certainly a period of consolidation and growth of Farington interests.

The division of the manor into two parts in the thirteenth century did not result in a simple division of Leyland into two segments. Rather, each set of fields was split. This obviously led to many disputes between the Faringtons and whoever held the rights to the other portion; in such disputes with the local people and tenants Henry Farington was quite prepared to resort to violence. A series of complaints brought against him in the Duchy Court of 1502-3 illustrates this well. When bailiffs appeared to collect rents which Sir Henry claimed to be his 'The said Henry with the assistance of his tenants and friends, to the number of 100 and above, with bows, arrows etc. set about to kill them'. Seth Sumpnor was struck in the face while drinking ale, and Thurston Cooper's pregnant wife was viciously hit in the stomach with a pot of ale by Edward Rutter, one of Sir Henry's servants.

The courtier was even prepared to intervene personally. He drove Edward Lykas from his marl pit 'On payne of my head', and after a visit and beating of William Sumpnor had failed to have the desired effect he waylaid him in the street, 'As I was going towards to the town of Preston to the market, the said Henry Farington was in the way, whether intentionally or not I cannot say, howbeit I understood from a gentleman named Jenkyn Farington that I was in danger. The said Faryngton took me by the bosom, drew out a long hynger a knife and said I should die, but I geld him and so escaped'.[4] By his cleverness, however, Sir Henry brought about a sequence of events which led to the family losing Farington and Farington Hall itself.

Sir Henry died on December 8th 1551, and an inventory drawn up at this time provides a fine description of the estates, possessions and heirlooms of a Tudor gentleman of means. In normal circumstances the estate should have passed to the only surviving son by his first marriage, Robert, who had left the priesthood and married Elizabeth Southworth of Samlesbury - a member of a staunchly Catholic family. However, Robert's eldest brother had left a daughter, Joan, who was married to Anthony Browne, a leading and clever lawyer and chief justice. For whatever reason, Robert was disinherited and Joan was named heir to Farington and the moiety of Leyland.

On Sir Henry's death Robert, the rightful heir and his wife were evicted from Farington Hall and ultimately imprisoned. At the same time Browne purchased the other half of the manor and so Joan's daughter, Dorothy, inherited the whole of Leyland Manor, Farington and Farington Hall, which on her marriage passed into the Huddleston family. They and Anthony Browne successfully fought off the claims of Robert Farington and in 1575 his son was forced to settle for £420 in compensation from the Huddlestons. Susan Maria Farington recorded this event, 'The date of the final decision against his claims is November 20th, 17th year of Elizabeth, and from that evil day to this, Farington has been in alien hands and we have not had a possession in the township from which we take our name as the cradle of our race. We had had it for about 370 years when it went away in 1575'.[5]

In 1549 in yet another settlement Sir Henry had named William (1537-1610), his son by a second marriage, as heir to the remainder of his estates. William Farington was thus the first head of the family to reside at Old Worden Hall which his father had acquired from the Anderton family, and henceforth the family were to style themselves Farington of Worden. Notwithstanding these events it is clear that the Faringtons did retain lands in Leyland, and in 1617 they were able to buy the manor back from the Huddlestons.

The question remains, however, of how this affair is to be explained, for as late as 1546 Robert was acknowledged by his father to be his rightful heir, and just prior to his death in 1551 he seems to have tried to reinstate him. Clearly the lawyer's role is as suspicious as it is central, and the changes in the succession were probably made at Anthony Browne's suggestion, whilst Sir Henry was by this time a man approaching eighty – a very advanced age for the times. Why disinherit Robert? The answer may lie in the turmoil of uncertainty following the Reformation: Sir Henry may have feared that Robert's Catholic associations might lead to the confiscation by the Crown of the entire estate and Anthony Browne might have suggested an apparent safeguard. Sir Henry's subsequent efforts to put things right were dismissed by the Huddlestons as forgeries.[6]

'The Old Comptroller'

WILLIAM Farington (1537-1610) 'The Old Comptroller', was only eighteen when these events unfolded. Apart from the inevitable land disputes his relations with the Huddlestons seem to have been quite good, but he has left a memo among the family papers entitled, 'A Note of Sondrie evill and subtyll dealings used by Sir Anthonie Browne . . . towards William Farington'.[7] Through his marriage he acquired both a fortune and a close connection with the Stanleys, the Earls of Derby and the great magnates of Lancashire. In 1561 he became secretary to the Earl, and from 1586-91 he was 'comptroller' (steward) of the household.

A trained lawyer, his remarkable diary and papers reveal him as a great man of business, like his father, and in his time the Farington estates expanded and were very efficiently administered. In spite of, or perhaps because of this, his family affairs were not so happy. Among his surviving papers and letters, he frequently complains of the extravagance of his sons, and he eventually settled his estates on his grandson to prevent Thomas, his son, from squandering them.

In March 1600 Thomas wrote to his father complaining that he was driving his friends away. 'My harte not being able to endure that thus hardly you should deal with me, only for that I matched myself in marriage without your consent, yet not in any way which is any disworshipp to you or your house or to myself'.[8] His younger brother wrote to Worden in 1608 describing the high life in London, whereupon, the 'Old Comptroller' wrote back urging him to mend his ways. 'I wish you to endeavour yourself to win over again the credyte you have loste in the worlde. Otherwise you shall never have my blessing or good torn while as your leiffe, and therefore, I wisshe you to so take hit for a warninge from henceforth . . . Your mother hath sente unto you one of her beste cheeses . . . and thus wishing unto you better than I fear you dow yorself I seace yor loving father if so you shall deserve, William Farington'.[9]

William Farington's attitude to the religious troubles of his day appears enigmatic. As Farrer wrote of him, 'In religion he was externally a conformist to the Elizabethan settlement, but reputed to be in secret its bitter enemy'.[10] The Rector of Wigan, writing to Queen Elizabeth's great minister Lord Burghley, noted the Catholic leanings of the Earl of Derby's council, 'Halsall is a lawyer, presented these last sessions as a recusant in some degree. Farington is as cunning as he: not anything sounder in religion, though much more subtle to avoid the public note than he. Rigby is as cunning and unsound as either, and as grossly to be detected therein as Halsall. All three of them as busy contrivers of dangerous devices against the peace of the ministry and free course of the Gospel and direct proceeding of justice, in all common opinion, as any that ever bore authority amongst us'.[11]

Accordingly Lord Burghley duly marked William Farington on the celebrated map which he had specially drawn up to show where all the prominent Lancashire Catholics lived. Critically from the point of view of the local people such a man would be unlikely to persecute local Catholics beyond that required for appearances' sake, and in Leyland much must have continued after the Reformation as before. Sir William's portrait painted in 1593 suggests a meticulous man of great authority, and is dominated by his penetrating look. The eyes of a man who scholars have suggested was the inspiration for Malvolio in Shakespeare's play *Twelfth Night,* and who was perhaps the greatest of the Faringtons. In his will dated June 1609 he mentions his houses at Worden (his 'capitall House'), Northbrook, Littlewood, the Lower Hall in Penwortham and Shaw Hall. Within a generation the loss of Farington had been more than made up for.[12]

William Farington 'The Royalist'

WILLIAM Farington ('The Royalist', 1583-1658) succeeded to the Worden estates on the death of his grandfather in 1610. Another man of business, his troubles were to come to him late in life. In 1636 he was appointed high sheriff of Lancashire, a signal honour but an onerous and expensive one. In addition to overseeing the operation of the county assizes in Lancaster, he was also expected to entertain on a lavish scale, as the accounts for his year in office make clear.

After listing the considerable amounts of beer and food provided (including 'two barrells of Aile for Morninge Draughts . . . two barrells of small beare for prysoners . . . ten stoane of Butter . . . Cold Redd deare pies and all other Baken Meats made and sente from Worden'), and household utensils ('twelve beddes', 'twenty dozen of Trenchers', and many items from Worden including the frying pan), the account describes a staff of fifty-six to run the sheriff's house and to feed the throng. Other gentry helped out by lending their plate.[13] Even the prisoners shared in this bounty, for the Sheriff 'Shall during the . . . assyzes releve the poor prisoners with some such broken meats as shall remaine after everie meal'.[14]

The list of prisoners reveals something of the crime and punishment of the day. Margaret Chambers was prosecuted by Henry Ashurst esq, 'Charged with the breaking of a certen dwelling house in the night time

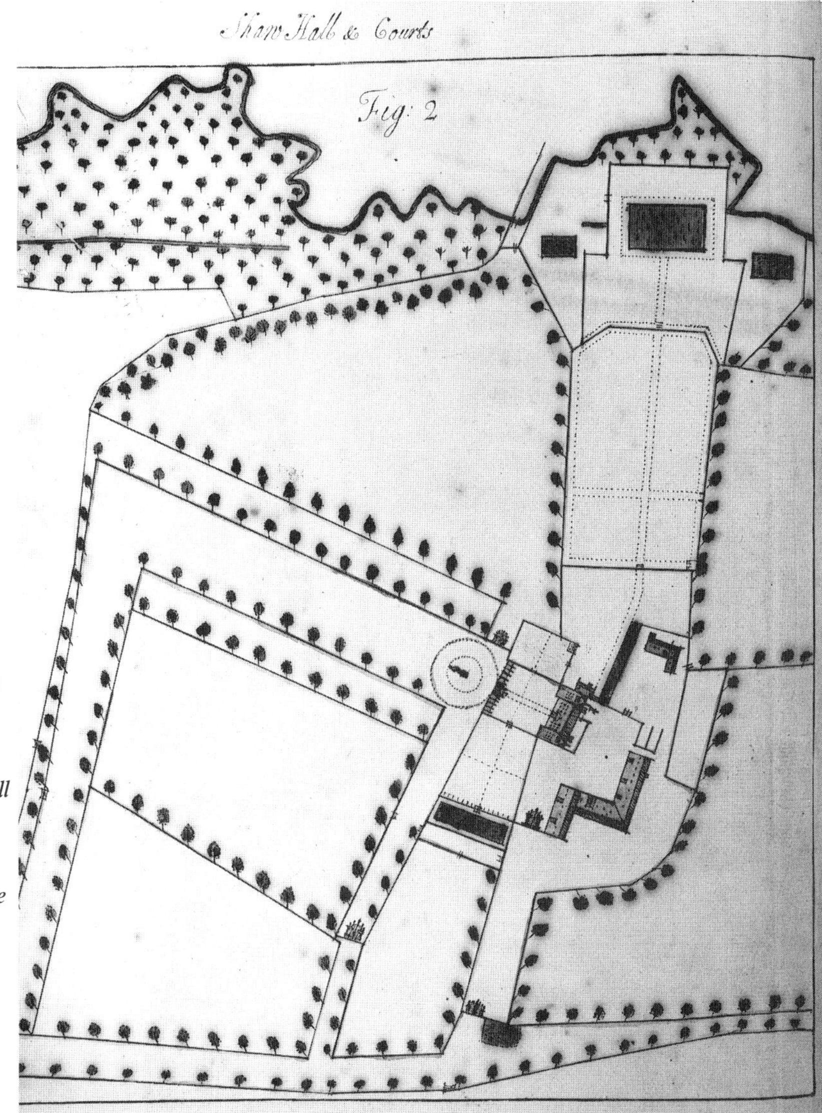

Estate Plan 1725: Shaw Hall (Present day Worden Hall).
Though a much smaller building in 1725 than the hall whose name it was to adopt in the 1840s, Shaw Hall was nevertheless an ancient family residence, and along with Northbrook and Charnock Hall was one of the ancient farm estates on the fringes of the townfields. At the foot of the plan can be seen the line of the 'Back Lane', the southern counterpart to Golden Hill Lane in the north. Ultimately closed to the public the lane was one of the four ancient trackways which surrounded the township. (Lancashire Record Office).

and with the felonious takinge of divers goods which she hath confessed. [Verdict] Giltie: whipped next Market day'. A party of witches also awaited his attentions.[15]

All this was bad enough, but the appointment was further complicated by long standing disputes between the holders of the sheriff's office and the assize judges. In particular the latter claimed that it was the former's responsibility to entertain and keep them during the Lancaster assizes, going as far as to fine him when all this did not come up to their expectations! It was thus rather inevitable that William Farington would fall foul of them, and in 1637 he was duly fined a total of £700 on three charges. The third charge was 'A ffyne of 100 markes for sufferinge the prisoners at lardge in the face of the

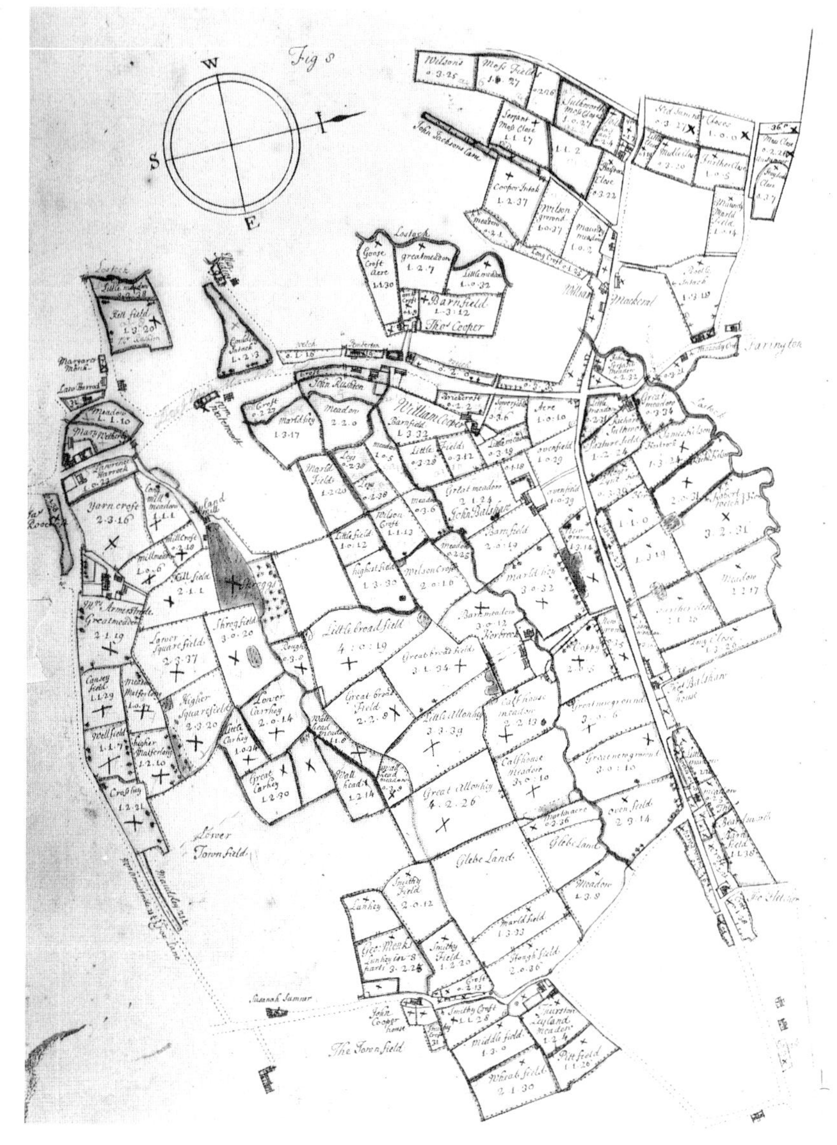

Estate Plan 1725: Farington holdings west of Towngate.
The 1725 Farington estate plan book contains the earliest known detailed maps of Leyland. This extract shows the family holdings to the west of Towngate and School Lane, broadly between Fox Lane and Golden Hill Lane, bounded to the west by Leyland Lane and a part of the moss holdings. The extent of the upper and lower townfields in 1725 can be seen, along with one of the ancient field strips (near the top of Fox Lane), and the sites of Leyland Mill and Northbrook. The coloured maps in this survey provide the name of each field and its area in acres, rods, and perches, whilst the accompanying register gives the name of each tenant, their holdings and rent. It is thus perhaps the most important single item in the historical sources of the town and is one of the treasures of the Lancashire Record Office in Preston. (Lancashire Record Office).

Courte to ye danger of ye Judge and ye courte',

> to which the former sheriff claimed 'Neither the Judge nor anie one in the Courte were in anie danger att all of the prisoners. Neither did anie prisoner at anie time offere voluntarily to move or stirr out of the dockes where they were, excepting a lunatick man which had irons made fast both to his hands and feete, and not he neither (to the best of my remembrance) out of the docks, nor in any assaultinge manner either upon the Judge or anie in the courte. But out of his mere lunacie would some tyme have been offeringe to come under the barr and tumble over, but that he was still thrust backe by some of my servants, and which supposed offence was not then faulted.[16]

In 1640 with Sir Gilbert Hoghton he represented the county in the Short Parliament, and so was about sixty when the Farington family's

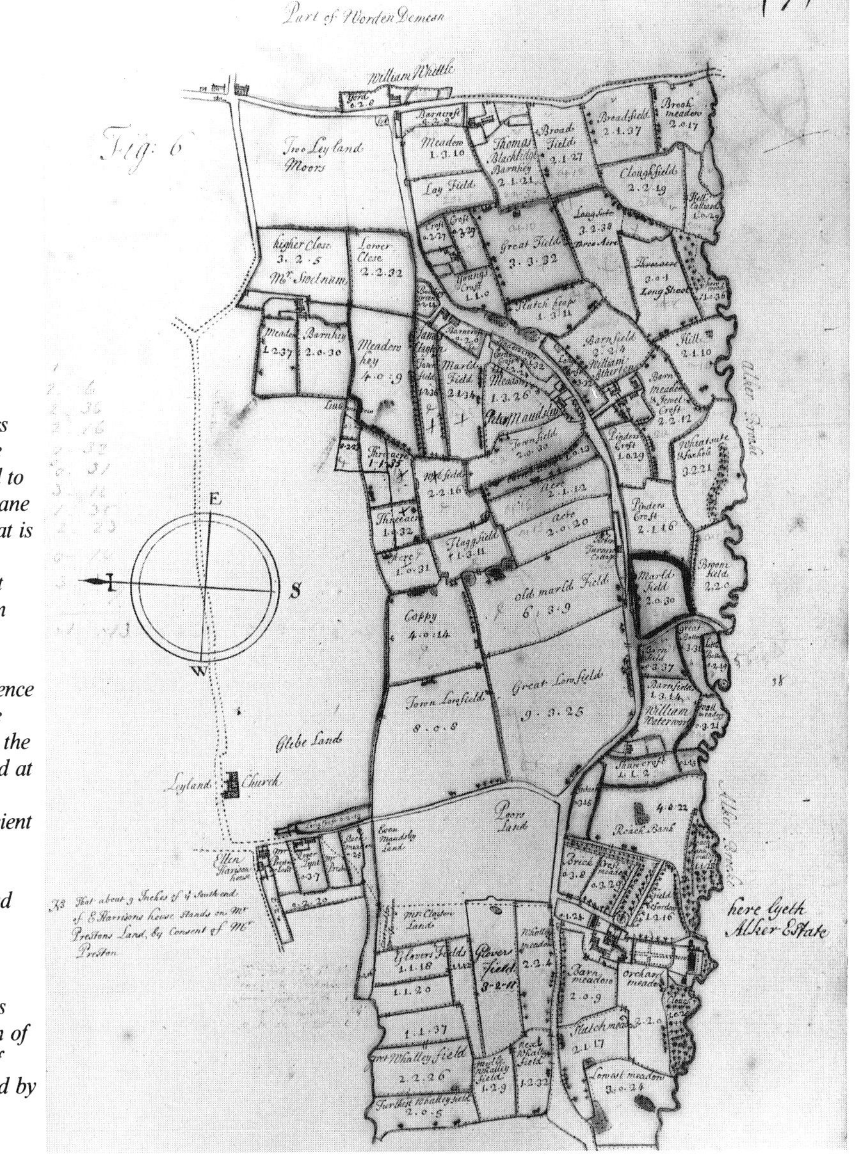

Estate Plan 1725: Farington holdings along Back Lane.
This map records holdings along Back Lane (Langdale Road) from the Wigan road to the junction with Worden Lane and continuing through what is now Worden Park towards Leyland Lane in the west. It clearly shows Atherton Farm and Shaw Hall. The field names are particularly interesting and provide evidence for the original extent of the townfields, the Poor's Land, the Glebe or Church Lands, and at the New Inn crossroads placename traces of the ancient Leyland Moor (the higher portion of the town). To the south along the Wigan Road can be seen the farm in the tenancy of William Whittle, subsequently known to generations of Leylanders as 'Rose Whittles'. To the north of Church Road the pattern of landholdings was dominated by the Charnock Hall estate. (Lancashire Record Office).

close connection with the Earls of Derby ensured their active participation on the losing side in the English Civil War.

In Lancashire, as elsewhere, the history of the conflict between the King (Charles I) and the House of Commons (Parliament', ultimately led by Oliver Cromwell) as to who should have the final say in the running of the country falls into two broad phases, the first Civil War of 1642-6, and the second of 1648-51. In the former both the Faringtons and the Hoghtons played leading parts on the Royalist side and suffered accordingly. Thereafter the Faringtons appear to have played little part in events, while the Royalist Sir Gilbert Hoghton was succeeded by his son Richard who supported Cromwell.

Beneath the overlying political issues of the day religion played an important part in determining where people's sympathies lay. In the south east of the county the emergent clothing towns with their puritan sympathies (Bolton was widely known as 'The Geneva of the North') supported the Parliamentarian side, whilst the more rural Anglican and Roman Catholic districts of the north and west were for the King. Yet although the Earl of Derby could rely on most of the gentry and the majority of the towns, the local Parliamentarian forces were much better organised and perhaps had the sympathy of the majority of the people.

Of course, in the time-honoured tradition, many people were fairly apathetic to politics. Many tried desperately to keep out of the conflict altogether while others - so-called 'sidechangers' - directed their loyalty wisely to whichever force was occupying their town at a given time, or, if they were tenants, by their landlord's position. Many of the gentry, one suspects, were fairly half-hearted, taking action only when forced to by circumstances. All these tendencies were greatly emphasised when local people witnessed at first hand the horrors of war, and particularly when they suffered at the hands of the participants in the Battle of Walton Bridge and Wigan Road in 1648.

None of the major battles of the first Civil War were fought in Lancashire and the local war effort took the form of skirmishes and raids to secure control of the towns on the main road through the county (Warrington - Wigan - Preston - Lancaster). All four towns changed hands on several occasions, usually when their garrisons were 'out' trying to capture one of the other towns.

In December 1642 Sir Gilbert Hoghton gathered a force and lit a beacon at Hoghton Tower: 'The signall to the countrey for the papists and malignants to arise in the Fylede [Fylde] and in Lealand hundred'.[17] By the end of 1643, however, most of the county was in the hands of the Parliamentarian forces, and the Royalists were besieged at Lathom House, the stronghold of the Earls of Derby. This was briefly relieved by the army of Prince Rupert, who also perpetrated the 'Bolton Massacre' and besieged Liverpool on their way through Lancashire en route for defeat at Marston Moor in July 1644.

Although the Parliamentarians rapidly recovered lost ground, a second siege of Lathom was only successful in December 1645. The Royalist cause fared even more badly in the Second Civil War of 1648. Amid much plundering of the locals by the Scots marching south, the Battle of Preston in 1648 resulted in the execution of Charles I, while a second Scottish and Royalist invasion in 1651 resulted in the defeat of Charles II at Worcester and the execution of the Earl of Derby in Bolton.

William Farington, 'In the beginning of these times . . . was a man of placable disposition, bending all his councells to accommodation and quiet of the countrey'.[18] He did, nevertheless, play a full part in these events. In 1642 he was with the King at York, and he was an adviser at the first siege of Lathon, whilst his son - another William - was also actively and deeply involved in the Derby cause. In his absence his estates were sequestered (temporarily seized), and his personal property amounting to £428-9-4d was taken by Parliamentarian soldiers, virtually stripping the house at Worden.

The list of these items (itemised room by room) includes furniture ('In the Higher Dininge room: one long table, fifteen plain Buffet stooles, three little tables with coverings, two chairs, four set Quishions, two covered forms and one chimney with furniture'), pots, linen, trunks, kitchen utensils, farm implements, crops and farm animals. At least a portion of the family heirlooms do, however, seem to have been spirited away before the soldiers arrived.[19] All this, and the virtual confiscation of estate and rents, meant hard times for Sir William's wife, Margaret, 'By reason therefore and of her said husbands absence she is left destitute of present subsistence for herself, children and familie'.[20]

Arrested on his way home to Leyland and imprisoned until the following May, William Farington was released on condition of his payment of a fine of £536 for the return of his estates and the end of their sequestration. His son William was similarly fined, as he was himself again in 1649, after which the family does not appear to have taken any overt part in the struggle, 'His long absence from home, the sequestrations and the fines had brought his affairs into a very embarrassed state, from which it took his descendants more than one or two generations to recover.[21]

Notwithstanding all these troubles, he took great pains to establish a new endowment of the Farington almshouses in 1649. About 1650 he wrote a very revealing letter to a friend, Father Bradley, Minister of Heapy, 'From my clossett at Worden – the strong and almost invincible inclination I have to solitude and retirement, with a natural aversion from ye controversies of this age, wherein ther is so little Christian candour, fidelity, ingenuity, and moderation to be found, hath given me no small satisfaction in my being presented hitherto from these vexatious conflicts which I see many learned and pious men involved in'.[22] He died, an old man, in April 1658, and his wife Margaret survived him only until January of the following year.

Chapter Four

The origins of modern Leyland 1550 - 1700

FROM the middle of the sixteenth century onwards, and particularly in the seventeenth century, the years of the Reformation and Civil War, the quality and quantity of surviving documents improve greatly and it becomes possible for the first time to see something of the lives of ordinary people. In addition to being able to identify most of the Leyland householders by name, it is even possible to explore their political and religious beliefs. Among the consequences of the Reformation was the need to establish new institutions to carry out tasks formerly undertaken by the Church, notably in the fields of education and support for the poor. In Leyland the Farington almshouses survive to the present day, and the Leyland Free Grammar School, closed in 1874 after three hundred years, still maintains its educational role as the town museum. The late-sixteenth and early-seventeenth century is thus as important and formative a period in the history of Leyland, as it is in Britain as a whole.

Parish registers, simple chronological lists of christenings, weddings and burials, are the most important historical source prior to the Births Marriages and Deaths Act of 1837.[1] They were first instituted by the great governmental reformer Thomas Cromwell in 1538, but were often improperly kept up or allowed to lapse due to negligence or perhaps persistent fears that they would be used as the basis for some type of poll tax.

The Leyland register, however, was duly begun on the 27th of April, 1538, and has been kept up ever since. Unfortunately the last that is known of the first register book is a reference to its being in the possession of Robert Abbot in a certificate signed by Edward Robinson in 1656 at the time of the ejection from office of Vicar Rothwell. So that apart from transcripts for the years 1622, 29, 30, 31, 37, 39, 40 and 41 the surviving registers extend back only to 1653. The registers contain many interesting items. Twins are mentioned quite frequently among the baptisms, and burials sometimes also give the deceased his nick name, '19 December 1653 Thomas Watkinson of

Leyland, Alias Ffoulebie.' Parish affairs are also referred to:

> 4th November 1664. It is concluded upon by Mr Rothwell vicar and the churchwarden . . . that the ringers appointed by them shall observe to ring in due time on Sundaies and take the benefit of ringing of Burialls and other items to be divided amongst them by equall portions.
>
> 8 September 1671. Collected in Leyland parish the sum of three pounds seven shillings and six pence towards the ransoming of our English subjects from Turkish slavery.
>
> Collected for the reliefe of Irish Protestants a 2d [second] time in the parish of Leyland the summ of two pound six shillings.[2]

Where registers are complete it is possible to lay bare the bones of family history and to gain some idea of the local population in the 11,000 parishes of England and Wales. In Leyland there are several periods - particularly in the upheavals of the 1650s and 1660s - when the register is incomplete. Also all births, marriages and deaths may not be recorded, for Catholics and other dissenters would tend to avoid having their children baptised at the Protestant parish church. Similar strictures apply to marriages. The list of burials (deaths) is usually a much more accurate guide to actual events since the Established Church had a virtual monopoly of consecrated ground. Ignoring the years where the records were not kept up (1658-63) the following are the average number of burials of people from Leyland township at Leyland parish church:

Average number of burials per year

1650-1660	22.6
1660-1670	14.6
1670-1680	20.0
1680-1690	17.1
1690-1700	18.2
1700-1710	14.8
1710-1720	15.9
1720-1730	27.0
1730-1740	20.6

In theory these numbers of deaths should represent a consistent proportion of the overall population, which may be estimated by multiplying the number of burials by thirty. For example, during the 1670s the average number of burials each year is twenty. Multiplied by thirty, this produces an estimate of the overall population of around six hundred. Obviously this can be little more than a rough guide since many deaths, particularly of babies and small children, may have gone unrecorded. Alternatively, the parish clerk may have forgotten to keep his books, whilst the death rate may have been higher or lower than the estimated thirty per 1,000 people per year.

Thus it is not surprising that the estimates for the population of Leyland produced for the years 1660-1730 fluctuate greatly - between 438 and 810. Such fluctuations also record actual changes in the death rate brought about by disease and bad winters. Notable in this respect are the winters of 1670-1, 1680-1, 1693-4, 1697-8, 1727-8 and 1728-9; from analysis of all the South Ribble registers it is clear that such harsh winters became apparent as early as September of the previous year. Sadly the Leyland register containing entries for 1631 has been lost, so that the plague of that year (which the Preston records reveal to have carried off over 1,000 people) is not recorded.

In 1642, on the eve of the Civil War, people were obliged to take an oath to uphold the Established Church settlement. The 'Protestation Return' of 1642 lists 189 males over eighteen years of age. Assuming that there was a similar number of females, this would produce a figure of 378 adults, to which must be added a number for the children. Nineteenth-century census studies suggest that this can be produced by multiplying the number of adults by 0.755. This is obviously of doubtful validity in a seventeenth-century context, but would produce a figure of 285 children and a total population of 683 people. Similarly, the local survey for the Hearth Tax of 1664 can be manipulated: Leyland township had 146 dwellings Assuming 4.5 people per house produces a total population figure of 657; if the average household size is taken at five people, one reaches a total of 730.[3]

In conclusion, this guesswork produces figures of between 438 (1660-70) and 810 (1720-30) from the analysis of burials; the Protestation Return of the 1640s indicates around 700 people; and the Hearth Tax of 1664 between 650 and 730 people. A figure of between 650 and 700 people, half of them children, may thus not be too far wide of the mark for the population of mid-seventeenth-century Leyland.

The town was still a dispersed township consisting of small houses and crofts strung out along the main tracks, with a cluster of houses around the parish church, familiar from medieval times. The west side of the township along the axis of Leyland Lane had emerged as a district, perhaps reflecting the systematic encroachment onto the moss, and entries in the parish register frequently refer to 'Leland Moss side', 'Leland Lane' and 'Leyland below ye town.' The Hearth Tax reveals something of the size of the 146 houses listed. 120 dwellings had only a single chimney, and only seven had more than three - Old Worden Hall had sixteen! The parish registers occasionally refer to people's occupations. Between 1650 and 1695, they record four Catholic priests, two thatchers, and single websters, spinners, blacksmiths, carpenters, shoemakers and wheelwrights.

Leyland wills and inventories

THE keenest insight into people's lives at this time is provided by their surviving wills and the inventories of their goods which are often attached to them.[4] From the Reformation onwards quite large numbers of Leyland wills and inventories have survived, with almost 250 available for the years 1545-1720 (140 from 1545 to 1620, 36 from 1621 to 1650, 82 from 1660 to 1680, 147 from 1681 to 1700, 34 from 1701 to 1720). At this time wills are very individual documents, inventories are quite detailed, and since wills were made immediately prior to death they are also very personal documents. During the sixteenth century they frequently consisted of three main elements: a religious introduction, the assignment of property, (ie the will of the deceased), and inventory that was often attached to it, (itemising the estate possessions and moneys due to and from the deceased). A fine example of the religious introduction to a will is provided by that of William Atherton, yeoman, dated 1673.

> In the name of God Amen, I William Atherton of Leyland within the Countie of Lancaster yeoman being sicke and weake in Bodie but of good and perfect memorie, praised bee God for the same, doe make publish and declare this my last will and testament in manner and forme ffollowing, (that is to say) ffirst and most principallie I commend my soule into the hands of allmightie God my maker and only Redeemer, trustinge assuredlie by the death and passion of Jesus Christe to have full pardon of all my sinns And my bodie to the earthe, there to remain till the generall resurrection of all fleshe and my Will is that the same may bee buried, att my parrish church of Leyland.

This section is usually followed by the division of the estate into three equal portions, to the deceased's wife, his son or heir, and to himself. The latter was to cover funeral expenses and any donations to charity. Peter Blackhurst's will, dated 1623, was divided in this way, with shares 'One unto Isabel, my wife, two unto Thomas my son, and the third part I preserve unto myself . . . my funeral expenses, mortuary [traditional payment to the vicar], and my dowle [a donation to the poor] shall be taken out of my own part. The dowle shall be twelve mettes [measures] of Barlie and be dealt upon Good Fridaie next after my death, at my own dwelling house unto the poor folkes in Leyland only.'

Jane Sumner, Spinster, left £4 to the poor of the township in 1638. 'To be distributed amongst them by my executors upon four Good Fridays next after my decease by 20/- a year.' John Silcock left 40/- in 1670 for the 'walling out' (the lining) of a well called Shorrocks Well in Leyland (near the Gables Hotel on Hough Lane), 'As long as Mr Farington and his heirs will ascent and permit the inhabitants of Leyland town to have the benefit and use of the water thereof and therein without stop and molestation.'

Peacock Hall. Sketch by David Grant, 1881.

This house was built by John Sumner on a piece of land taken in from the 'waste' along Leyland Lane in 1628. The Faringtons' steward, he is perhaps best remembered for his letter to William Farington written on a visit to London, informing him of the Gunpowder Plot. (Leyland Museum).

The legacies and related details often reveal a good deal about family life. William Atherton mentions 'John Atherton, my loving sonne,' and 'Alice, my lovinge wife,' hoping she will be fortunate enough to remarry. William Rigby in 1608 left 'Everyone I am godfather unto 6d apiece.' Jennet Monk who lived in a house on the site of the present 'Tudor House' by Leyland Cross, in 1670, made many bequests to her children and grandchildren, including, 'The little house in the back-side commonly called the Jepp house and half of ye backside in the garden to the pippin tree' to her grandson.

Above: *Fleetwood Hall. Sketch by David Grant, 1881.*

Fleetwood Hall stood on Chapel Brow and was acquired by Edward Fleetwood of Penwortham in the middle of the seventeenth century. A sale notice dated 1804 outlines the extent of the Fleetwood Hall estate, lying between Turpin Green Lane, Chapel Brow, Moss Lane and Bow Lane, including the Bow Field, Turpin Green Croft and the house 'consisting of two parlours to the front, middle kitchen, large back kitchen, pantry staircase, rooms over the whole'. The list of outlying lands included 'one baulk of land in the Higher Townfield, called the Town Field Butts' and moss lands adjoining the 'Minnagate', including 'The lower moss room and the higher moss heads'.

The will and inventory of Evan Whittle, a cooper, contains a simple room-by-room account of his goods, including books valued at 13/4d, a spinning wheel and the work items of his trade, worth in all £87, but also the following clause, 'I the said Evan Whittle for and in consideration of twenty-four-years service my sonne done unto me which I must acknowledge hath made him these ye remainder of my goods, not as a gift but as a debt.'

The long and very interesting will of Roger Southworth (1670) reveals his concern 'To be interred in or near unto the place where my father and mother were interred in the parish churchyard of Leyland.' An 'upper' servant of the Faringtons, he left an estate worth £288-0-1d, including bills and bonds worth £184-5-11d – a very large sum indeed for the time. In the tradition of the day, he left 2/- each to his fellow servants, and 'To Mr Farington my master 10/- to buy him a ring.'

By contrast Jane Gramdage of the almshouses left a very simple will in 1676. The inventory of her household goods contains only nineteen

Left: *Dunkirk Hall, Dunkirk Lane, Moss-side c1900.*

This fine building is firm evidence for the early development of the potentially highly fertile mosslands to the west of the River Lostock. The Western Primary Route now passes in front of this building, which has been converted into a public house.

items worth just £1-16-7d, but in addition she had debts due her of £4-13-0d, in all an estate of £6-9-7d. Robert Addison and his wife Jennett Farington had married on May 8th 1671, Jennett had died on January 17th and Robert on the 20th, perhaps the victims of an epidemic; they were clearly poor, Robert's estate being worth a total of just £5-17- 9d.

The wills also reveal much of the society and economy of the times. The series of great Farington wills list the estates and possession of the gentry, and many of the vicars of Leyland were very well-off. Thurston Breres, vicar from 1604 to 1611, left a will (5th February 1611) and an enormously detailed inventory (12th March 1611) itemising his possessions room by room, including 'in Parlour one mappe,' 'in his study all his bookes £16,' 'the maid's chamber' etc. Among his possessions are listed twenty-nine items of bedding, thirty-nine of 'Lynnen', clothes worth £6 in the maid's chamber, horse and cart gear, a spinning wheel, farm animals (three cows, one heiffer, one nag, thirty sheep, one sow, five pigs, two young swine) and beef and bacon in the buttery. Of particular interest is the list of his silver valued at 5/- per ounce, 'one trencher salt, thirty-eight oz, £9-1-0d,' 'one salte and tune double gilt' (a dish) £8-13- 4d' and 'two dozen silver spoons, thirty-seven oz [ounces], £8-3-6d'. His estate, in all, was worth £248-11-6d.

The farming interest is well represented by the wills of the local yeomen. For example, William Atherton had;

	£	s	d
Seaven Kyne, 2 steares, 3 stirks, 3 calfes	38	0	0
Two mares and one horse	17	10	0
Corne and Haye	26	13	6
Cowp timber and wheel timber	5	0	0
Three swine	2	5	0
In butter and cheese	2	0	0

The raw materials of the textile trade were also produced locally, and several yeomen seem to have had interests in the trade. William Rigby (1608) sold flax, Alexander Park (1671) had fustians worth £28, and Edmund Machon (1638) left 'In linen yarn, wool and toe, 50s' Edward Fleetwood, gentleman of Fleetwood Hall, which stood on Chapel Brow, had (1667);

	£	s	d
2 acres of wheat on the ground	7	0	0
Hay in the barn	3	10	0
2 acres of barley, beans and oats	4	0	0

However, Richard Nelson, a yeoman of the Seven Stars district, had left Leyland to fight in the Civil War under the command of Captain Mawdesley, 'making a will when a soldier in February 1648 and death being a possibility'. The will was proved at Richmond on October 22nd 1649, so he had probably been killed somewhere in the North.

In the absence of banks most people with cash in hand seem to have loaned it out. Vicar Breres (1611) had bonds worth £66, and Jennet Wilson, spinster (1625), had twenty-two debtors owing her £79-16-9d including Mr Henry Farington 16s, William Farington £6-10-0d and William Hesketh £20 – all prosperous men. Clearly informal as well as formal mechanisms existed for the supply of capital.

Of great interest are the prices of everyday items which are occasionally given. Two ladders 2/- (1588), one irone potte 1/4d (1583), a fouling piece (gun) 12/- (1667), stockings and shirt cloth 8/4d, tobacco 6d (1622), coals and cannel 3/4d (1639), cooper's working tools 6/8d (1633), one ewe and lamb 6/8d, one brass mortar and pewter bowl 3/- (1638), one swine 16/-, one bible 5/- (1670), Spinning wheel 8d (1664) and, in one well-stocked household, 138 lbs of butter worth £1-11-0d (1638).

The wills and inventories thus provide an informative and colourful picture of life which is familiar to us today: in 1664 Thomas Snart left £318-17-0d to his daughter Thomasin. By her death four years later she had managed to spend all but half of it.

Troubles: Reformation and Civil War

THE Reformation of the previous century cast a long shadow and the Faringtons were not alone in suffering its eventual consequences, both political and financial, as well as benefiting from the various opportunities if offered. How far the local people were affected, is much less clear. The Elizabethan Church settlement of 1559 was comparatively liberal for the time, for although attendance at church was supposed to be compulsory, fines were not great, and magistrates, if not Catholics themselves, were often willing to turn a blind eye to their neighbours and tenants absenting themselves from church.

Away from the south east of the county, Lancashire remained strongly Catholic for at least a further century. A series of events brought about a shift in this situation and a less tolerant attitude on the part of the authorities. Of particular importance was the deteriorating relationship between England and Spain towards the end of the sixteenth century, culminating in the Spanish Armada and fears of a landing on the Lancashire coast. The visit of Edmund Campion to Hoghton Tower and Samlesbury Hall, as part of a Jesuit mission to win back England for the Church of Rome, appeared to give credence to such fears. In this tense atmosphere the attitude of the local gentry - in effect the local legal, civil and military authorities - was all important in what was still in some respects a distant and remote corner of England.

In Leyland the position of the Faringtons seems to have been equivocal - ostensibly the well-rewarded upholders of the Reformation and loyal supporters of Church and State, actively prosecuting overt recusants (people refusing to attend Anglican services), yet strongly rumoured to have Catholic sympathies. A very sizeable proportion of the local population seems to have retained Catholic leanings without undue interference by the authorities.

A clear insight into this situation is provided by the Protestation Returns of 1642; in Leyland the oath to uphold the established Church and State was administered to 189 men, perhaps in the Old Grammar School, and eighty-three refused to take it. 'The names of such persons inhabiting within the townshippe of Leyland which hath taken the protestation' include two of the local gentry, Richard Clayton and

David Grant's sketch of Charnock Hall 1881 (Also known as 'Old Hall' and 'Leyland Hall').
One of the ancient estates or large farms in the centre of the town, this was long the home of the Catholic Charnock family, and it lay at the centre of one of the more discreditable episodes in the religious history of Leyland. During nineteenth-century 'restoration' work priest hiding holes were claimed to have been discovered. Located on present-day Balcarres Road, close to the line of a planned link-road, the house is an important link with Leyland's ancient and disappearing past. (Leyland Museum).

William Farington ('The Royalist') with eleven of his servants. The same surname is occasionally found on both lists. For example John Jackson senior took the oath and his son John Jackson junior refused.[5]

Whatever the implications of this for individual family loyalties (given the possible advantages of the family property having a foot in both camps in a time of uncertainty), two important points are clear; that as late as the 1640s a very sizeable minority of the people of Leyland remained attached to former ways, and that no serious local efforts were made to coerce them into conforming to Protestantism. So long as local Catholicism was less than open, ostensibly secret and underground and local Catholics were peaceable and seen to be loyally law-abiding, it was perhaps convenient for the local magistrates to overlook them. Problems arose only when the law was confronted head on, and recourse could be had to powers outside of the local community and its attitudes. Particular problems arose from the fact that proven Catholics were not allowed to own land, and technically their estates could be confiscated by the state. It has been seen that this fear may account for the disinheritance of Robert Farington by his father in the late 1540s.

A celebrated instance was the affair of Charnock Hall – Leyland Hall or 'Old Hall' as it is now known, in Balcarres Road. The Charnock family were staunchly Catholic and Robert Charnock, though outwardly a landed gentleman, was in fact 'Mr Manley', a priest trained at Lisbon and ministering to local Catholics. He wished to leave his estate for Catholic use, 'In case the catholique religion come again to be established in England the same should go to Jesus Chappel in Leyland Church', so he left the estate in trust to his housekeeper and confidant, Grace Bold. On her death she left the Leyland Hall estate to relatives, ignoring Robert Charnock's wishes in the matter.

Mr Charnock's 'co-religionists' discussed this and in 1686 a case was brought against the inheritors, which found, 'That Leyland Hall was conveyed to Grace Bold in trust for the support and maintenance of priests in the Romish religion in the county of Lancashire'. The lands were forfeited and confiscated by the state, and ultimately granted 'To the poore vicar of Leyland'.[6] When the house was restored last century a number of 'priest's holes' or hiding places were discovered. Exactly how many tacit understandings between Anglican and Catholic neighbours and friends were carried out without incident will never be known, but several others are to be suspected in the township.

The events of the Civil War also had far-reaching consequences for the people living in the district, who, irrespective of any direct involvement they may have had, obviously suffered at the hands of external military forces. One of the most important leaders on the Parliamentarian side was Edward Robinson of Buckshaw Hall (the neighbour of the Faringtons at Old Worden Hall!), who took a significant part in several actions in the county. During the Commonwealth period he exercised very considerable local authority effectively replacing that of the Faringtons, and on the restoration of the monarchy he was arrested but subsequently released. It has been suggested that he was the author of the *Discourse of the Warr in Lancashire,* one of the main historical sources for the period.

By contrast William Rothwell, the vicar from 1650 to 1675, was driven into hiding by the extreme Puritans and had to endure much hardship and persecution, only resuming his duties at the Restoration. The various confiscations by the military must have greatly disrupted the running of the Farington estate and greatly harmed the livelihood of the tenants. Some idea of the extent of this can be gained from a valuation for the year 1643/4:

> . . . Taken from Littlewood [Ulnes Walton] . . . In oats which did growe there the same yeare upon eight acres of ground and two acres of barley . . . £20-10-0d.
>
> '. . . In the month of August 1644 certain souldiers . . . did take out of ye demayne lands att Worden and Norbrook (Leyland) six oxen, one heifer and one steare value of . . . £24-0-0d.
>
> 'In the same yeare certain troopers under the command of Major Robinson did take out of the demanyne grounds att Penwortham one and twentie steares att three years old valued att . . . £73-10-0d.

In all the crops and animals taken come to £650-0- 0d, lands to £263-0-8d, and rents to £46-0-11d, in all £959-1-7d.[7] The Civil War did not mark the end of these difficulties. Religion and politics remained inextricably linked, and times were very tense during the Glorious Revolution of 1689/90 and the pro-Stuart Jacobite risings of 1715 and 1745. Yet the laws against the diminishing number of local Catholics seem to have been rarely enforced, and only then for motives which often had little to do with religion.

Leyland Grammar School

AMONG the functions of the un-reformed Church in Leyland were the provision of education for the young and assistance to the poor.

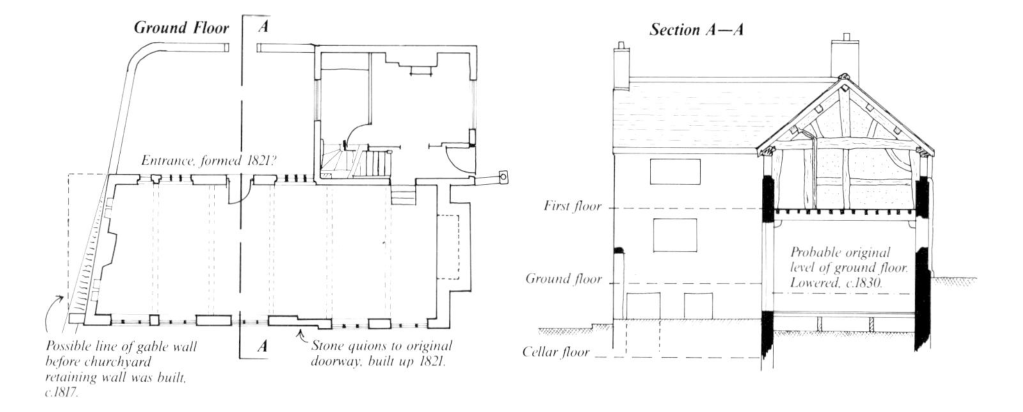

A sketch plan and drawing of the Grammar School, now the town museum, by Peter Barrow. Here we can see the timber-frame construction and the overall layout of the building.

After the Reformation, institutions had to be re-established to provide these services, most notably in the case of the town's grammar school and the almshouses.

In the corner of the Leyland parish churchyard stands one of the most remarkable buildings in the district, the former Leyland Free Grammar School. Now the South Ribble Borough Museum, it was, for two hundred years, the sole educational establishment in Leyland, and is the fourth oldest grammar school in Lancashire. Originally established in the church itself in 1524 the present building was probably erected between 1580 and 1620. Although the exterior is of seventeenth-century hand-made brick, the interior is much older and may be the remains of a timber-framed and largely wooden building. The main feature of the schoolroom is an enormous ingle-nook fireplace and chimney formerly bricked up but exposed during recent restorations.

An extension was added to the original building to house the schoolmaster, erected 'By the liberal contributions of the gentlemen of this parish and others in the year 1790'. Writing in about 1680 Dr. Kuerden described it as 'New re-edified . . . fairly built with brick and hansomly adorned with wyndows'.[8] The entrance to the school was originally from the west, churchyard side, but in 1821 a new east door was provided. Several of the former schoolmasters are buried in the adjoining churchyard.

In 1524, as Sir Henry Farington carefully drew up the deeds for the establishment of his chantry at the parish church, he was perhaps more concerned with the good of his soul than the foundation of the school.[9] Yet when the chantry was abolished in 1546 the school was allowed to continue. Although the salary of the master, Thurston Taylor, was to be reduced from £4-5-9d to £3-17-0d per year in future, it was at least made fairly secure by being paid from the revenues of the Duchy of Lancaster. During the following centuries an endowment to add to the master's wages was built up through bequests - Peter

Leyland Free Grammar School, on the edge of the parish churchyard, c1910.

This photograph clearly reveals the L-shaped plan of the building: to the left is the oldest timber framed part, dating from perhaps as early as 1580, and to the right the Schoolmaster's house added at the end of the eighteenth century. (Leyland Museum).

The Schoolmaster's House c1910.

From the churchyard gate a network of paths formerly extended through the Vicars-fields towards 'Back Lane'. This photograph also shows one of the fine rows of trees for which the churchyard was famous, and the houses on the opposite side of Church Road between Sandy Lane and Balcarres Road removed to make way for a major traffic junction in the mid-1980s. (Leyland Museum).

Procession c1920.

Following the closure of the school in 1876 the building wa used for parish activities, and the schoolmaster's house continued to be inhabited into the 1950s. (Leyland Museum).

To become a car park c1970.
No longer occupied or used, the building had deteriorated considerably by the 1970s. Plans to demolish it to make way for a car park, however, were fought by the local community and following restoration work and re-roofing, the old Grammar School was re-opened in 1977. As the South Ribble Museum and Exhibition Centre, it houses the town's museum. Remarkably, nearly all of the original timber work was intact, a fine inglenook fireplace was discovered and visitors can still see clearly the local staff and daub construction techniques. Opening times, however, are restricted. (Leyland Museum).

Burscough left £100 in 1624, as did Andrew Dandie in 1672 – so that by 1800 interest was available from a fund of £708. From an early date, therefore, incumbents at the old Grammar School were poorly paid.

The list of twenty-two masters from Thurston Taylor to John Westley in 1874 is fairly complete. Throughout the seventeenth century the school prospered, the educational quality of the masters seems to have been very high, and many of them were men of the highest quality.

William Walker, 'Batchelor of Musicke', who died in 1588 and whose celebrated gravestone still survives by the parish church, instructed 'That everie one that is a scoler at Leyland scole at the tyme of my death shall have one halfpenny in silver', whilst Hugh Bonkin (master 1671-81) left a fine description of the school which had 'No bookes save a Dixionary which is Gaudman's workes; which the churchwardens of the Parish of Leyland hath for the use of the schoole'.[10]

In the 145 years from 1716 the school had only three masters, Thomas Moon (sixty years), Edward Marsden (fifty-six) and John James (twenty-nine years). Thomas Moon's gravestone, recently broken up, read,

> In memory of Thomas Moon, a gentleman, who died January 4th, 1776. A man of sound learning, wit and probity. An instructive companion and a sincere friend, to whom a good conscience was more dear than accumulated wealth. He was for sixty-two years an indefatigable schoolmaster, and was sixty years master of the Free Grammar School.
>
> He seldom grieved at worldly loss
> Gold he esteemed as gilded dross
> No change of fortune did destroy
> His peace of mind and heartfelt joy.

From the school generations of scholars went out to make their mark in the world. Among them was Richard Kuerden, whose parents are buried by the church. With Christopher Townley he amassed a great collection of historical documents, which he planned to publish in a five-volume history of the county entitled *Brigantia Lancastriensis Restaurata*. The work was never published but the collection remains an important resource for historians. As a provincial, Kuerden has never been accorded the recognition his efforts merit. He was a scholar prior to his going to Oxford in 1638. Notwithstanding a distinguished academic career and his vast antiquarian interests he maintained close links with the school, for in 1673 he was listed as a 'Governor of the Skoole'. John Woodcock, the Catholic martyr and now saint, was probably also educated here.

The location of the buildings did not lend itself to expansion and it is doubtful if the school ever had more than fifty pupils, probably far fewer; we know, for example, that in 1809 it had only twenty-four and in 1826 thirty pupils. Nor does the structure appear to have been very well maintained by the churchwardens. In 1826 it was in poor repair and extensive work had to be undertaken in 1827-31. After 1865 nothing was done to the building and its poor condition in 1874 was perhaps a factor in the closure of the school.

By this date education in other establishments was available, Samuel Crook's Moss-side school was established in 1770, but of greater significance was the founding of Richard Balshaw's school trust in 1782 which emerged as a well-financed alternative. The infants' school in Fox Lane was built in 1837 at a cost of £300, and a great expansion of local school provision followed the 1870 Education Act.

By the middle of the nineteenth century the grammar school was something of an anachronism, and the suggestion was put forward that it should be merged with Balshaws School. Mr Bryce, Assistant Commissioner of the Enquiry Commission, perhaps hoped to facilitate this by writing a critical, if colourful, description of the school in 1865,

> Leyland, although it gives its name to one of the hundreds of Lancashire, is only an inconsiderable village. It contains a so-called Grammar School, which has, for a long time, been virtually an elementary school. Reading and spelling were not very good, five boys were fair in arithmetic; the head girl could not do . . . an easy sum in the addition of money. Geography and English grammar were poor, the children showing very little intelligence . . . The scholars seem to be socially of a higher class than is commonly found in such a school: of thirty-five present, ten stated to be children of people with independent means, professional men and land stewards, nine tradesmen, eight of farmers, eight of working men.[11]

The children had twenty-seven hours of school time per week, with six weeks' holiday a year, while discipline was maintained by corporal punishment, exercises and detention.

Following the closure of the school the endowment was used to provide 'exhibitions' for deserving scholars at Balshaws School and the building was closed. John Stanning, the local bleacher, purchased it for use by the church as a parish hall, the floor of the schoolroom was lowered to provide greater headroom and the adjoining master's house was sub-let as accommodation.

In the early years of the twentieth century the building was used for choir practices, catechism classes and as a store for May festival props, while the house continued to be occupied into the 1950s. Thereafter no longer used, it fell into disrepair and a prey to vandals: its windows which so pleased Richard Kuerden three hundred years earlier were bricked up in the mid 1960s. By the early 1970s its condition was precarious, but amid fears that it was to be removed to make way for a car park, moves began to effect its preservation. Restoration was undertaken through the Jobs Creation Scheme, and in December 1978 it was reopened by the Mayor, Jack Marsden, as the museum and exhibition centre for the South Ribble Borough, and it entered the third phase of its life. In March 1989 the centre had its 50,000th visitor.

The schoolroom where Hugh Bonkin and Thomas Moon sweated the principles of Latin grammar into the sons of the local gentry and yeomen now displays monthly exhibitions of artwork by local people, though the grooves worn in the stone fireplace by the sharpening of generations of slate pencils can still be seen, and many pupils have succeeded in boring their initials on the ceiling beams. The small timbered-framed staff and daub-walled rooms above the classroom house the borough's museum collection begun by its first curator, Mrs May Knowles, which is a popular objective for the many groups of local schoolchildren who annually visit the centre. Thus Leyland still possesses one of the finest surviving examples of a Tudor timber-framed grammar school in the country, and one that still fulfills a function well in keeping with the intent of its founder almost five hundred years ago.

The Farington Almshouses

THE Farington almshouses provide another link with the turbulent times following the Reformation. The original houses stood at Seven

The Farington Alms Houses c1905.

Originally located at Seven Stars, the houses were rebuilt in Fox Lane in 1849, on a site nearer to the church. In the foreground can be seen the original narrow track that was Fox Lane prior to road widening. The development of the Church Road to Fox Lane through-route was an important consequence of motorised transport, altering the balance of the town's plan, and accounting for the difficult transit around Leyland cross. Since previously the main route at the cross had been north-south along Worden Lane and Towngate, the roads here were never intended as a crossroads, and do not literally form one. (Leyland Museum).

Stars on Leyland Lane, and are known to have had an inscription 'Will Farington, Worden 1607',[12] which is now preserved in the museum. In 1849 the houses were rebuilt on their present site near the top of the lane. The exact origins of the almshouses are now obscure. They appear to have been re-established on several occasions, but perhaps the most important benefaction was that of 1661, when William Farington provided for six houses, allowing the inhabitants £6 per year and new gowns worth twenty shillings every third year. The rent from fourteen acres of land at Old Worden was used for their upkeep, and the almspeople received ten shillings every Good Friday and St. Thomas's day and four loads of turf annually. To be eligible they had to be born in Leyland, be regular attendants at the parish church, and to wear the letters W.F. on their coats. Proving 'distasteful to the inmates' the latter was dispensed with in 1781.

Susan Maria Farington seems to have taken a close interest in the running of the houses and has left a vivid description of them: and the various duties the almspeople were obliged to perform.

> They must actually reside in the houses, must keep them clean and neat, and take their share in keeping the garden tidy, and they are expected to live in peace and goodwill with each other. They are removeable for misconduct or if wholly unable to take care of themselves or to find anyone to take care of them, in this case the workhouse is the remedy. They are nominated by the founder's representative, by whom, from time to time, bye-laws are made. We find that it does not answer to make the almshouses too much of an infirmary . . . very deaf or great invalids are very inconvenient, as they are a perpetual burden on the other inmates.

By this time, the middle 1860s, the inmates, who were mostly former handloom weavers, were allowed three shillings per week, the dark blue gowns, coals instead of turf, and vegetable seeds for the garden. And in addition, 'Besides the coals we have given them for some years a meat pie at Christmas, and seed for their gardens, and occasionally once in two or three years they come to the hall for tea.'[13]

Chapter Five

Progress in farming
The later Faringtons of Worden

OLLOWING the death of William Farington 'The Royalist' in 1658 the succession of the family, though complicated, calls for little comment. The income of his son William 'Captain' Farington (1612-73), who had shared the tribulations of the Civil War with him, was estimated at a healthy £1,000 per year in 1660. Towards the end of the century the family again became enmeshed in national politics, this time as supporters of the Jacobite cause. Captain Farington split the estate between his two sons, Henry, the eldest, at Worden, and George at Shaw Hall. Although this practice was fairly widespread in the North at this time, Susan Maria Farington later commented; 'This plan of giving younger sons large shares of property as their fortune was not to be commended and if continued would have made mere yeomen of us all'.[1]

George Farington and his son William (1675-1718) were all staunch Jacobites, supporters of the Catholic James II. The 'Mock Corporation' of Walton-le-Dale, which met at the Unicorn Inn in Walton, was ostensibly a drinking club parodying the Corporation of Preston but, in fact, had strong Jacobite leanings. A number of important national figures were members, including the Earl of Derwentwater, who was executed for his part in the 1715 uprising.

Meetings were marked by great formality; the list of court officials was very long, with the honourable offices of 'champion', 'poet laureate', 'jester', 'custard eater' and 'slut kisser' etc. The first holder of the high office of mayor in 1701 was William Farington of Shaw Hall. He subsequently held the office in 1708 and also served as bailiff (1702) and mace bearer (1704). His cousin William of Worden was less illustrious, being 'house groper' (1702) and 'huntsman' (1706-14), though briefly elevated to 'master of hounds' in 1709. Another member of the family, Dr. Valentine Farington, was 'physician' (1704-11) and mayor in 1712.[2]

The Catholic interest in the family again appears to have been strong at this time. Henry's eldest son who had died both young and

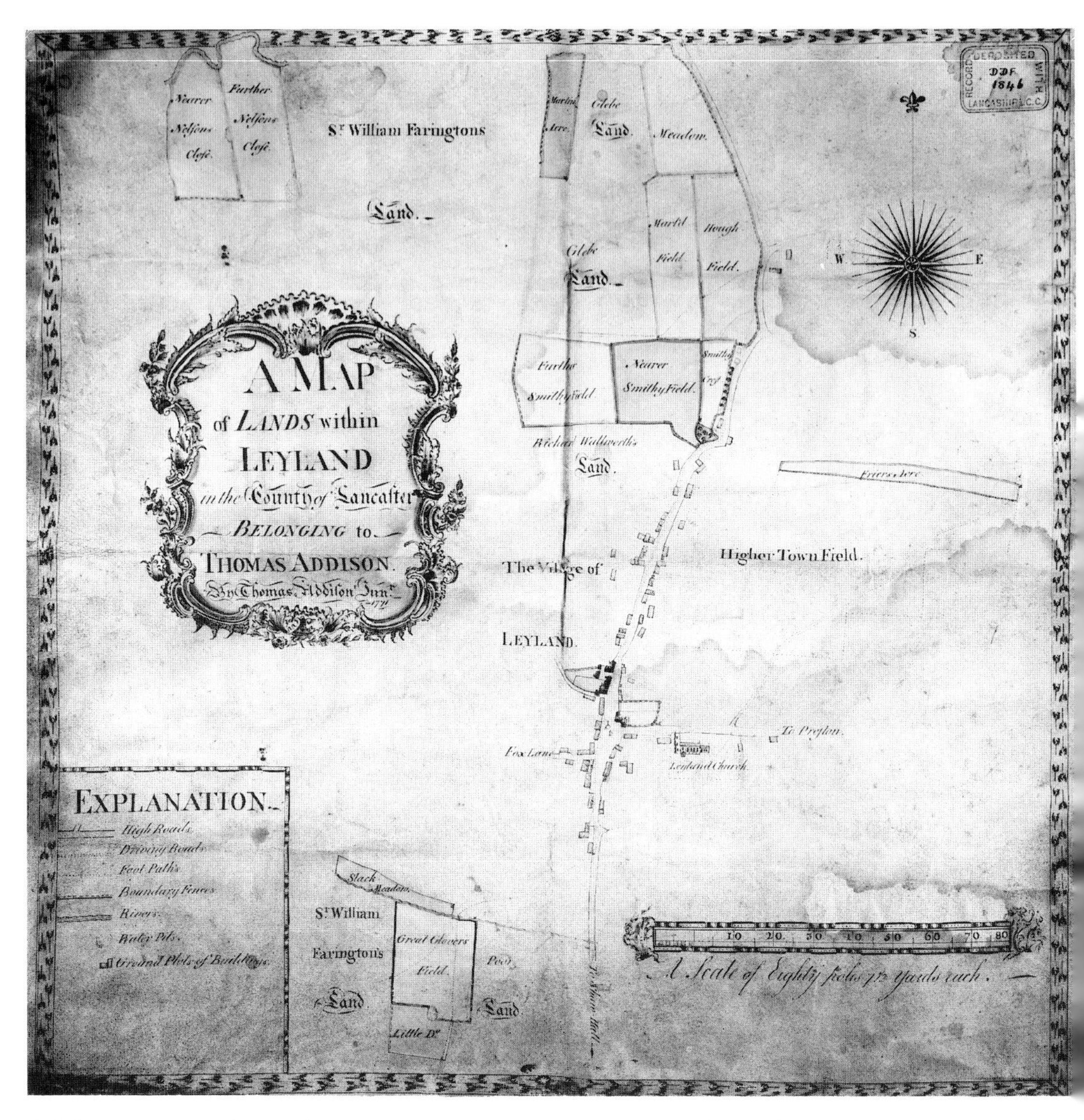

Map of Leyland by Thomas Addison 1771.

One of two surviving maps drawn by Addison. Leyland remained a small rural farming centre straddling Towngate, between the Upper and Lower Townfields. The map shows the family holdings in the townships, and of particular interest is the solitary field strip owned by them in the Higher Townfield.

childless was married to Agnes Dicconson. Susan Maria Farington's judgement of this liaison is to the point, 'The Dicconsons were Roman Catholics, but their strongly Jacobite principles would, I suppose, endear them to the Faringtons. We have no proof that she became a Protestant . . . and considering the weight of a mother's influence, it is a blessing she was childless, or her descendants might possibly have lapsed into popery again'.[3] How closely members of the family were involved in the occupation by, and defeat of, the Scottish Jacobites at Preston in 1715 is obscure, but they appear to have taken no part in the Young Pretender's march south through the township a generation later in 1745.

With comparitively dangerous political leanings and the division of the family estate, the Farington inheritance passed through a

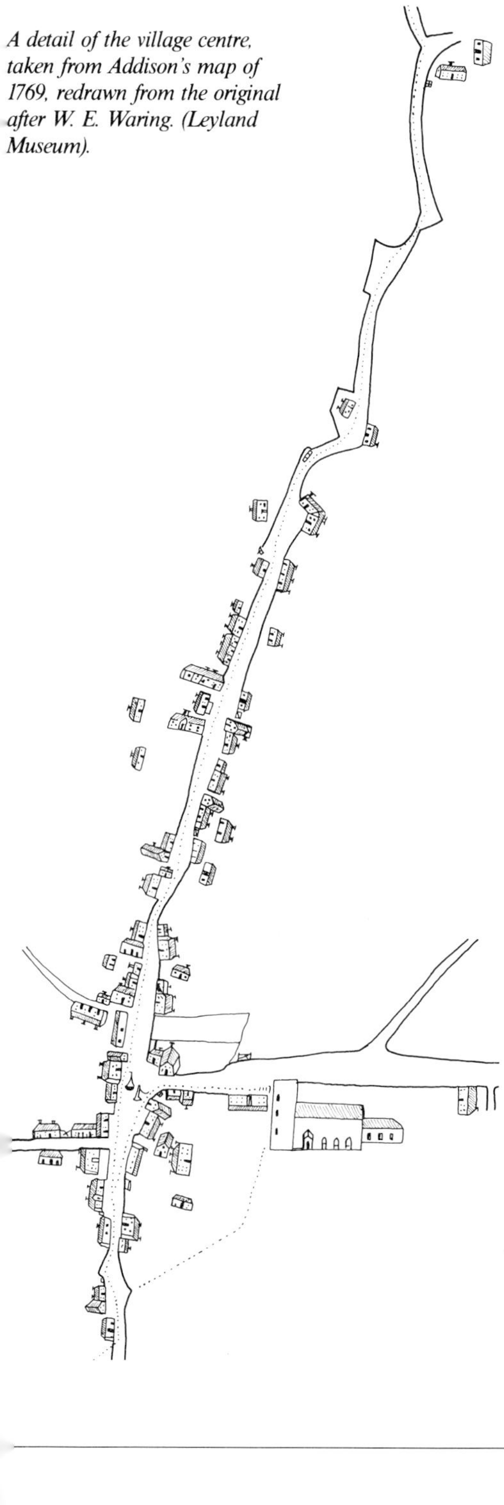

A detail of the village centre, taken from Addison's map of 1769, redrawn from the original after W. E. Waring. (Leyland Museum).

potentially dangerous phase at the end of the seventeenth and early in the eighteenth century. In the event Henry's heirs died childless, and the estates passed to his brother George's family. Shaw Hall and Walton Mains were restored to the estate, and since George's family had lived at the former, it was Shaw Hall and not Worden that was henceforth the family home.

George's grandson, another George Farington (1697-1742), began to dismantle Old Worden, which now became little more than a farmhouse, and its fine timber panelling was removed to the 'Oak Room' at Shaw Hall. At the time of his death in 1742 George Farington's property was estimated to be worth £1,500 per annum. Susan Maria Farington has left a colourful description of him:

> George was a most respectable country gentleman . . . he was addicted to field sports and was much valued by his circle of acquaintances . . . His large family pressed on his by no means large income, and he lived bitterly to repent the sale of Pennington, his wife's inheritance, though he probably never knew what mineral wealth he threw away in the valuable coal which lay beneath the green fields of which, alone he thought.[4]

George Farington's lasting importance in the local history of Leyland lies in the great series of maps of his estates which he caused to be produced. 'A survey of the Manours of Norbrooke, Worden, Shawe Hall, Littlewood with the Lordships of Leyland, Ulnes Walton, Penwortham. Walton-le-Dale estate. Belonging to George Farington of Shaw Hall . . . By Henry Bankes of Winwick, Writing Master A.D. 1725'.[5] This provides a clear outline of the estates and a guide to the size of the landholdings. Taken in conjunction with Addison's map of 1769 and the tithe survey of 1838, it provides materials for a very detailed analysis of the township, as well as containing the earliest, and some of the most intereting, maps of Leyland.

The estate in 1725

THE Farington estate in 1725 comprised about 3,500 acres, with 1,800 in Leyland, 800 in Ulnes Walton, 800 in Penwortham, sixty in Walton-le-

Dale ('The Mains') and sixty in Euxton ('Alker').[6] Landholdings in Ulnes Walton and Penwortham were clearly very important, and Littlewood and Crookings Farm rivalled Worden itself in size. The typical farm was fairly small - forty-nine holdings were under ten acres, twenty-five of ten to thirty acres, and just ten of over thirty acres. By contrast five large farms accounted for over 700 acres in Leyland; in addition to Mrs Armestridings (fifty-eight ac.) and Athertons (sixty-five acres), the three largest farms were the old medieval 'demesnes' of Worden (382 acres), Shaw Hall (125 acres) and Northbrook (eighty-four ac.). Though the centre of family affairs had shifted to Shaw Hall, Worden thus remained the most important property, and of 1,800 acres in Leyland just under half was farmed in comparatively large units - a critical factor in estate finances.

In his *General View of the Agriculture of the County of Lancashire*, published in 1792, John Holt noted the general situation: although few common fields remained, both the resulting enclosures and the average holdings were too small, factors he considered largely to blame for the general backwardness of agriculture. In spite of the efforts of the improving landlords, the introduction of root crops and improved grasses spread slowly, though potatoes were grown as early as the late-seventeenth century. Cereals were extensively grown, both wheat and barley, but cattle were particularly important on the grasslands around Preston, and cheese making was an important local occupation. William Atherton's farm on Back Lane, Leyland, (Langdale Road), may be taken as illustrative of a relatively large local holding by contemporary standards. In addition to a house, outhouses, orchard and vegetable garden the farm comprised:[7]

Field	*Acre value in 1746*	*Acre value in c. 1800*
Calfcroft	?	110/-
Nearer Pinders Croft	45/-	110/-
Further Pinders Croft	30/-	80/-
Barn Meadow and Jewel Croft	50/-	130/-
Wheatearth and Fox Hole	28/-	100/-
Broom Field	30/-	70/-
Hill	25/-	100/-
Long Croft	45/-	120/-
Barn Field	30/-	90/-
Long Shoot	28/-	?
How Wood	20/-	?
Three Acre	25/-	?
Rent	**£43-16-0d**	**£97-17-7d**

In addition, William Atherton also rented an adjacent holding, 'Youngs', which added a further 12 acres. From subsequent leases it is possible to estimate the changing value of the rent, which more than doubled between 1746 and around 1800.

The mid-eighteenth century, when George's son William (1720-81) inherited the estate, was a period of innovation and change, but old customs continued. For example the 1725 Map of Ulnes Walton is marked 'N.B. that the worshipfull George Farington Esq. hath as

The Gallery at Worden c1900. The Gallery housed antiques purchased by Sir William on his 'Grand Tour'. In addition, he took great pains to develop the pleasure grounds and park around the house, which, further improved by James Nowell Farington in the 1840s, ultimately became Worden Park and as such were opened to the public in 1951. (Leyland Museum).

much land within Hugh Charnock's land as a workman can mow in one swath'.[8] Although rents were largely paid in money, service dues (the number of days the tenant had to work for the land, ditching, reaping etc.) were listed as late as 1730, and tenancies were still taken out, not for a specified number of years, but, according to the ancient custom, for particular people's lifetimes.[9] William Atherton's lease of 1742 was for just one life, that of his daughter, Johanna, then aged twenty-four. John Balshaw of Golden Hill acquired a lease for two lives, Adam Balshaw, aged six and John Balshaw, aged four. Clearly the younger the lines the longer security the tenant had. James Calderbank, landlord at the 'Sign of the Rose' ('Rose-Whittles'), had a lease of Whittles Farm in 1729 for three lives, but by 1746, two of them had died. More typical of the smaller holdings was that of William Rigby, which comprised:[10]

	£ per year
House, outhousing, folds and intack, garden, orchard	3–10–0d
Barnfield, 2 acres	4– 0–0d
Meadow, 1 acre	2–16–½d

for two lives, William, his son (aged 36) and Thomas Croston, his grandson (aged 12).[11]

The remainder of the century was a period of rising prices, which must have meant hardship for the tenants. At the time of William Farington's inheritance the annual rentals per acre in Leyland ranged from 25s to 60s, with townfield strips worth 26-30s, new moss ground 25-30s, woodland 20s, and with the majority of fields in the range 40-

Shaw Hall (print) prior to rebuilding in the 1840s.

To the left may be seen the gallery built by Sir William Farington in the latter half of the eighteenth century, adjoining the much older house to the right.

50s. By 1800, spurred on by the Napoleonic Wars, inflation and rising urban demand, prices were much higher, 50-100s per acre, and strips on the lower townfield for example were now worth sixty shillings.[12]

William Farington's income, like his father's before him, thus came from a small number of medium-sized farms and a large number of very small ones. Through his portraits, journals, letters and cash books he is today one of the best-known members of the family. 'He liked great people all his life, and in his friendships with men of his own position, thorough gentlemanliness and good character seem always to be essential points with him'.[13] A knight and sheriff of Lancashire, he continued his father's work of enlarging and embellishing Shaw Hall, adding a gallery to house the classical antiques he brought back from his Grand Tour in 1765, and laying out gardens and temples along the Shaw Brook. In his time Shaw Hall became one of the showhouses of the county, as the surviving visitors' book makes clear, and the cultivated centre of an eighteenth-century gentleman's estate.

Amid these pleasures, however, there can be little doubt that a considerable amount of Sir William's time was taken up by estate matters, which at this time meant the affairs of much of Leyland. This is made clear by the detailed cashbooks in his own hand which have survived. The household cash book (1744-80)[14] reveals that apart from the final decade of his life his household was run at a cost of £200-£250 per year, perhaps not a large sum since his father had planned to retire on £340 per annum in 1742. Several entries provide colourful insights into his domestic affairs and the luxuries he allowed himself:

28 April, 1744:	Paid to Will. Thornley, his ¼ year's wage	£1- 2- 6d
18 June 1744:	Mrs Chorley for a gallon of rum	10/-
	Mrs Chew for a pound of chocolate	4/6d
4 March 1754:	To Mr Baldwin for 6lbs of caviar	13/-
23 April 1756:	To Christopher for a pound of green tea	16/-
23 November 1765:	To my brother, Slater, for a Hogshead of Port	£17-11- 0d
12 November 1767:	836 Baskets of Standish coals	£8-14- 0d
28 December 1769:	To Mr Willson for 60lbs of butter @ 6½d a lb	£1-12- 6d

His great estate cash book, of receipts and debits for the years 1742-73,[15] is a major historical record of the agricultural affairs of the township in the early years of its transformation by the development of the textile industry. Farm rents were paid half yearly, and accordingly the finances of the estate were balanced by bonds and loans, and occasional land sales or purchases. For example, in January 1747, Sir William received £2,600 for lands in Ulnes Walton; this was immediately paid to Sir Thomas Booth 'In full of his mortgage of £2,500 and interest of £100' Under his father's will he also had to make payments to his brothers and sisters, '25th September 1753. Received from Mr Grimshaw a bond to discharge the whole principal of Brother Henry's fortune and part of Brother James, £250'. The half yearly 'small' rents paid at Michaelmas 1743 were worth £212-17-2d, Worden was worth half yearly £85 in 1753 rising to £100 in 1773, Littlewood £125 in 1754 and £152-10-0d in 1772, whilst Northbrook was worth £43 in 1772, fishing rights £120 and the Leyland Corn Mill and farm £10-2-6d.

The list of 'out' payments supplements the details in the household cash book, recording such items as doctors' bills for the servants, presents for their children ('24/Dec/1757. What I gave Addison's little boys for New Years Gifts amongst them 4/6d'), the Window Tax (£4-16-0d), presents of cheese to the tenantry ('24/Dec/1761. To Ellis Sumner for 567lbs of cheese, £6-5-0d'); even the gift of one shilling for the chimneysweep's boy. Of special interest are references to wages paid and work done on the house and gardens, some of which can still be identified today:

23 December 1749:	To James Leyland for 147 days labouring @ 10d per day	£1–19– 2d
23 March 1753:	To Ralph Barton for teaching a dogg 18 days at 1/– a day	18/–
22 September 1755:	To Wm Rigby and Thos Allanson for spade-work about the waterfalls	£1–17– 6d
26 September 1757:	To Thos Seed and Ralph Fish for building my Triumphal Arch	£2– 5– 0d
17 August 1763:	To John Balshaw 4/– for the bells for the Chinese House	4/–

Sir William died, a bachelor, in 1781, and was succeeded by his brother James (1733-1800), and ultimately by his nephew William Farington (1766-1837). It would appear that James Farington was something of a disappointment to the family, as Susan Maria Farington recorded.

> Our Grandfather was decidedly the black sheep of his generation . . . he married the respectable widow of an innkeeper, who happily died soon and left no family . . . he then ran off to Scotland with Miss Nowell, the only daughter and heiress of Roger Nowell of Altham . . . she was worthy of a better husband if she had not vexed her parents by eloping with the handsome captain . . . he sank into a low, sporting and drinking sort of a fellow . . . and although his companions were not always gentlemanly, he could, no doubt, be gentlemanly enough when the occasion suited him.[16]

His son William (1766-1837) was kept away from bad influences by his grandparents, and took over the running of the estate in 1787, by which time it seems to have become neglected and in need of repairs and attention.

Agricultural improvement

WILLIAM Farington was sheriff of the county in 1813 and was keenly interested in agricultural improvement. The early years of the nineteenth century were a period of major changes in the economy of Leyland, with the development of the handloom weaving industry and agricultural prosperity engendered by high prices during the Napoleonic Wars. The tithe survey undertaken in the year of his death, 1837, and 'published' in 1838 provides a very detailed account of his estate, as well as revealing something of the developments following the survey of 1725. Tithes were the contentious and irksome payment which every householder was obliged to pay for the upkeep of the Church. Reckoned at one tenth of a farmer's produce, these payments

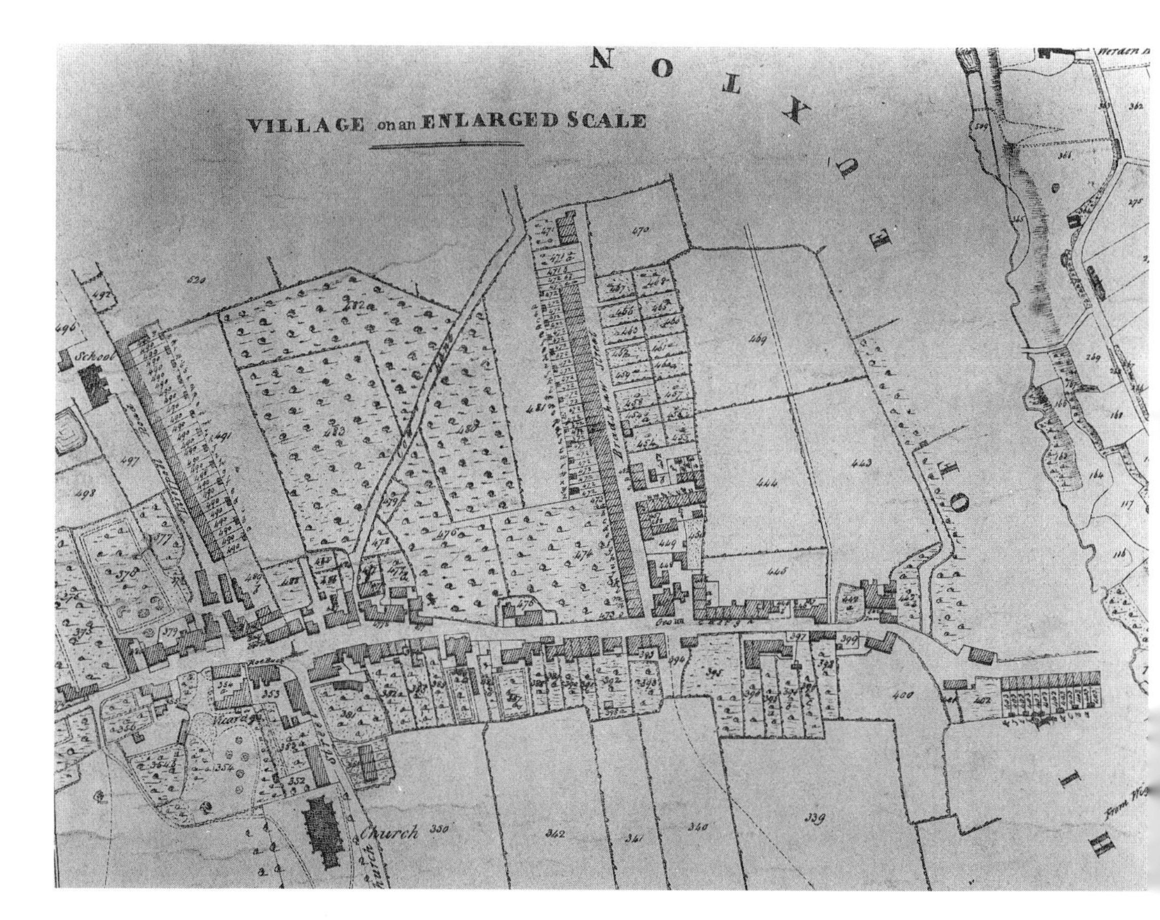

were usually made in kind and stored in a tithebarn (Leyland's one stood close by the parish church). When tithes were eventually commuted into cash payments, maps were drawn up to show each person's liability. These maps remain a very important source of information, especially when compared with the 1841 census.

Leyland township was estimated to contain 3,533 statute acres, and tithes were payable on 3,143: 943 acres were arable land, 2,200 meadow or pasture land, and no tithes were payable from the remaining 371 acres of uncultivated moss and nineteen acres of woodland.[17] Of the 3,500 acres of the township, 2,600 (74%) were owned by fourteen landowners, of whom James Nowell Farington was by far the largest, owning 1,369 acres (39%). J. Mitchell esq. owned 286 acres, Hugh Dawson 150 acres, Robert Snell 120 acres, and the vicar, the Rev. Gardnor Baldwin, 104 acres, including forty-four acres of church glebe; the remaining landowners each owned less than one hundred acres.

Left: The Leyland Tithe Map 1838. Extract of centre. Although a much consolidated pattern of field strips is still clearly apparent, particularly to the east of Towngate, the development of the local weaving industry had clearly transformed the social structure of the town centre in the first decades of the nineteenth century. This map also illustrates the large number of gardens which so impressed visitors. Between 1790 and 1820 a rural farming community had transformed itself into a bustling weaving and textile finishing centre which may might well have grown to a considerable extent if the Leeds and Liverpool Canal had been routed through the town as its proposers originally intended. Since each loomshop may have held up to four looms, the town's textile output, even on a weekly basis, must have been considerable. Tithe and survey maps are an important aid to local historians since they indicate each landholding and house, with details of the tenants, field size, crop and field name, for most parishes in England. The local examples are available for inspection in the Lancashire Record Office, whilst the Leyland map is also available in the Local History Centre at Leyland Library. (Leyland Museum).

The size of the Farington estate in Leyland was thus considerably reduced from what it had been in 1725 by the sale of quite significant holdings, particularly within the arc of the Longmeanygate at Moss-side. To some extent these losses had been made good by subsequent enclosure beyond the Longmeanygate, whilst the holdings away from the moss had been consolidated and were much more compact.

Land sales had been undertaken in such a fashion as to leave the larger farms intact, and smaller holdings had been disposed of. Out of the forty-nine holdings of under ten acres in 1725, only twenty-five remained, but the large units remained. Old Worden had been split into two farms, of 164 and 173 acres, the Shaw Hall estate had been enlarged slightly, and a holding of fifty-two acres held by William Moore had been created by amalgamating pieces of the moss. Thus, notwithstanding a net loss of 450 acres in Leyland, the area of land in the 'large' farms remained more or less the same (704 acres in 1837, 714 in 1725). Overall, almost a third of the township was in farm units of over fifty acres, and there were eighty-three farms of over twenty acres. Despite the emergence of the local cotton industry, Leyland thus remained a largely agricultural district: 'A lovely, green-swarded and rurally situated spot'.[18]

The medium-sized and larger farms were essentially self-contained units, with areas of arable for cereal growing, and pasture and meadow for cattle. Under the influence of steadily increasing demand from the neighbouring industrial towns, particularly Preston, clear progress had been made, with extended land drainage, and improved crops and the introduction of new breeds of animals. The pattern of small family-run farms, with dairying and cheese production, was to remain familiar well into the twentieth century, when the very smallness of the farms which had so aroused the criticism of the agricultural improvers was to aid their survival through the disastrous depression of the 1930s.

An important agent of agricultural innovation in the nineteenth century was the 'Leyland Hundred Agricultural and Horticultural Society'. In September 1847 the *Preston Pilot* newspaper informed its readers, 'The collections of horticultural and other productions exhibited at the Leyland meeting may be properly said to be unrivalled by those of any other society'.[19] Prizes were awarded for a variety of categories of produce and animals, and improved types of machinery – much of it locally-made – exhibited. The event was usually given considerable prominence in the local press. 'Next came the stand laden with the most luscious of fruits, grapes, melons, peaches, pines, apples, peas etc., etc., and calling forth the exclamation, 'Did you ever see the like!. The 'squeeze' round this portion of the exhibition was sometimes too much for crinoline, and some of the ladies' dresses went into rather smaller compass than when the fair wearers entered the room'.[20]

William Farington and his son took an important lead in these affairs, and James Nowell's estate was described in the Report of the Royal Agricultural Society as 'A good example of what might be done by perseverance and skill, combined with a liberal and judicious outlay of capital.'[21] Such improvements could not be achieved without considerable cost, and the drive for greater efficiency and mechanisation led to a reduction in the number of farm labourers required. The repeal of the Corn Laws in 1846, allowing tariff-free importation of cereals from abroad, strengthened these tendencies. At the Leyland agricultural meeting of 1847 amid the usual junketings, the vicar, Mr Baldwin, proposed a toast to 'The Agricultural Labourer' since, 'That individual was now in a very different position from the one in which he was formerly placed, but let him not be cast out as useless to society'.[22]

The twin themes, of the drive to greater farm efficiency and the drift of labourers from work on the land, dominate the agricultural history of the nineteenth century. In 1855 Jonathan Swann won the prize at the Leyland show for the best cultivated farm. On his holding along the north side of Fox Lane and Leyland Lane, 'He has fourteen acres of wheat, twelve acres of potatoes, two acres of beans, two acres of turnips, one acre of vetches, three of old meadow, one acre of gardens, orchards etc. An excellent dairy cheese is made on the farm.' In 1858 Thomas Strickland of Crookings Farm, Penwortham, a very large farm of 210 acres, was commended for the large amount of fertilizer, imported guano, night soil etc. used on his fields.[23]

In the face of increasing underemployment in the countryside from the 1780s onwards, large numbers of labourers and smallholders began to supplement their income through weaving at home on the handloom. Few of the 147 landholdings of between one and twenty acres listed in the tithe survey can have provided much of a living from farming alone, whilst many of the remaining 402 holdings of under one acre were in fact occupied by handloom weavers. As we shall see, weaving thus became an important element in the town's essentially rural economy, and was to remain so in the Leyland Hundred well into the second half of the nineteenth century.

James Nowell Farington

JAMES Nowell Farington (1813-1848) thus had a very considerable

Mr and Mrs Edmund Farington at Worden c1908. (Leyland Museum).

Front of Worden Hall c1920. This view clearly shows the stark if regular lines imposed on the building by the architect Anthony Salvin during the reconstruction of the 1840s. (Leyland Library).

inheritance for a young man of twenty-four, and also had clear ideas as to how his estate might be further improved, 'As a landlord he was in high repute: and considering the interests of his tenants identified with his own, he spared neither pains nor expense in improving his estates and adding to the comfort as well as the resources of the occupiers of the soil'.[24]

Shaw Hall was shortly afterwards discovered to be in a precarious state due to dry rot, and an extensive and expensive programme of rebuilding was embarked upon. Anthony Salvin, a noted architect of the day, was engaged to rebuild the hall and lay out the gardens and maze, and between 1840 and 1845 over £12,000 was spent. The old house was demolished, leaving only Sir William Farington's Grecian gallery, the 'Derby Wing' built by George Farington earlier in the eighteenth century and various farm buildings. To the great confusion of all ever since, it was decided to rename Shaw Hall 'Worden Hall', in honour of the old family seat. The original Worden was, by this time, merely a farmhouse, and was subsequently referred to as 'Old Worden'.[25]

It was perhaps just as well that in 1847 James Nowell married an heiress, Sarah Esther Touchet, an event marked by celebrations which have perhaps only ever been exceeded in Leyland by the 1951 Festival of Britain. The wedding was one of the great county events of the year, and the celebrations spread over three days. On the wedding day itself (a Thursday) sports were held on the vicar's field, and the list of events included an ascent by balloon. A grand dinner at the Union Hall ended with toasts to 'Worden – root and branch', followed by a ball which was attended by six hundred people. On the Friday the local schools organised an enormous 'Children's Treat', for almost 1,500 pupils, and the following day meat left over from an ox roast, together with suitable liquid refreshments formed a repast for the 237 poor of the township. Mr Morrell, steward of the estate and one of the organisers, wrote to the young squire on his honeymoon informing him of the success of these events.

Mary Hannah Farington. A gifted natural scientist, Mary Hannah accumulated a renowned collection of sea shells in the Worden Hall Museum. Both the sisters of James Nowell Farington were, therefore, essentially ladies well ahead of their time, excelling in fields which in Victorian England were still the preserve of men. (Leyland Library).

> It was really thought by the oldest inhabitants in the village that there never were so many people in Leyland at once before, it was crowded over to excess, we compared it to Preston Guild . . . the people say they would be glad if Squire Farington would be married every year. On the Saturday . . . the fireworks and lamps were splendid . . . the village was literally all of a blazing light by the illumination from the windows, for everyone appeared to enjoy the thing and desired to pay a compliment to Mr and Mrs Farington. There was scarcely a respectable house in Leyland that had not friends either from Liverpool, Manchester, Bolton, Preston or other distant towns. Your tenantry enjoyed it much, for all attended . . . all was conducted in a manner much like you wished it, no drunkenness, no quarrelling or other disagreeable work, to be seen or heard.[26]

Dogged by poor health all his life, James Nowell died just eight months later, to be succeeded at Worden by his widow and two sisters, Mary Hannah, who was a gifted natural scientist, and Susan Maria, a much-respected historian. In their lifetimes the traditions of the estate, the manor courts and so on, were maintained. Susan Maria soon proved herself to be a formidable administrator of the estate, as well as exerting considerable influence on Leyland affairs, the church, local charities and the Local Board (the predecessor of the Leyland Urban District Council). The last surviving member of the main Farington line, Susan Maria did more than most, through her extensive historical researches, to perpetuate their memory.

The church of St. James at Moss-side was built in memory of their brother with money donated by his widow, a school was built, and both sisters played important parts in organising relief for the unemployed factory workers during the Cotton Famine. On Susan Maria's death at the age of 85 in 1894 the main line of the family came to an end. 'She was a wonderful woman, clever, capable and good; beloved in her home and village. Her whole heart and soul was given to Worden and its well-being. She survived her sister, Mary Hannah,

Susan Maria Farington.
The last surviving member of the main line of the Faringtons of Worden, Susan Maria was a much respected historian and a shrewd administrator of the family estate. (Leyland Library).

by eight years, and left a will arranging as far as she could that the beloved estate should always be owned by a Farington'.[27]

On her death the estate passed to an eight-year-old boy, William Edmund Farington, of the Isle of Wight branch of the family. When twenty-one he married and the young couple moved into Worden Hall amid celebrations not seen since James Nowell's wedding. He died the following year (1908), followed by his wife shortly after. The estate then passed to the Wigan branch of the family, and from 1910 to 1947 Henry Nowell Farington was squire at Worden.

Remembered as 'The Last Squire', Henry Nowell was a solicitor and noted meteorologist, and had the public-spirited foresight to place the enormous and irreplaceable family and estate archive with the Lancashire Record Office. His lifetime saw the acceleration of the breaking-up of the Leyland estate after the First World War and the fire at the hall in 1941 which was eventually to lead to its demolition. Shortly after his death a public auction was held in the remains of the hall and a treasure-trove of furniture, paintings and heirlooms was dispersed. An artistic and historical heritage accumulated over centuries was thus lost to the town, representing perhaps the greatest cultural disaster in its history.[28] The estate passed to the present Sir Henry Farrington, of Somerset, who in 1951 sold the remains of the hall and the park to the Leyland Urban District Council.

It thus fell to Councillor Frank Marsden, as Chairman of the Council, to open the park to the public in 1951, and so herald in the post-war history of Worden and Leyland. Extensively re-developed in recent years, the remaining buildings house an arts centre and the local branch of the Council for the Protection of Rural England. The surrounding park, effectively saved from post-war building schemes, is maintained to the highest standards by the parks department of South Ribble Borough Council, providing a leisure resource of great beauty and inestimable value for ever.

Chapter Six

The handloom weavers of Leyland

ODAY Leyland is closely associated with the motor industry, and the importance of textiles as the spearhead of the town's industrial revolution is largely forgotten. In the half century from 1790 to 1840, however, nearly all the houses apart from those of the well-to-do had at least one resident handloom weaver. In addition, four specially-built rows of step-houses had been constructed, probably in the period 1802-10, each with a loomshop in the basement and with plenty of large windows to admit as much natural light as possible. These rows comprised Union Street (the surviving houses at the top of Fox Lane), Bradshaw Street (now Spring Gardens, demolished), Water Street (on Towngate, sometimes called Finch's houses, demolished), and Heaton Street (on Golden Hill Lane at Earnshaw Bridge).

In addition the town had warehouses - including one belonging to Horrockses - bleachworks, and a rising class of 'manufacturers'. With the coming of the railway the very large mill at Farington was built. Mills also developed along Leyland Lane, and finally, in the 1870s, Brook Mill was opened. Handloom weaving continued for a surprisingly long period and the textile industry remained a mainstay of the local economy throughout the nineteenth century, despite the effects of the Lancashire Cotton Famine, and was to remain an important local employer into the 1960s. The textile industry thus profoundly shaped the town's fortunes for over two hundred years.

The growth of the population of Leyland parallels the rise of the weaving industry; from a level of perhaps 1,000 people in 1700 it had doubled by 1801, the year of the first national census:

Year	Population	Increase	Increase as %
1801	2,088		
1811	2,646	558	27%
1821	3,173	527	20%
1831	3,404	231	7%
1841	3,569	165	4.8%
1851	3,617	48	1.3%

Right: 6" Ordnance Survey Map, Leyland c1840.

Although the railway had been recently completed, in 1838, this extract provides a clear picture of Leyland before the development of the local cotton mills and the industrial zone at the eastern end of Golden Hill Lane, and most of the fields mapped by the 1725 survey are still familiar. The rows of weavers' houses can clearly be identified, as can the sites of the town's two bleachworks at Northbrook and Shruggs.

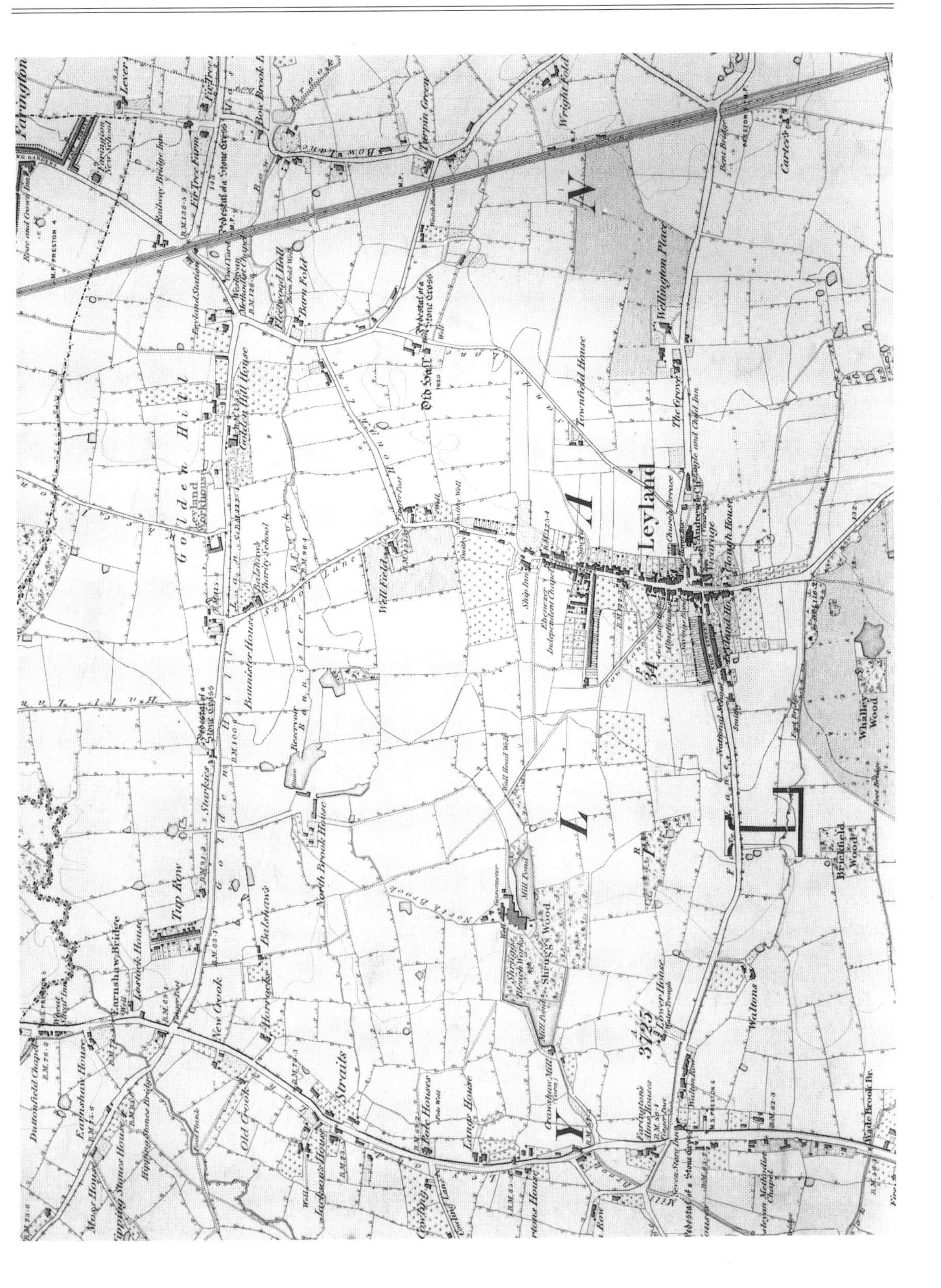
Farington
Leyland
Golden Hill
Golden Hill House
Leyland Workhouse
Townfield House
The Grove
Wellington Place
Old Hall
Well Field
School Lane
Balshaw's Charity School
Bannister House
North Brook House
Reservoir
Tip Row
Starkies
New Crook
Horrocks
Balshaws
Old Crook
Straits
Earnshaw House
Earnshaw Bridge
Duttonfield Chapel
Lower House
Shruggs Wood
Shruggs Bleach Works
Mill Pond
North Brook
Waltons
Whalley Wood
Brickfield Wood
National School
Ship Inn
Ebenezer Independent Chapel
Church Terrace
Rough House
Eagle and Child Inn
Carter's
Bent Bridge
Turpin Green
Wright Fold
Bow Lane
Fir Tree Farm
Railway Bridge Inn
Leyland Station
Barn Fold
Lane House
Pole Houses
Jacksons House
Moss House
Wade Brook Br.

The censuses show that Leyland was growing spectacularly in the first decades of the nineteenth century, particularly in the years 1801-10, when Union Street and Bradshaw Street were built. Between 1800 and 1830 - the highwater mark of the handloom industry - the population of the town increased by over a half. Thereafter the rate of growth slackened until the 1870s, when it again exceeded 25% per decade, as Leyland embarked on the second phase of its industrial development.

Although the construction of the great rows of loomshop-houses greatly altered its social complexion, the town centre remained a very compact place, a loose ribbon of houses linking the cross and Water Street along Towngate and still surrounded by fields of medieval date. Away from the centre, cottages straggled along Leyland Lane, the moss-lanes, Bow Lane and Turpin Green. These changes were therefore firmly rooted in the countryside. After 1850 new centres of development began to emerge around the railway station, Seven Stars and Earnshaw Bridge.

Early textile production in Leyland

TEXTILES were an important local industry from the earliest times, and Preston, Bolton and Blackburn had emerged as centres during the Middle Ages. The tools and raw materials used in the spinning and weaving of flax and wool are frequently mentioned in the wills of Leyland people. The inventory attached to the will of William Walker, dated 1588, included 'One stone of Wolle, One Spinynge Wheele, One pare of Cards, One pare of Wolle Combes,' worth 5/-. At his death in 1671 Alexander Park, yeoman of Leyland, had fustions to the value of £28, and, of thirty-eight debts owed to William Rigby in 1608, twenty-two were for flax supplied by him to linen workers: 'Debt: Roger Cocker of Clayton, five stone of flax 36/-'.[1]

For the years 1722-6 following 'Mr Chancellour Gastrell's direction', the Leyland parish register also records people's occupations and a sample of the years 1722-4 provides a rough guide to the importance of textiles throughout the parish. Of the fathers of children baptised, it is significant that fifty-one were textile workers (mostly weavers), and out of a total of 174 only fifty were agricultural workers. Textiles employed half these fathers in Clayton, Cuerden and Heapey; eight out of twenty-one in Whittle; in Leyland itself, eighteen out of seventy-two; but in Euxton only four out of thirty-seven. This, of course, takes no account of spinning, which was usually undertaken by female relatives, whilst an early bleaching industry was emerging, for the entries for Leyland township include three 'whiteners' or 'whitsters', Ralph Boardman, Lawrence Almond and John Waring. It is clear, therefore, that as early as the 1720s a lot of people in Leyland were making at least a fair proportion of their living from textiles.

Like much of the North West, Leyland was thus well placed to take advantage of the technological innovations and economic benefits related to the mechanisation of the textile industry in the late-eighteenth century, and in particular the 'take-off' in demand for the wonder product of the nineteenth century – cotton.[2]

Although the marked developments in the industry during the years 1780-1850 are usually recorded as the 'Industrial Revolution', their origins clearly lie in changes in economic organisation apparent from Tudor times. Rather, these years saw the intensification of processes long established, and the rising importance of the textile industry in the economy of Leyland at this time was the outcome of gradual and cumulative growth. That is not to say, however, that development in this period was not rapid and intense, for, as will be seen, it was clearly both, and did indeed indicate something of a revolution in the town's affairs.

The attraction of weaving as a trade is fairly straightforward. It was a long-established local handicraft using local resources. Weaving did not require an enormous outlay of capital, nor great strength or skill. It could be readily learnt and could be undertaken in the weaver's own home. Moreover, the efforts of all the family, from young children upwards, could be utilised in some way, be it spinning, winding bobbins, fetching and carrying, or taking a turn on the handloom. Thus even if the head of the family had another main source of income, such as an acre or more of land, other members of the family could supplement the funds. Weaving on the handloom was thus ideally suited for integration within an agricultural economy that was marked by small land-holdings of limited potential, periods of seasonal inactivity, and an increasing degree of underemployment. In the present day similar factors have assisted the survival of the handloom tweed industry in the Highlands and Islands of Scotland, where the clacking of the handloom is still to be heard as it once was along the streets and lanes of Leyland.

The arrival of cotton

THE emergence of the cotton industry in Leyland must be seen in the context of its development in mid-Lancashire as a whole, and particularly in the district around Preston. Preston developed as a major cotton town in the early-nineteenth century largely due to the availability of a plentiful supply of labour which it was able to absorb from the surplus population of the agricultural Fylde and other neighbouring areas. Although the town did not enjoy the natural advantages of the mill towns on the Lancashire coalfield, it did have much lower labour costs, perhaps in the region of ten per cent below those of its rivals.

That an extensive cotton industry would develop at all in Leyland might at first appear unlikely, since throughout much of the eighteenth century it was predominantly an agricultural centre, dominated, as has been seen, by the Farington estate. The town centre had no strongly running rivers to power machinery and was not a road or canal centre.

Yet Leyland and the surrounding villages of the Leyland Hundred were also able to develop within the orbit of Preston, principally through the availability of relatively cheap and plentiful labour. In the absence of employment in other industries such as iron, mining or shipbuilding people were forced in increasing numbers as time went on to turn to weaving for their livelihood. Fortunately, the improvement and increasing rationalisation of agriculture coincided in the late-eighteenth century with the golden age of the handloom weaver.

The development of handloom weaving in Leyland was thus very closely related to developments in agriculture, a point frequently alluded to by contemporary observers. The relative cheapness of agricultural labour in the Leyland Hundred, away from the main manufacturing towns, was noted by Holt as early as 1795. 'The rate of wages is in proportion to the distance of the townships from the seats of manufacture: eg. at Chorley the wages of a common labourer 3/- with ale, at Euxton 2/- or 2/6d, at Eccleston, 1/6d or 2/- at Mawdesley and Bispham (in harvest time!), 1/2d or 1/4d'.[3]

The impact of the early manufacturing industry on land values can also be seen, as Dickson observed, 'The great range of fine land between the Ribble and the Mersey, is in general let off at a higher rent than any of the others, in consequence of its population, markets and other causes. In the parishes of Walton-le-Dale, Chorley and Leyland, the rents run from about 40/-, 50/- to £3-10-0d [per acre], some a little higher near the towns and adjoining manufacturies. Around Penwortham, Croston etc., from 35/- to 50/-, but little higher than that rate. In the neighbourhood of Preston from £2 to £3-10-0d as farms: but for the convenience of trade, at £6 or £7 and sometimes more the customary acre for grassland'.[4]

Indeed the great extension of handloom weaving first became apparent on the farms themselves, as Lawrence Rawstorne of Penwortham recalled in 1843. 'At the time when weaving was at its tip-top price, it was introduced into the different farm houses, when all other considerations gave way to it. A good handloom weaver would then earn his 30/- a week or even more: he would perhaps work half the week and drink the remainder. Farms by these means become sub-divided: cottages were built; a large shop was attached to every building. The houses both of the farmers and the cottagers were occupied by as large families as could be procured and these paid an enormous rent from the profits of the loom.'[5]

The history of the local handloom weaving industry falls into three main phases: a period of steady development up to 1780 as a cottage industry dominated by fairly independent yeoman farmers; a period of rapid growth fed by the availability of cheap factory-spun yarn and the development of foreign markets, resulting in high wages and investment, for example, in the Leyland stephouse rows; and a long, slow period of decline after 1810, as demand for goods was unable to keep pace with the rising throng of weavers, and wages fell accordingly.

The early power-looms were relatively crude and for many years their threat was largely psychological, but after 1840, with improvements to the machinery, handloom weaving began to be obsolete for all but the very finest yarns.

From 1800 onwards, if not before, weavers lost their independence from the middle men – the 'putters-out', merchants or 'manufacturers' – who supplied yarn and ordered and collected the finished 'pieces'. Given the frequently isolated nature of the work weavers were generally unable to organise themselves effectively to resist the downward pressure on wages, and since weaving required little apprenticeship, they were unable to control their own numbers, the supply of cloth, and therefore their wages.

Memories of an earlier phase of prosperity thus haunted the later years of the industry, which came to be synonymous with long hours, low wages and poverty. Many weavers turned to political action to redress the situation, and Richard Marsden, a handloom weaver from Club Street, Bamber Bridge, became a leader of the Chartist movement.

In many areas of scholarship and science self-taught handloom weavers were acknowledged authorities. In 1830 when nationally their numbers perhaps exceeded 300,000, a Royal Commission set up to inquire into the depression in the industry could only recommend emigration as a cure for the industry's ills, urging weavers to ensure that their children did not enter the trade. In the Leyland Hundred handloom weaving was to survive for a further thirty years, by which time, however, a very substantial mill-based industry had emerged in Leyland.

Throughout the district the 1780s was a period of great advance in the organisation of the local textile industry. The firm of Livesey, Hargreaves amd Co. directly and indirectly employed large numbers of handloom weavers in Preston and South Ribble. They had their own mills, bleaching grounds and warehouses in Manchester and London, and offices in Manchester in what was recognisably a modern firm, directing all levels of manufacture right through from purchase of raw materials to sales. When the firm was declared bankrupt in 1788 they claimed to be 'The means of giving bread to near 20,000 persons in the district.'[6]

Although weaving was to remain largely a home industry until the 1840s, it was thus integrated with the other textile processes, especially spinning and bleaching. The rapid success of John Horrocks (1768-1804) in Preston after 1791 was largely due to his effective organisation of the industry.[7] The series of spinning mills he built in the town during the 1790s supplied the needs of local weavers, and the list of his warehouses in the towns and villages around Preston, including Leyland, Longton, Chorley, Ormskirk and Croston, illustrates the geographical extent of the Preston-centred industry.

Horrockses clearly had considerable influence in towns such as Leyland. By the mid-1790s the firm had a warehouse in the town, occupied by Edward Martin, and by 1819 two houses and a warehouse, the latter located at the rear of the buildings on the west side of Leyland Cross, at the top of Fox Lane. Yet much of the initiative in Leyland seems to have come, not from any large industrial concern but from the plethora of small 'manufacturers'. In 1819 Mr Pollard and William Sergeant owned warehouses, and the heirs of the latter still owned a good number of weavers' houses in Bradshaw and Union

Streets well into the 1840s.

In Edward Baines' *County Directory* of 1825 Henry Norris and Francis Serjeant Pilkington of Union Street are listed as 'manufacturers', and Thomas Readet as a 'manufacturing agent'; all three owned warehouses and numbers of houses (and therefore loomshops) as late as 1838. Thomas Jackson, John Hall and Thomas Finch are also listed as 'manufacturing agents', Thomas Forshaw as a muslin manufacturer and Caroline Isherwood as a linen draper. The Finch family also had interests in bleaching, and the Water Street houses were once known as 'Finch's Houses'. Significantly, Baines in 1825 does not list any factories in the town, the first of which only appeared about 1850 when F. S. Pilkington opened his Earnshaw Bridge Mill.[8]

Right: *Union Street, Leyland c1905. (Top of Fox Lane).*

The weavers' step houses were erected, under the auspices of an early form of building society, upon one of the townfield strips adjoining Fox Lane. The buildings were essentially two up and two down cottages built over loomshops. At a later date as the home weaving industry declined, after about 1830, the cellars were often sub-let to poorer tenants. (Leyland Museum).

The Leyland step-houses

THE model for the Leyland step-houses, Union Street (Fox Lane) and Bradshaw Street, and possibly also Water Street and Heaton Street, seems to have been the Longridge Terminating Building Society. Such a society was simply a club for the building of houses which were to be distributed by ballot among the members, after which it terminated – in contrast to the permanent building societies of today. Hence the frequent use of names such as 'Club Row' or 'Club Street', although the first Leyland houses adopted the more genteel 'Union Street'. Often the 'clubs' had rules and a constitution to regulate their subsequent use. At Leyland these are lost but at Longridge a member should not 'suffer his tennants to lay, any ashes, dung, manure or other nuisances, at the front of his own, or any other house belonging to the society'. New ideas were welcome, 'but nothing shall be admitted tending to alter or destroy the external uniformity or regularity of the buildings, which is inviolably to be adhered to.' Any member divulging the 'secrets' of the society was to be fined 5/-.[9]

The Longridge Society established in 1793, is popularly believed to be the earliest building society in the world. In Leyland the medieval field strip alongside Fox Lane on which the Union Street houses still stand was purchased by George Bretherton of the Bay Horse Inn in 1794. An indenture for two of the houses, dated 1802, states that 'Daniel Barron, [the owner of this particular pair] and others, all members of a certain society established *some time ago* in Leyland for the building of houses, have contracted and agreed with George Bretherton for the purchase of the said land, the price being £254-7-0d' (my italics). The precise dates are thus unclear, but the initiative in Leyland was very early.

By 1802 members of the society had built houses in a series of blocks, ultimately of four, twelve and six houses, at 'joint and equal expense', to form the row which, though still unfinished in 1802, was 'to be known as Union Street.' Members of the society had also made 'an equal division amongst themselves, by ballot, of the several houses

One of the stephouses on Union Street today – a good example, showing the cellar window partially blocked up. Good light was essential for the weavers and large windows were a feature of handloom weavers' cottages throughout Lancashire and West Yorkshire.

Far right: *Sale notice, House in Bradshaw Street 1810.*

Following the commercial success of the Union Street houses, a similar development was undertaken in nearby Bradshaw Street (Spring Gardens), and the society houses were soon changing hands for quite large sums. Many of the cottages had gardens (large enough to be worthwhile – but not too large to distract the inmates from weaving), providing an important source of food during the not infrequent 'hard times' experienced by the early textile industry. (Leyland Museum).

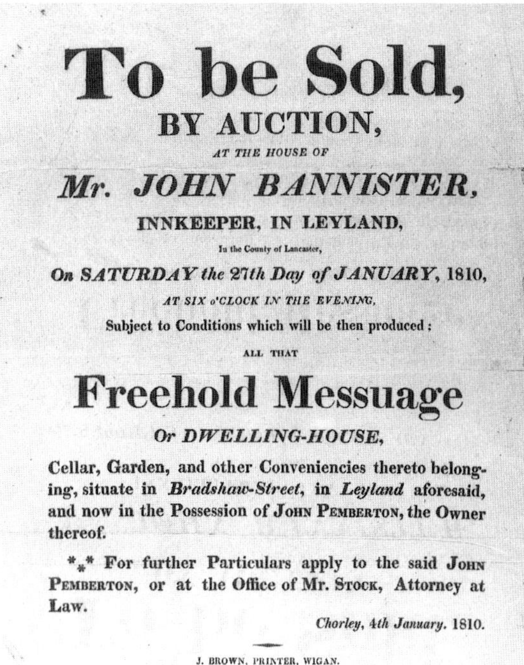

To be Sold,

BY AUCTION,

AT THE HOUSE OF

Mr. JOHN BANNISTER,

INNKEEPER, IN LEYLAND,

In the County of Lancaster,

On *SATURDAY the 27th Day of JANUARY*, 1810,

AT SIX o'CLOCK IN THE EVENING,

Subject to Conditions which will be then produced:

ALL THAT

Freehold Messuage

Or DWELLING-HOUSE,

Cellar, Garden, and other Conveniencies thereto belonging, situate in *Bradshaw-Street*, in *Leyland* aforesaid, and now in the Possession of JOHN PEMBERTON, the Owner thereof.

***** For further Particulars apply to the said JOHN PEMBERTON, or at the Office of Mr. STOCK, Attorney at Law.**

Chorley, 4th January, 1810.

J. BROWN, PRINTER, WIGAN.

and plots of land', with Daniel Barron receiving his two houses ('No. 10 is 35 yds. 2' in depth, 6 yds. wide and in the possession of George Halstone; No. 11 is 34 yds. 1' in depth, 6 yds. wide, and in possession of Thomas Woods') including all rights, especially cellar light.

Union Street today, little changed from when it was built.

Union Street from Towngate c1895.

The owner of the Bay Horse Inn (on the right of this photograph) seems to have been a prime mover in the establishment of the Union Street Building Society. In fact, much of the capital for the expansion of the Leyland weaving industry in the late-eighteenth century seems to have been derived from the sale of beer. The building to the left is Occleshaw House (now a medical practice), a timber-framed building dating from the early-eighteenth century, but on a plot occupied since medieval times.

Two of the houses still have metal insurance plaques, one of which, No. 198555, for the Royal Exchange Insurance Co. (now Guardian Royal Exchange), was issued 'for a house in Union Street, Leyland', on March 3rd 1803.

Where, one might ask, had the capital for this pioneering housing venture originated? John Norris of Rufford, the original owner of the strip was a maltster – and it could therefore be said that this corner of Leyland floated into the industrial age on a tide of beer![10]

The Union Street houses proved to be a great success, being large enough to sub-let, and with whole families confined to the cellars, by the 1820s they were changing hands for upwards of £200 each. So profitable did they prove for their owners that in 1806 a second club was formed to build houses on another of the Lower Townfield strips, the 'meadow' just a few hundred yards to the north, to be known as Bradshaw Street. A memorandum of 30th November 1818 confirms the title of William Farington of Moss-side to No. 19 Bradshaw Street which he had recently purchased from the club, and states 'A club or society was formed in the year 1806 for the purpose of erecting houses at Leyland aforesaid and proper rules and orders were made for the regulation of the said club and a committee appointed for the government thereof and a certain plot of land was purchased for the said houses and houses were accordingly built thereupon'.

The club had a committee to oversee the houses and 'Edmund Halliwell of Leyland and Henry Riding of Chorley were the committee of the said club'. The houses may well have been named after their builder, for the document also states 'Memorandum: John Bradshaw of Leyland, builder, is not to erect nor build any thing whatsoever, nor make any fence whatsoever within the space of 5 yards to the front or north side of the premises, as specified in the contract or agreement bearing day 26th July 1806'. Sadly it has not yet proved possible to trace the deeds of the smaller Leyland step-houses.[11]

Bleaching and finishing

LEYLAND also developed an important bleaching and finishing industry very early, and the works at Northbrook and Shruggs, with their supplies of clear spring- and well-water, may have originated in the 1780s. Important innovations in the industry were made locally at Mosney in Walton-le-Dale, and at Mr Clayton's works at Bamber Bridge. Although the survey of 1819 does not mention Shruggs, a works was certainly established at Northbrook at this time. In 1825 Baines lists two bleachers in the town, John Bainbridge and Robert Brindle. By 1837 William Finch was living at Northbrook and James Fletcher at Shruggs. In the 1851 census Fletcher is described as a 'bleacher of cotton goods employing 132 men' and was tenant at both places. The temporary closure of the Shruggs works in the early 1860s, leading to great distress in the town, seems to have been due in part to a legal dispute over the tenancy. Northbrook seems to have closed in the 1870s, becoming the residence of the Forrester family, stewards to the Faringtons. During recent alterations, one of the great wells was temporarily uncovered.

John Stanning and Son took over the Shruggs works in 1871, and under their guidance the firm became one of the leaders in the industry, instrumental in the formation of British Bleachers in 1900, and a major employer in the town. The Leyland works seems to have had links with the great firm of Ainsworths of Halliwell founded in 1739, for Halliwell was the birthplace of James Fletcher, James Holt (manager in 1861), and the two John Stannings. John Stanning senior, who took over the works in January 1871, had been a partner in the Ainsworth firm. His son John was to be a leading figure in Leyland during the late-nineteenth century.[12]

The scale of the works in the 1830s is well illustrated by the following advertisement which appeared in the *Preston Pilot* newspaper in

August 1835:

> To Bleachers, Sizers and Others, to be sold or let, all those extensive buildings and premises, called the 'Shruggs', situate in Leyland, lately used as bleach and sizing works, with the steam engine, machinery, lodges and outbuildings: together with the excellent messuage or dwelling house, stables, gardens and orchard, and 3 acres of land adjoining containing seven acres, one rood and twelve perches and thereabouts.
>
> The Premises are eligibly situated in the neighbourhood of a great manufacturing district, and within a very short distance of the new line of the railway between Wigan and Preston, and the steam engine and machinery are in perfect order and almost new, and the whole are well adapted for carrying on an extensive business. The above are held on a lease, of which about seventeen years are unexpired, and immediate possession may be had.[13]

Leyland by 1830 was thus a community very dependent on the handloom weaving trade, with very large numbers of weavers in the surrounding farms and cottages, large purpose-built rows of weavers' houses over loomshops, a bleaching industry and warehouses. This great concentration of activity in a single industry made the town very susceptible to downturns in trade and the cyclical economic

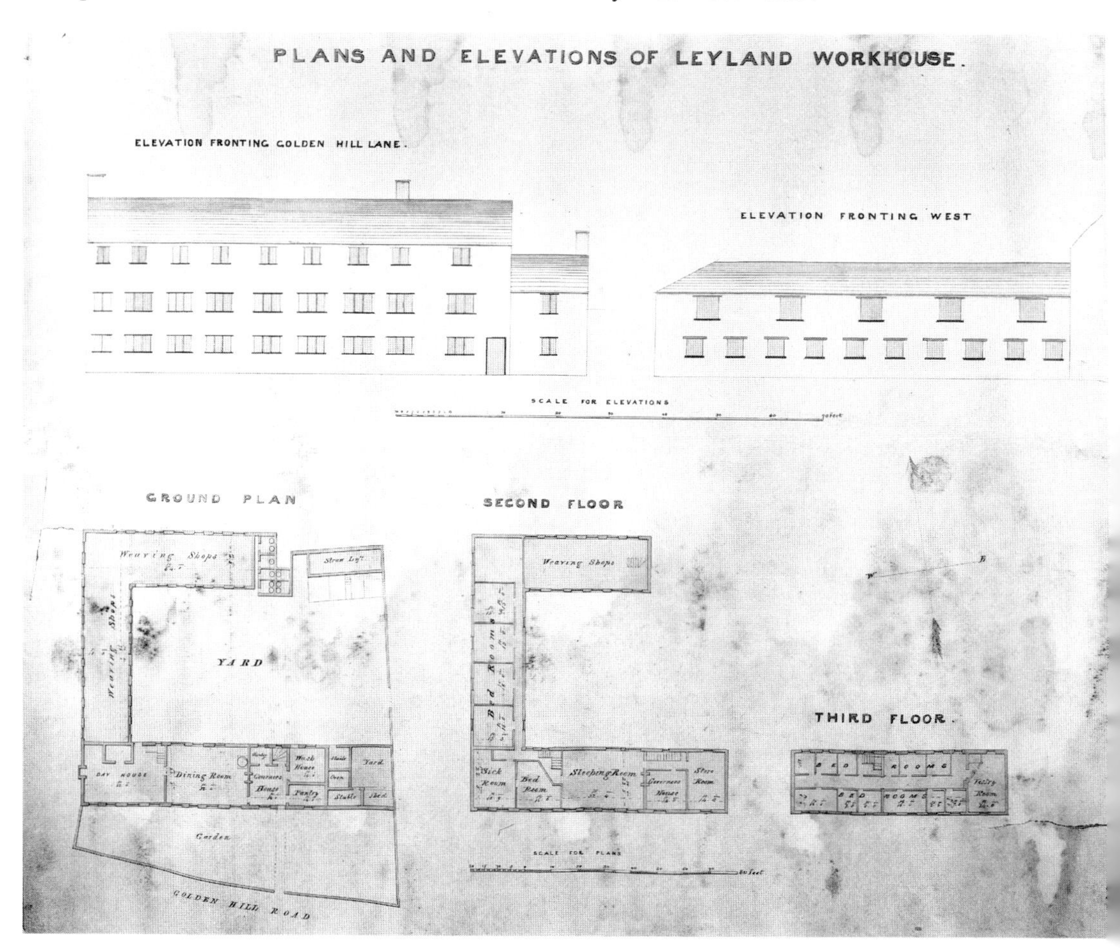

depressions of the early-nineteenth century.

The 1831 census recorded that 'In the Hundred of Leyland, Chorley contains 1,200 males employed in the cotton manufacture, the township of Leyland 400, and the residue of that parish in various townships collectively 2,300: in other places 450'.[14] But in 1835 Baines reported that although factory workers were working seventy hours a week, 'The handloom weavers employed in making plain goods, on the contrary, are in a deplorable condition, both in the large towns and in the villages, their wages are a miserable pittance and they generally work in confined and unwholesome dwellings'.[15]

The Royal Commission set up to investigate the crisis in the industry in 1830 took evidence from townspeople. In 1838 the *Preston Chronicle* newspaper revealed the crisis in the town, 'Handloom Weavers at Leyland – The handloom weavers, residing at Leyland, who comprise a majority of the population of that beautiful village, complain very much of the hard times, wages have been very low for some time past, and but for the facilities which many of them have for growing potatoes, etc., and the assistance given by their neighbours, who are better off in the world, their situation, particularly during the winter months, must have been truly distressing'.[16] The first detailed census, that of 1841, thus records the industry when it was already in marked decline.[17] It provides a clear, if late, picture of the spread of weavers throughout the township.

Left: *Plans of the Leyland Workhouse, Golden Hill Lane, c1820.*

Like most of the surrounding parishes, Leyland had a workhouse from an early date. With the great demand for weavers in the early years of the nineteenth century, the local poor (very elderly people, the sick, mentally ill, orphans etc.) were put to work for long hours handloom weaving in what was really a small factory. So successful was this scheme that some workhouses were almost able to pay their way. Skill in managing the weaving trade seems to have been a useful qualification for an aspiring workhouse master, and Heyes Hunt of Walton-le-Dale certainly does not seem to have found his experience at Leyland a handicap in the accumulation of his fortune. The workhouse plans reveal the scale of the weaving enterprise in the building; notice also the large number of windows in the weaving shops.

	Weavers	Weavers: Heads of Houses	Weavers: Family & lodgers
Water Street	25	6	19
Bradshaw St. (including Spring Gardens and Orange Square)	109	51	58
Union Street	14	5	9
Towngate (West Side)	57	7	50
Towngate (East Side)	57	7	50
Town Centre total	**262**	**76**	**186**
Golden Hill Lane	27	7	20
Bow Lane	14	7	7
Turpin Green Lane	35	14	21
Hough Lane	12	8	4
Leyland Lane (East Side)	20	11	9
Leyland Lane (West Side, i) (Ulnes Walton to Seven Stars, incl. Slater and Dunkirk Lane)	89	49	40
Leyland Lane (West Side, ii) (Seven Stars to Earnshaw Br., including Longmeanygate and Midge Hall)	23	14	9
The Workhouse (Golden Hill)	21		21
Total	**503**	**186**	**317**

In addition to a quantitative survey of the industry the 1841 census also provides direct information on individual weavers and their families. By this date more fortunate workers had found alternative employment, and were able to supplement their incomes by sub-letting their cellar loomshops to weavers, often leading to great overcrowding. The following entries are fairly typical:

Name		Occupation	Age
Union Street			
Edward Hesketh	(head)	Painter	30
Jane Hesketh	(wife)		30
Edward Hesketh	(son)		4
William Wood	(lodger)	Joiner	20
Thomas Adamson	(lodger)	Weaver	35
Elizabeth Adamson	(wife)		40
Richard Adamson	(son)		8
Andrew Adamson	(son)		3
Bradshaw Street			
Thomas Gregson	(head)	Weaver	70
Ann Gregson	(daughter)		30
Mary Gregson	(daughter)	Weaver	15
Ellen Gregson	(daughter)	Weaver	10
Mary Gregson	(daughter)		4
Jane Walmsley	(lodger)	Weaver	40
Jane Walmsley	(daughter)		4
Alice Cross	(lodger)	Weaver	50
Elizabeth Cross	(lodger)		25
John Cross	(son)		6
Water Street			
Richard Livesey	(head)	Bleacher	25
Ellen Livesey	(wife)		20
William Marsden	(lodger)	Weaver	20
Ellen Marsden	(lodger)		20
Alice Marsden	(lodger)		1 week
Heaton Street			
Jno. Swindlehurst	(head)	Tailor	50
Jane Swindlehurst	(wife)		55
Thomas Swindlehurst	(son)		20
Alice Swindlehurst	(daughter)		10
William Bradshaw	(lodger)	Weaver	60
John Cattrall	(lodger)	Weaver	20

In the rural areas handloom weaving remained very important, being well suited to large farming families. This example is from Golden Hill:

Robert Cocker	(head)	Farmer	55
Margaret Cocker	(wife)		60
Jane Cocker	(daughter)	Weaver	20
Helen Cocker	(daughter)	Weaver	20
Robert Cocker	(son)		15
Mary Clitheroe	(lodger)	Farm servant	10
William Cocker	(lodger)	Weaver	25
Helen Cocker	(lodger)		20
James Cocker	(lodger)		6 months

By the time of the next census in 1851 the number of handloom weavers had fallen markedly, and though significant numbers remained in the country areas and in Bradshaw Street, many of the weavers' children had found work in the factories, as the following examples reveal:

Union Street

Ellen Norris	(head)	Housekeeper	72
Richard	(son)	Handloom weaver	45
Lucy	(daughter)	Warper in mill	43
Ellen	(daughter)	Warper in mill	38
William	(son)	Handloom weaver	35
Henry	(son)	Book-keeper in mill	31

Water Street

John Bennett	(head)	Agricultural labourer	42
Elizabeth	(wife)	Labourer's wife	45
Ann	(daughter)	Power-loom weaver	21
William	(son)	Power-loom weaver	19
Ellen	(daughter)	Power-loom weaver	17
Elizabeth	(daughter)	Power-loom weaver	15
John	(grandson)		2

Heaton Street

Thomas Bradshaw	(head)	Power-loom weaver	39
Elizabeth	(wife)	Power-loom weaver	36
Elizabeth	(daughter)	Power-loom weaver	17
John	(son)	Power-loom weaver	15
Margaret	(daughter)	Power-loom weaver	14
Richard	(son)	Scholar	11
Ann	(daughter)	Scholar	9
Thomas	(son)		6
Jane	(daughter)		2

Relatively few handloom weavers are listed in 1861, but in the Golden Hill area the trade survived into the 1870s. By tracing one family through a number of censuses it is possible to see the impact these economic trends had on real people's lives. In this example

Margaret	(daughter)		4 months
Thomas Charnley	(lodger)	Handloom weaver	30
Margaret	(lodger)		30
Margaret	(lodger)		3 months

1851

James Hunt	(head)	Handloom weaver	36
Nancy	(wife)	Handloom weaver	35
Alice	(daughter)	Steamloom weaver	19

James Hunt	(son)	Steamloom weaver	16
Nancy Hunt	(daughter)	Steamloom weaver	16

1861

James Hunt	(head)	Handloom weaver	54
Ann (?)	(wife)	Handloom weaver	53
James	(son)	Handloom weaver	26
Thomas Bennet (son-in-law)	(lodger)	Power-loom weaver	29
Alice Bennet	(lodger)	Power-loom weaver	28
James Bennet	(lodger)	Scholar	
Margaret	(lodger)	Scholar	
Jane	(lodger)	Scholar	

1871

James Hunt	(head)	Labourer	67
Nancy	(wife)		64
James	(son)	Hosepipe weaver	37

From the 1830s onwards Leyland was clearly changing rapidly. By 1841 the great factory at Farington had opened and most families in Union Street, for example, were no longer dependent on weaving. By 1851 many people had found work in the factories, and after 1860 a new range of industries had begun to develop. Only in the rural areas and the poorer parts of the town such as Bradshaw Street did handloom weaving remain important after 1851. As we shall see, however, although one sector of the town's economy was in decline. At the same time, marked growth was underway in others.

Chapter Seven

Cottonopolis: The story of Farington

AFTER 1840 the fortunes of Leyland and Farington became inextricably linked, both to each other, and to the railway. Following the opening of the Wigan and Preston line of the North Union Railway Company – ultimately to become part of the main line between London, the North and Scotland – a new Leyland and a new Farington began to develop away from the ancient core, in the vicinity of the railway station, Farington village, and eventually Hough Lane. In this zone were to be laid the foundations of modern industrial Leyland, and central to its growth was the railway and the town's new-found prime location upon it mid-way between London and Glasgow.

The construction of a railway between Preston and Wigan was proposed as early as 1830, the year that the Manchester and Liverpool line was opened, but it was not until June 1834 that resistance from local landowners was overcome and the company's engineer was [illegible]

a distant part of Penwortham parish with moated manor house and mill, rather than a centralised settlement in its own right with ecclesiastical and civil functions.[3]

Ploughlands in Farington also formed part of the lands given by Warine Bussel to Evesham Abbey in the establishment of Penwortham Priory. When John de Farington married Warine's daughter Avice, acquiring lands in Leyland, Farington formed the bridegroom's share of what was to become the Farington family estate.

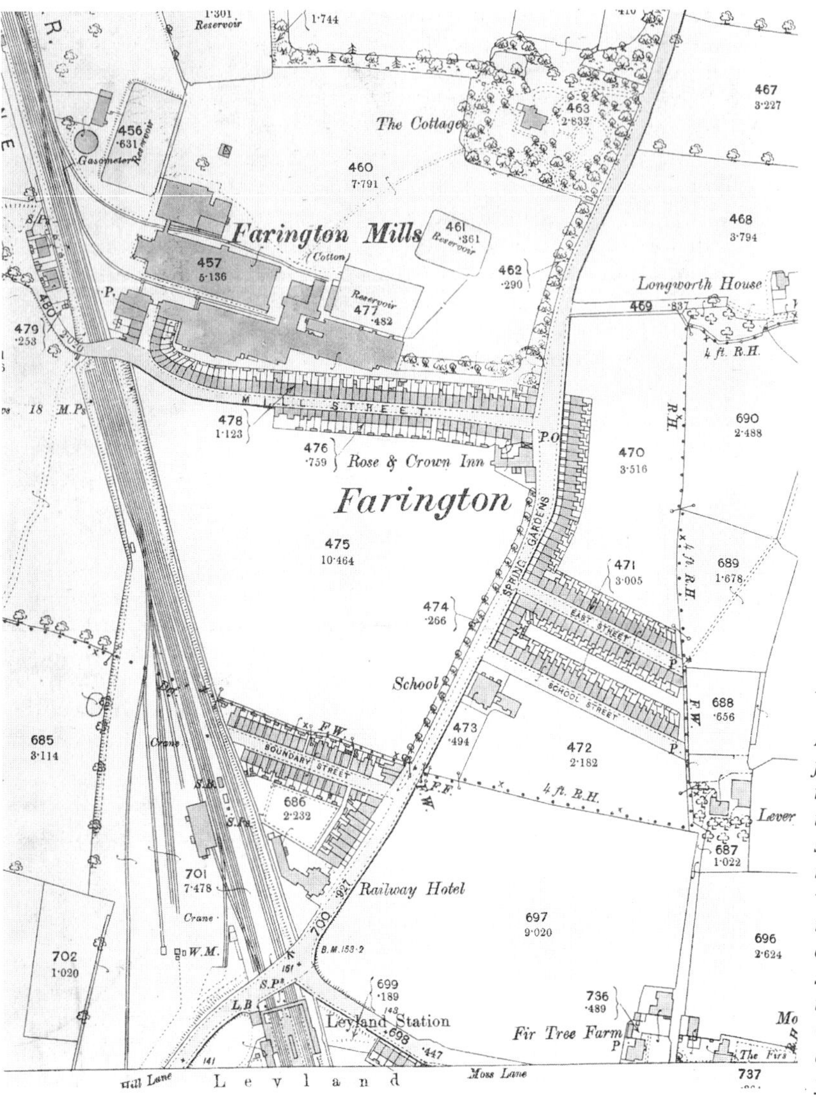

1893 O.S. Map, Farington area. This map clearly shows Bashall and Boardman's factory estate, a planned and model village of the 1840s. The importance of the railway is shown by the spur lines running into the factory yard. It was along these sidings that the mill people pushed wagons of cotton amidst much hymn singing and rejoicing to herald the end of the Lancashire Cotton Famine, an event commemorated until recent years by an annual walk.

Many writers have taken this marriage to mark the beginnings of the history of Leyland, as well as the start of the Farington interest in the district, but it is interesting to note that the joint estate was long known as the 'Manor of Farington'. The principal family in the district for seven hundred years thus took their name from the township, and the centre of their estate was Farington Hall. Nothing now remains of this ancient and important historical site which for three hundred years was virtually the political and military centre of the district. Following Sir Henry Farington's enigmatic will in the mid-sixteenth century the family moved to Old Worden Hall and Farington passed to the Huddlestons.

As Catholics and Royalists their history during the Reformation and Civil War is as interesting as that of the Faringtons. John Huddleston, born at Farington in 1608, assisted Charles II to escape after his defeat at the Battle of Worcester in 1651. He became a Benedictine monk in 1660, and in 1685 he reconciled the dying King to the Catholic Church, dying himself in 1698 at the age of ninety. Thereafter the estate passed to the Pennington family.

An important theme in the history of Farington from the earliest times is the reclamation of the area's very extensive mosslands, and many references to this process have been made in the earlier account of Leyland. As late as 1851 Mannex's trade directory could record, 'In the township is a considerable quantity of unreclaimed land, called Farington Moss, connected with the bogs of Leyland, Hoole and Longton. Farington and Longton mosses were formerly six miles in length and four in breadth, but large portions of them have been drained and cultivated. Numbers of oak and other trees have been found here, emerging from their peaty bed, and frequently in regular layers, as if a whole range had been swept down by one simultaneous operation'.

Prior to the coming of the railway and the opening of Farington Mill the township was therefore a sparsely populated agricultural district developed along the receding fringes of the moss: in 1666 the township had only fifty-nine hearths (fourteen of them in just two houses), and by 1801 the population was just 382. Occasionally gruesome murders and memories of fugitive priests apart, Farington enjoyed what the Rev. Townson called 'centuries of peace'.[4] All this was to change dramatically in the 1830s when the new village became a byeword for rapid and extensive industrial development, and again in the twentieth century when it was to become home for one of the greatest manufacturing companies in the world.

An account of 1851 recorded that;

> 'Farington township extends from about 2½ miles to 5 miles south of Preston, and has a modern thriving village, with an extensive cotton manufacture, at which about 1,000 hands receive constant employment. This factory belongs to Messrs. Bashall and Boardman, who may be said to have brought the village into existence. The North Union railway passes by the village, and has a station contiguous, where there is a good inn, very conveniently situated for the convenience of travellers. The East Lancashire [illegible]
> acres of lan[illegible]
> 1831, 672 [illegible]
> extraordina[illegible]
> the latter ye[illegible]

Bashall's Mill

WILLIAM Bashall was established at Cuerden as a cotton spinner from the early-nineteenth century. A trade directory of 1816 records the firm of Wm Bashall and Co., 'Cotton Manufacturers of Bamber Bridge'. Conditions in the early factories were harsh. In 1825 during agitation surrounding the repeal of the Combination Laws (which

The McMinnies family. Mr McMinnies was manager and later a partner in Farington Mill, and duly led the workforce in their annual cricket match with John Stanning's Leyland Eleven. (Leyland Museum).

forbade the 'combinations' or 'unions' of workers) the workforce of Cuerden joined the strike, and the *Preston Chronicle* of January 15th 1825 reported that, 'The Spinners of Mr Bashall's near Leyland have given up their situations'.[6] Something of this tradition seems to have continued at Farington, and the mill was to play a significant part in the history of labour struggles in the Preston district.

The factory that the firm planned at Farington was to be on a much greater scale than any hitherto seen in the district. Indeed, it was virtually to create a new town on a green field site. Work on the mill seems to have been underway by 1835, contemporary with the adjacent railway line. The mill ledger began in December 1834 and lists early payments for work undertaken by contractors:[7]

6 January 1836:	Bach and Young, Preston. By lead, plumbing and glazing	£898- 5- 4d
11 June 1836:	Sam Woods, Preston. By stone work for mill, cottages, etc.	£587- 4- 0d
7 July 1838:	Betty Morris, Wheelton, By flaggs, steps, side stone etc.	£513-16-7½d
25 November 1836:	Tomlinson and Todd, Preston. By brickwork for 18 cottages, Gas Tank, Gas House etc	£168-17- 3d
2 December 1836:	Galloway & Co., Preston. By gasometer compleat	£410
31 December 1837:	Thos Grundy, Preston. By machinery as per sundry accounts	£13,649-15- 2d
6 April 1840:	Davison and Price, Blackburn. By looms	£945

The spinning mill began running in July 1836, and in 1838 winding, warping and sizing rooms were added. This structure blew down in a gale and had to be rebuilt – 'with a wing on the east side to strengthen it. The mill was powered by two beam engines, later compounded by a horizontal engine made in Bolton by the firm of Hicks.'[8] In the 1850s new machinery was acquired, for the accounts include payments;[9]

4 March – 20 Nov. 1855:	to Platt Brothers, Oldham	£4,101- 0- 8d
24 November 1855:	John Elce and Co., Manchester	
	22 pair self-acting mules,	
	1,200 spindles @ 3/8d	£4,480- 0- 0d
	44 looms and other apparatus	£70- 8- 0d
	Other machinery	£47- 1- 7d
	Total	£4,957- 9- 7d

A surviving ledger of goods exported provides an indication of the mills, markets and agents about 1840, listing Ker Rawson and Co., Singapore (Goods worth £1,409-8-0d); Leach Kettlewell and Co. (£4,717-9-11d); Eglington and McClure and Co., Calcutta (£1,688); Fox Rawson and Co., Canton (£11,027-0-2d); Morgan Melbourn and Co., Batavia (£3,858) and Joseph Hagan and Co., Valparaiso. The number of 'pieces', their value, and the name of the boat for each consignment is listed. The sailing ships include *Euphrates, Kestrel* and *England's Queen.* On February 11th 1845, for example, a consignment of 10,005 pieces of shirtings worth £6,465-15-0d was shipped aboard the *Lady Bute* bound for Messrs. Fox Rawson of Canton. Farington Mill therefore formed a link in the chain of early-Victorian trading prosperity which bound the cotton fields of the southern slave states of America with the developing markets for finished goods in the Orient.[10]

The firm was very progressive, as the scale of their investment and their appreciation of the likely benefits of the railway would suggest. Around the mill they developed an industrial village to house their workforce – Mill Street, Spring Gardens, East Street and School Street. A rent list of 1903 indicates the scale and value of this investment:

	2/-	*2/4d*	*2/6d*	*2/9d*	*3/-*	*3/3d*	*3/6d*	*3/9d*	*4/-*	*4/6d*	*4/9d*
Mill Street*	2	16	59	10	2	1					
Spring Gardens †			4	5		7	15				
East Street			2	1	2	6	29		1		
School Street			1	2		12	10				
Brigge Cott., High Ash								1	3		1
Total, 197 rents	**2**	**16**	**66**	**18**	**4**	**26**	**54**	**1**	**4**		**1**

* 90 cottages, 1 shop. † 33 cottages, 1 pub, 1 shop

'The above (without water charge) equals £29-3-1d per week and £1,516-0-4d per annum.'

A large school was built by the firm in 1843, which in 1880 'still generously supported by the firm, evinces their deep interest in the moral and social progress of the people', and an account book for the years 1900-3 lists school fund payments for salaries, cleaning, coke, 'drilling' the children and milk.[11]

The development of Farington was thus a very considerable enterprise, and a very profitable one for the firm (subsequently Bashall and Boardman, and after 1905 G. and R. Dewhurst), and an important local source of labour, contrasting markedly with the condition of the handloom industry in Leyland, which in the late 1830s appeared to be returning to its pre-industrial state. Central to this success and the future prosperity of the district was the railway.

The North Union Railway

EARLY difficulties overcome and sufficient capital raised, work on the railway began in earnest in 1835, but estimates of how long it would take and what problems would be encountered were consistently over-optimistic.[12] In all 2,202,030 cubic yards of rock, sand, clay, marl and earth were removed from cuttings and a similar amount deposited for the embankments, at a cost of just over £500,000, or £21,000 a mile.

During the summer months 3,000 men worked on the line, in shifts, 'One party relieving another in succession, and all engaging in such operations as were adapted to each one's skill, tact or labour'. Work was contracted to be finished by March 31st 1838, with stiff financial penalties for the contractors. Accidents, with almost weekly fatalities, were the outcome;

> An inquest was held on Monday last at Chorley on the body of James Riddle. From the evidence of James Pilkington, it appeared that the deceased was a labourer on the North Union railway line, at Charnock Richard, and that on the Tuesday preceeding, when he had care of the waggons, one of the hooks caught him and dragged him for about ten yards, and crushed his hand. Lockjaw ensued on the Friday following, but left him on Saturday just before he died. The jury returned the verdict – Accidental Death'.[13]

Work was let by the company in three contracts.

> First, the Ribble Contract, extending 2½ miles south of Preston, including the Ribble Valley and the viaduct across the river, was taken by Messrs. Henry Mullins and McMahon of Dublin, for the sum of £80,000.
>
> Second, the Yarrow Contract, commencing at Farington School and continuing southwards as far as Coppull Summit, a distance of eight miles, was taken by Mr Wm. Mackenzie of Liverpool for £76,000.
>
> Third, the Douglas Contract, extending from Coppull to Chapel Lane in Wigan a length of five miles, was let first to Mr Wm. Hughes of Glasgow for £60,000 but, being unfinished, was re-let to Mullins and McMahon for £50,000.

In September 1835, the company minutes reported that 'considerable progress has been made with the works in some places, but they are not generally in as forward a state as the board hoped to find them'.[14] Worse was to come, for in October 1837 a timber viaduct and earthen embankment across the valley of the Yarrow was swept away, causing extensive flooding in Eccleston and district. During the winter of 1838 fears of a similar fate arose for the great Ribble bridge. On February 3rd the *Preston Chronicle* informed its anxious readers,

> The thaw which set in at the early part of the week, has been so mild and gradual, that the fears which were entertained last week as to the fate of the Railway bridge, from the expected pressure of the ice, have happily not been realised. A considerable mass of ice still remains in the pool

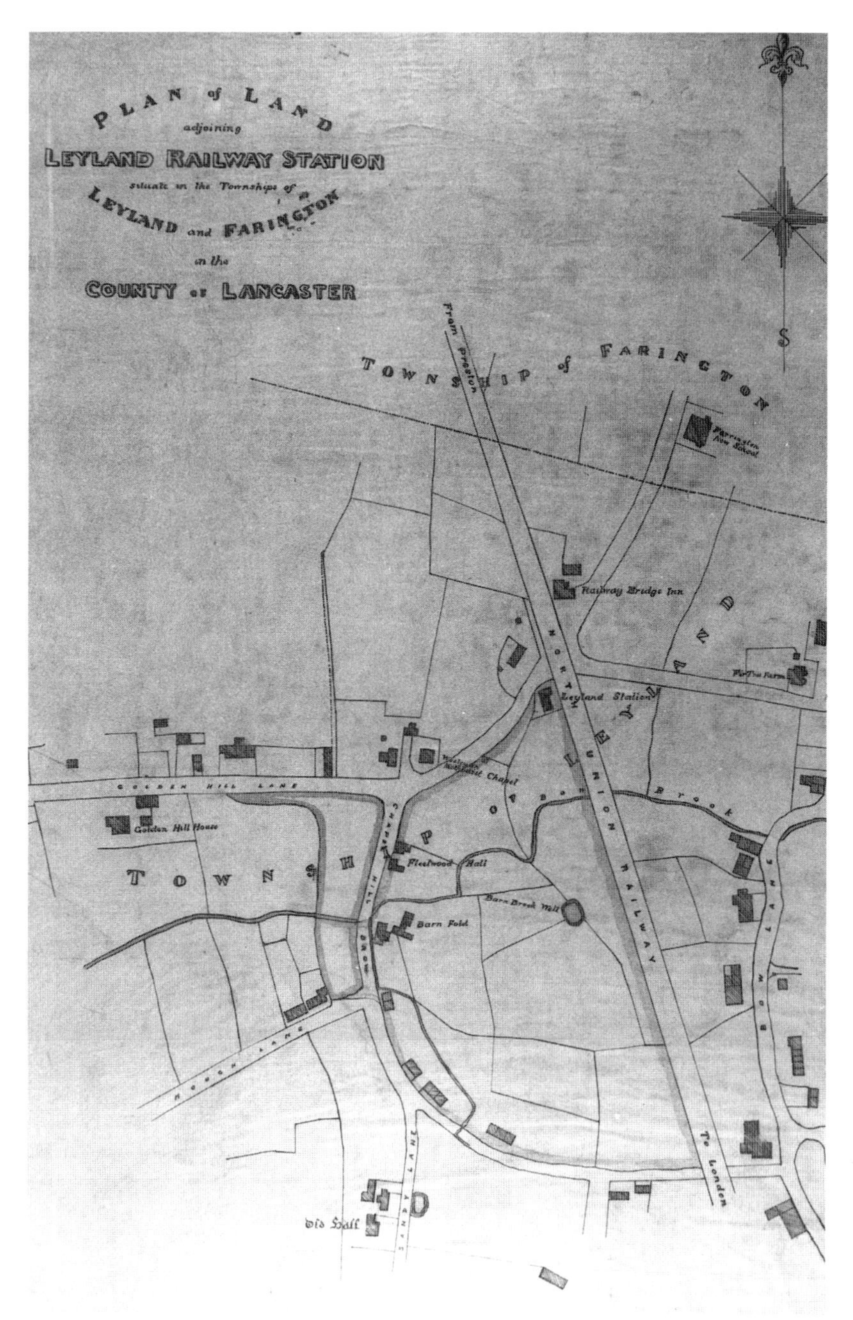

n early map showing the
oute of the North Union
ailway through Leyland.

between Walton Bridge and the Railway Bridge, but we trust there is no further ground for apprehending danger. Every precaution has been adopted to prevent the occurrence of any disaster.

The ice began to break up on March 3rd, and a week later did a great deal of damage and swept away the service bridge. By April work was again being pushed on. 'The spirited contractors on this line of railway, whose labours have been so much impeded by the protracted

Farington Railway Station c1860.

Few forces in the whole of English history were to transform society much as the railway did, and in both Farington and Leyland new industries were to grow up at this mid-point on the west-coast, Glasgow to London, line. Notice the station master's fine apparel and the line of plants. (Leyland Museum).

Leyland Station and Level Crossing, 1878.

This sketch by William Dawber shows the railway prior to the construction of the bridge over the lines. (Leyland Museum).

frost of the winter, are straining every nerve to effect an opening of the line into Preston, in August. We hope that they may be successful in the attempt, as we understand a premium is dependent upon its realization',[15] and by June 'The operations on this line of railway are now proceeding with extraordinary activity. The fine weather appears to have given a stimulus to the more rapid progress of the works, and an immense number of workmen are engaged in them throughout the respective departments.'

The scale of engineering on the line through Leyland was impressive. The Ribble Viaduct, 872 feet long, rising sixty-eight feet from the bed of the river to the parapet, and constructed at a cost of £40,000, is a spectacular monument to the railway pioneers. South of the bridge the line entered Penwortham cutting, one and a half miles long, thirty-eight feet deep and requiring the excavation of half a million cubic yards of marl and clay and the construction of four bridges, the largest being at Bee Lane. The railway then ran up an incline of 1/100 for 1,200 yards along the Lostock embankment to Farington, 'Contiguous to the railway, on the left, are also the newly erected mansions of Messrs. Bashall and Boardman, whose factory the traveller passes before he comes to Golden Hill in Leyland. The factory is approached by a handsome brick bridge over the railway'.

Passengers alighted at Golden Hill station (the present Leyland station), 'The Cuerden, Clayton and Blackburn road crosses on the level of the railway; and to the south-west, in the immediate propinquity, is situated the beautiful and sequestered village of Leyland'. Leaving Golden Hill there was a rise of 1/100 for 700 yards and then the line entered a cutting one mile long through Leyland sandhill, and on to Packsaddle Bridge and Euxton Station.[16]

In November 1838 the line was opened, with great ceremony, and large crowds gathered by the bridge to witness the event and to have a grandstand seat for any mishaps, particularly, it was thought on the Ribble and Yarrow bridges. Spraying ashes and cinders in all directions Number Two engine left Preston:

> Twenty miles per hour was the rate of her course, but on reaching the Ribble Viaduct, which is not yet completely finished, the speed was slackened. In ten minutes we reached Farington Station and in a quarter of an hour were at Golden Hill Station in Leyland. Here was a short stoppage, and Captain Pollard was admitted as a passenger. Down the incline to the Yarrow Valley, the engine dashed away at thirty miles per hour, and the wooden viaduct over the Yarrow was securely traversed. The noise made by crossing the bridge, resembled the rumbling of thunder among the steep rocks of hills and mountains. Through a mistake of the guards, instead of stopping [at Spendmoor], the journey was pursued to Coppull Chapel, where it was discovered that our progress had been impeded by a brake having locked the wheels of the vehicles.

A stagecoach journey of three hours was thus reduced to twenty minutes. However, on the return journey, 'The lazy automaton so laboured up the incline of one in one-hundred, between Mr Rylance's factory, and the Boar's Head, that passengers had to push it onward. Several of them, impatient of delay, cried out for donkey carts, and in their jocularity, deprecated railway travelling'.[17]

The Battle of Farington

THE construction of the line through Farington was marked by disturbances between the locals and the railway navvies: 'After centuries of quiet in Farington, one can easily imagine how disturbed the country folk would be by the invasion of so many strange and rough labourers . . . not only was it risky for women and children to be out after dark, but even men ran some danger'.[18]

On the 26th of May 1838 the *Preston Chronicle* informed its readers:

> Dreadful and Revolting Outrages: With loss of life. The inhabitants of Penwortham and Farington during the night of Monday last, were placed in the greatest state of alarm, owing to a severe conflict having taken place,

> between some of the villagers and a number of Irish labourers, who are employed at the north end of the North Union Railway, from Preston to Wigan, especially that portion of it in the neighbourhood of Farington school, about two miles and a half from this town. The conflict was of a very serious character, and as the sequel will show, was attended by the most disastrous consequences. The following day, Tuesday, was employed by both parties in preparing for battle, and as the night approached, the most serious results were apprehended.

The riot and subsequent inquest were reported in full by the press. What seems to have happened was this:

Saturday – payday on the railway. The local shopkeeper in Farington refused the labourers further credit. All paid their debts except Owen and Peter Deans, who blamed a local, John Mayor, for the shopkeeper's action.

Monday – between six and seven o'clock in the evening the two Deans visited Mayor's house, ostensibly looking for their friend Barny Kelly. 'They proceeded immediately to destroy all the furniture they could lay their hands on. The windows were dashed out, and the floor was strewed with the fragments of broken tables, the clock, crockeryware etc.'. They retired to the Blue Anchor pub and with five of their countrymen drove out about a dozen spinners who were drinking upstairs. In turn the spinners armed themselves and drove off the Irish, 'several broken heads were the consequence of this affray, and the Englishmen retired across the fields to collect their neighbours and fellow labourers, in anticipation of a general assault from the Irish labourers on the railway.' The Irish returned to the pub for a drink of rum, threatening to kill all Englishmen, 'On their road towards Tardy Gate, and to the railway, they so inhumanly beat two men named William Miller, of Walton, and Richard Livesey, of Farington, that they are now lying in a very precarious state'.

Tuesday – The rest of Monday evening and Tuesday both sides spent

St. Paul's Sunday School procession on Croston Road, Farington.

preparing for battle. 'Nothing of moment seems to have occurred until the hands turned out from Bashall's factory at half-past seven on Tuesday evening, when some hundreds of spinners and labourers went in a body towards the railway, cheering as they approached near to the Sumpter Horse in Penwortham, the headquarters of their opponents, and occasionally discharging, it is said, in bravado, fire-arms with which several had provided themselves'. Estimates of the crowd varied. Thomas Sims saw three or four hundred in a lane near Tardy Gate; Joseph Thornber a railway constable saw seven or eight hundred mostly boys eight to eighteen years of age, and William Birley, constable of Penwortham claimed around five to six hundred.

What happened next is uncertain. Both sides seem to have gathered around the house of Peter Smith, near Bee Lane. John Fitzpatrick, Overseer of Preston, testified, 'I saw a great crowd of persons coming towards Smith's house, shouting and huzzaing. Robert Robinson was one of the persons, and when he came right opposite Smith's house he called out, "Put out your lights, you soft devils, stand, and we'll drive the whole of them [meaning the Irish] out of the place". After Robinson and the party along with him had passed Smith's house about twenty yards, Robinson called out to them "fire". I saw the flash, and heard the report of three guns, which were fired in the direction of Smith's house. After further shooting I found two men lying upon the ground, a little above Smith's house. Pat Smith was then protecting them [the wounded], and said that no man should meddle with them. Smith at that time had not any gun with him. None of the Irishmen had any guns with them but about forty of them had sticks.' John Trafford, a labourer, had been shot dead and at least nine wounded. 'A bloody rencontre succeeded the death of this unfortunate young man: and it is computed that of English and Irish, from thirty to forty were more or less wounded'.

Wednesday, Thursday – On Wednesday the local magistrates met to consider what to do, and 'a detachment of military from, we believe, Burnley Barracks, paraded about in the neighbourhoods of Penwortham and Farington: but for their timely appearance it is more than probable that other breaches of the peace would have taken place. It is next to impossible to ascertain how many of the Irish are wounded, or to what extent, as great pains have been taken to conceal those who received injury.'

Smith was acquitted of the shooting and after eight hours the jury returned a verdict – 'Manslaughter against some person or persons unknown'. One June 2nd it was reported that Robert Robinson had been arrested, and his brother was being sought to stand trial at the quarter sessions. Feelings between the two sides seem to have been running high for some time for George Robinson, when asked to disperse the mob, replied, 'No, we are not willing, we have received so much injury from the Irish, that we are determined to have revenge.' The Irish had been armed with blackthorn sticks, cudgels and pieces of iron, the English with up to fifteen guns, scythes, hedge stakes and sticks.

Even by today's standards, the Battle of Farington was quite a large affair, and so the North Union Railway became associated with mob warfare, in addition to the terrors of timber bridges collapsing into raging torrents, and the press contained copious details of horrendous fatalities on the neighbouring lines, 'bodies exploded', 'leg torn off', 'boiler exploded at fearful speed' etc.

A Golden Age?

THE 1840s was a very difficult period in both agriculture and the cotton industry. The 'laissez-faire' government policy of the day precluded its interference in economic affairs, which were believed to have laws of their own. The most disastrous effects of this policy were seen in Ireland during the potato famine. In Leyland and district agriculture, as well as the declining handloom weaving industry, was badly affected. A letter to the press from a labourer in Farington complained,

> During a period of twenty years I have passed through a course of such incessant toil, and have been rewarded with such scanty fare for my wages, as few men have done without repining . . . I have worked most of my time for the farmers, and in the present depression of agricultural wages I was glad this last spring to hire myself to a neighbour for the season. For the first time in my life I find my spirits greatly depressed, and myself no longer entitled to the soubriquet of 'Happy Jack' with which my neighbours have designated me. I have today mowed ½ an acre of strong meadow grass, reached seven loads of hay, and cut in trusses another for the market tomorrow. I have been eighteen hours at work, and as my aching limbs deny me the comfort of balmy sleep, I have set down . . . to write this.
>
> Perhaps Sir, it may catch the eye of my masters, and induce him to have mercy on his slave, or of those who may, before it be too late to discover that the rate of taxes at present rung from the hard hands of peasants compels them to treat their servants as if their frames were of cast iron, and not of flesh and blood – *John Smith.*[19]

Right: *O.S. Map 1893 Extract showing Mount Pleasant Mill at Seven Stars.*

From the middle of the nineteenth century mill communities began to develop on Leyland Lane along the western fringe of the town. This extract also shows the site of the ancient manor water mill (Crawshaw Mill and Mill Pond), and Lower House, an important farm on the Farington estate noted for its fine cheese. Notice also that the Leyland Lane end of Fox Lane was known as Brook Street.

One political outcome of the economic depression was the growth of the Chartist movement which, through the submission of enormous petitions to Parliament, sought to bring about moderate political reform as a prelude to economic reform and ultimate revival. An important and essentially democratic reform movement, events frequently got out of hand with large crowds of desperate people attending meetings, and the absence of a professional police force to maintain law and order. Confrontation between the army and 'the mob' often resulted in bloodshed. On August 13th 1842 during a general strike demonstrators were shot dead during disturbances in Preston. At about 12 noon on the 17th word reached town that marchers were on their way from Chorley. People climbed the tower of the parish church to see them, and troops were put on the Ribble bridges:[20]

> The mob having started from Chorley, made to the factory of Messrs. Bashall and Co. at Leyland, where they obliged the hands to turn out, pulled out the plug of the boiler, and extinguished the fire. Bent, however, upon further mischief, they did not content themselves with this, but

Right: *Mount Pleasant Mill from Seven Stars c1900.*

A scene little changed today, although the mill chimney has gone. As late as 1939, Andrew Berry and Sons' mill had over 1,100 looms. (Leyland Museum).

Atherton Farm
Lostock Vale
Dunkirk Cottages
MILL STREET
W. M.
Reservoir
Alma Cottages
Crawshaw Mill
(Corn)
Mill Pond
Mill Lane
Mount Pleasant Mill
(Cotton)
GROVE STREET
Original Seven Stars
(P.H.)
Seven Stars
(P.H.)
Pedestal of
Stone Cross
BROOK STREET
Lostock Grove
Preston

levied contributions on some of the inhabitants of Leyland and the farmers in the neighbourhood, sweeping larders and pantries of their contents, and also enforcing pecuniary contributions.

Having visited the mills at Bamber Bridge and Walton this force, 'A large body of navigators, as they are called, that is, excavators employed in making the railway, colliers, weavers and others', armed with 'Bludgeons and other deadly weapons such as large iron bolts, iron bars, knives and scythes', and four or five hundred strong, was dispersed by the military on Walton Bridge.

Preston Lock Out

ONE of the most important industrial disputes of the nineteenth century was the thirty-week Preston Lock-out and Strike, from October 15th 1853 to May 13th 1854. Most of Lancashire's mill workers had won a ten per cent increase in wages, but, resisting the claims of local spinners and weavers, the Preston Millowners' Association closed the mills, locking out the operatives. Donations were collected from workers in those towns which had won the ten percent, enabling the unions to pay 7/- weekly to spinners, 4/- to weavers and 2/6d to cardroom hands. This enabled many strikers to avoid having to try to claim poor-relief from the Preston Board of Guardians.

Bashall and Boardmans do not appear to have been members of the Masters' Association but locked their workforce out anyway, presumably as an act of 'solidarity' with the Preston millowners. Given the lack of alternative employment in the area, and the fact that they were not party to the union payments, the Farington operatives were soon in a very sorry plight, having to walk daily to Preston for relief from the Guardians. Almost immediately they appealed to be allowed

Earnshaw Bridge Mill c1910. Leyland's first cotton mill, located to the north of Seven Stars at the junction of Golden Hill Lane, Leyland Lane and Longmeanygate. By the outbreak of the Second World War, the mill had just under 800 looms. Both Leyland Lane mills, Brook Mill and Farington Mill, weathered the economic disasters of the late 1920s and 1930s fairly well, and the industry in Leyland did not contract as rapidly as that in other Lancashire towns and in nearby Bamber Bridge and Walton-le-Dale. Although the chimney has been demolished, much of this site remains intact; worthy of particular note is the elegant engine house built for the mill steam engine.

to return to work, but the company refused to have them back.

In a change of tactics to break the unions the Preston owners re-opened the mills in December, expecting the workforce to return to work. Only those at Farington did, however, leading to their bitter denunciation as 'knobsticks' by the great majority of the workers who now went on strike.

The tactic having failed, the owners again closed the mills and the Farington workforce was again locked out. During bitterly cold winter conditions they had a daily walk of six miles to and from the stoneyard at Preston. In January the Royal Sovereign mill in Preston was re-opened and despite intimidation many hands from Farington found work. When all the mills were re-opened a second time in February 1854 the Farington workforce gladly returned to work. In Preston only one in twenty returned to work and the strike was not crushed until May 15th.[21]

The Cotton Famine

THE next great crisis in the local cotton industry was that of 1862-4, the Lancashire Cotton Famine. Speculation and disruption to the cotton supply caused by the American Civil War coincided with a steep cyclical trade depression caused by the over-supply of cotton goods and the collapse of Far Eastern markets. Farington was perhaps the worst affected community in Lancashire, and local people endured very considerable hardship. The mill seems to have closed in September 1862 and did not re-open until midway through 1864. In both Farington and Leyland 'relief committees' were established to channel funds from central appeal committees in London and Manchester. The Rev. Townson wrote of the Farington Committee,

> In the thirty-seven weeks during which the distress was at its worst Mr Power [the vicar] who acted as Secretary, received and distributed £2,027-4-9d. Of this large sum of money the Lord Mayor of London sent from the Mansion Hall fund £892: the Manchester Relief Committee sent £765, and £350 was raised in the neighbourhood.[22]

So badly was the village affected that frequent accounts of local conditions were published by the contemporary press. In December 1862 the annual garden party for the Sunday School Clothing Society was held: Mr Bashall, the owner, members of his family, the mill manager and three or four hundred local people attended. In contrast to earlier events, 'It was very pleasing to see the sympathy existing between these kind gentlemen and the people . . . repeated cheers were given for the liberal treatment which the people of the village are receiving from their kind employers'.[23]

In January 1863 the *Preston Chronicle* included a special report on the village, where 1,700 people were now in receipt of poor relief. Private charitable relief had been extensive, and the paper listed the range of articles donated,

> 100 pairs of sheets, 100 counterpanes, 350 flannel singlets, 150 petticoats,

500 shirts, 500 pairs of stockings and socks, 120 coats, vests and trousers, 120 gowns, 120 shawls, forty boys' suits, 200 pairs of blankets, fifty girls' dresses and 500 pairs of shoes. They have also got 300 pairs of boots and shoes repaired for the poor. This is a pretty substantial list for a place so small as Farington.[24]

The improvement in trading conditions, and particularly rising demand for goods, resulted in the re-opening of the mill amid much celebration, an event long remembered in local folk-lore, and until recently commemorated by an annual procession. As the *Preston Herald* reported on April 30th 1864:

Messrs. Bashall and Boardman's mill, at Farington, had been stopped for a year and a half when at last an intimation was given on a certain Wednesday that cotton was on its way from Liverpool, and that work was about to be resumed. All that day the villagers looked anxiously for the arrival of their old acquaintance – cotton. It was nearly noon, however, on Thursday before a couple of wagons of cotton were deposited in the mill siding. The shouts and acclamations of the spectators at once announced to the inhabitants the glad tidings. Soon the village began to evince signs of rejoicing, and Union Jacks, flags, shawls, etc., were hung gaily from almost every window. About one o'clock a large number of women, preceded by music, went down to the railway siding, and with hearty vigour pushed the wagons with their welcome freight up the steep and curved incline into the factory yard. This done, the crowd, numbering now some hundreds, sang the doxology to the tune of the 'old hundred', and then gave many rounds of hearty cheers, which were heard far away.

This was not to be the end of the trials of the workforce. On July 3rd 1867 the factory caught fire and was destroyed, the heat being so intense as to burn grass in the surrounding fields; 'Many . . . did their duty that day as brave Englishmen, and they did it the more willingly because they loved and respected the masters, whose loss and grief that day was great'. As the flames destroyed 50,000 spindles, William Boardman was reported to cry, 'What will my poor workpeople do now?'[25] Rebuilt, Farington Mill was to run for a further hundred years, closing only in the 1960s.

Hard times and boom times in Leyland

BY the 1860s, Leyland still had just a single mill – Mr Pilkington's Earnshaw Bridge Mill, with five pairs of spinning mules driving 6,600 spindles: Farington Mill had forty-five pairs and 57,800 spindles.[26] Yet in Leyland Parish the Cotton Famine seems to have affected many more people, the local relief committee distributed money and goods worth £4,400, against £2,000 in Farington. Clearly, much distress appears to have been caused in the township by the closure of the bleachworks. It is difficult to assess the overall local situation since Farington was a part of the Preston Poor Law Union, whilst Leyland was part of the Chorley Union. In Preston detailed statistical analyses were prepared by the workhouse authorities, the police, and the trades unions and these have survived. Such information does not appear to be so readily accessible for Chorley, but working largely from newspapers it is possible to gain at least an impression of events in Leyland.

By May 1862 the Chorley Board of Guardians was relieving almost eight hundred people in the parish of Leyland; by the following January this figure reached a peak of almost 2,000, and only fell below 1,000 again in August 1864. By late 1865, almost 500 people were still receiving poor relief. On September 22nd 1862 'A meeting of the inhabitants of Leyland was held at the Constabulary station, Leyland . . . to consider the best means of affording relief to the distressed operatives of the parish. It was the opinion of the meeting that an extraordinary effort was quite necessary. Ultimately, the parish, which is a very extensive one, was divided into districts, and visitors were appointed to ascertain the amount of distress etc. The meeting was then adjourned to Monday next, pending the report of the visiting committee'.

At the following meeting it was decided to distribute money in the form of tickets which could be exchanged in shops for goods, and the committee would reimburse the shopkeepers. A sewing class was to be set up by Mr Morrell, and for attending, women were to receive 6d per day. But more to the point 'Before the meeting broke up it was announced that £66 had been subscribed in the room'. The following week 'An Industrial School for distressed females was opened in Leyland at the Union Hall on Monday, 129 attended'. To be open four days per week, the school was conducted by Mrs and the Misses Farington, Mrs Eccles, the Misses Master, Mr Hargreaves, the Misses Burdon, Mrs D. Swann, Miss Riley and Mrs Norris. Subscriptions had reached £100, and the committee met on Tuesdays 2-5 pm to scrutinise claims for help. 'Relief was granted in some cases . . .'[27]

By the end of November the press had reported that 'The distress in Leyland continues to increase. Upwards of 700 persons are now on the books of the relief committee and receive relief at the rate of from 6½d to 7½d each per week'.[28] The Walton-le-Dale committee seems to have managed to provide 2/- to 3/- per person but since the Leyland committee's papers have not survived, it is difficult to be certain of the significance of this small sum. It may, for instance, have represented a bonus on top of payments from other sources. The final monthly report of the committee was published in full by the *Preston Chronicle:* of 730 cotton workers in the district, 105 were working full-time, eighty-five part-time and 540 were still entirely unemployed. The London committee had sent Leyland £1,640 that in Manchester £1,866, and £905 had been raised locally.[29] In addition, a soup kitchen is said to have been organised at Worden Hall for the unemployed, and the Faringtons were very much involved in the local effort. Despite the large number of people still unemployed, the press report was optimistic,

> Messrs Bashall and Boardman having commenced work at their mill at Farington, and no inconsiderable number of factory operatives having obtained other employment or left the village, very little distress now prevails in Leyland. It is also expected that the bleachworks will shortly be in full operation, and if so, matters will be still better. One drawback still remains, Mr F. S. Pilkington's mill, at Earnshaw Bridge is still stopped.

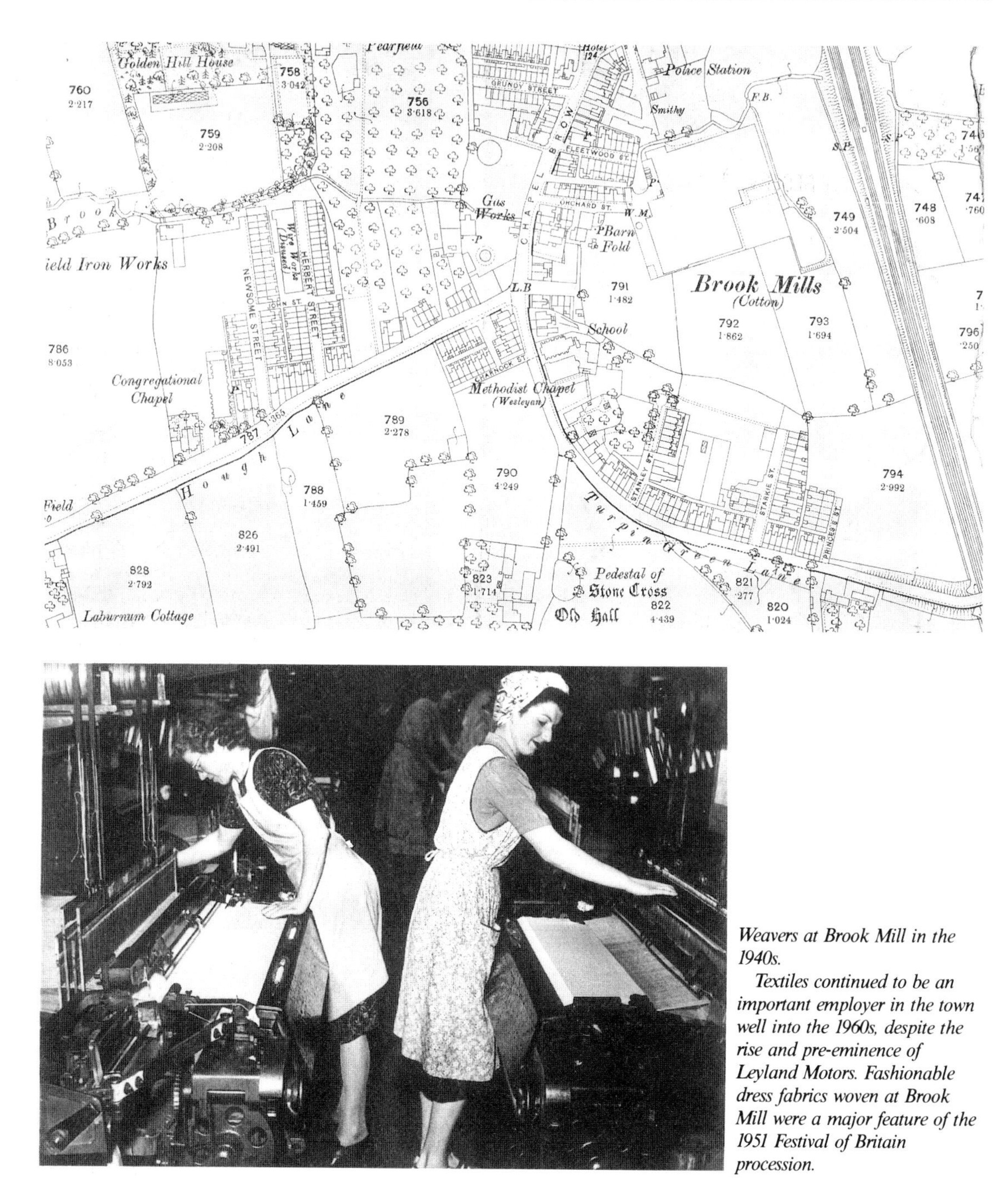

Weavers at Brook Mill in the 1940s.

Textiles continued to be an important employer in the town well into the 1960s, despite the rise and pre-eminence of Leyland Motors. Fashionable dress fabrics woven at Brook Mill were a major feature of the 1951 Festival of Britain procession.

The relief committee ceased their operations about a month ago.

The committee had operated for eighty-nine weeks.[30] The scenes witnessed at Farington were echoed at Leyland in August 1864, when the bleachworks re-opened after a legal dispute:

'Re-opening of the Shruggs Bleach Works - Great rejoicings at Leyland'

Left: O.S. Map 1893 Chapel Brow extract showing Brook Mill.

The last of the town's cotton mills to be opened, in the 1870s, Brook Mill was also the largest. The map shows the comparatively undeveloped nature of much of Hough Lane at the start of the twentieth century, and the site of Charnock Hall. Housing in Herbert Street and Newsome Street was largely occupied by rubber workers, and the Rubber Company was probably the town's largest employer at this time. This end of Leyland was thus still seperated from the old centre around the cross by open fields.

Great rejoicing took place yesterday at Leyland, the occasion being the taking possession by the new proprietors, Dr. Pilkington and Mr T. Holt, of Chorley, of the Shruggs Bleach Works, which they have lately purchased, and which are shortly to resume work. The news that there was a prospect of employment being again afforded at this establishment has caused great satisfaction in a striking manner, as was lately done at Farington, when the cotton mills of Messrs Bashall and Boardman resumed work. In accordance with previously arranged plans, a procession was formed shortly after 8 o'clock in the morning. It was composed of the workmen and their wives, in all nearly 200 in number. The Leyland brass band took its post at the head, and was immediately followed by three men, each bearing a broom: testifying that a little of the party spirit, caused by the late litigation concerning these works, still remained. All being in readiness, the band struck up its enlivening strains, flags and banners were enthusiastically waved, and the procession proceeded on its way to the railway station. Two mottos borne in the procession were, 'Welcome to the new proprietors' and 'A heart that can feel another:' the latter was painted on a piece of wood cut in the shape of a heart. The people were almost beside themselves with joy: many of them have suffered deeply for a long time, and we hope, with them, that yesterday commenced a new era of prosperity. On reaching the railway station they expected to meet the new owners of the mill, but these gentlemen had left the train at Euxton, having probably heard what awaited them at Leyland, and probably not desirous of receiving such an ovation. On returning from the railway station the procession halted at Mr Robinson's, The Ship Inn, who acted very generously towards them. Afterwards they proceeded by way of the village to the works, where many of them danced in the field adjoining. At intervals throughout the day the bells of the Parish Church rang out their merry peals, and there was many a fervent wish expressed yesterday, not merely by the workpeople, but by the other inhabitants of Leyland for the prosperity of the firm.'[31]

Within ten years a large and prosperous factory-based textile industry had developed in the town. Seven Stars Mill was developed with Earnshaw Bridge Mill on Leyland Lane; Brook Mill was opened on the edge of the old village, but close to the railway; and the Stannings had taken over the Bleachworks. Within thirty years an extensive cottage-based handloom industry had been superceded, and Leyland, though still essentially a rural district, had many of the attributes of a mill town.

By the 1870s it is also possible to trace the origins of the town's next industrial revolution, which was to transform it so completely during the twentieth century, in the very early development of the rubber industry. Yet right through the exciting developments of the early-twentieth century, it is important to realise that large numbers of townspeople were employed in textiles; that textiles were to remain an important staple of the local economy well into the 1960s. Although the Lancashire cotton industry fell into decline after 1921, all the Leyland mills were to survive the Second World War, and Farington Mill, Brook Mill and John Stanning's bleachworks were to survive well into the post-war period. Some idea of the size of the mills and the range of their products can be gained from the Lancashire Textile Industry Directories which were published annually, as in this example for 1939:[32]

John Stanning and Son Ltd: Bleachers Association Ltd., Leyland

Bleachworks; Bleachers, dyers and finishers of cotton and rayon material; specialists - poplins, cellulars, spun viscose fabrics, permanent organdies, and the crease-resisting finish. Manchester office, 20 Kennedy Street, F.L. Barnett, Manager.

Andrew Berry and Sons (1920) Ltd., Mount Pleasant Mill: 1,113 looms: Embroidery, cambrics, casement, umbrella, balloon and typewriter cloths, drillettes, warp satins and poplins etc.

John Pilkington Ltd. (1900): Earnshaw Bridge Mill: 771 looms: fine cambrics, downproofs, spun rayons, muslins, nainsooks and aircraft fabrics. John Pilkington, Managing Director, Secretary and Salesman.

Brook Mill (Leyland) Ltd. Brook Mill: 1,000 looms: rayon goods, plains, fancies, crepes and brocades in 100 per cents and mixtures: plain and striped cotton poplins, casement cloths etc. R. A. J. Berry, Managing Director, William Marland and J. Ferneley, Salesmen.

The textile industry thus profoundly shaped the development of Leyland for over 200 years. Yet, whereas other towns were to remain largely based on a single industry - cotton - which by the 1920s and 1930s was facing massive contraction, other sectors of the Leyland economy were able to develop to produce the very rapid growth of the present century: one of the most remarkable features of the history of Leyland.

Chapter Eight

Life in Victorian Leyland

HE rapid growth of Leyland in the early decades of the nineteenth century was not maintained thereafter, and the population, having risen to over 3,000 people in 1821, did not exceed 4,000 for a further half century. For much of this period the rate of growth between the ten-year censuses was generally below five per cent. After 1871 this picture changed radically: between 1871 and 1881 the population increased by almost thirty per cent, from 3,389 to 4,961, from 1881 to 1891 by twenty per cent to 5,972, reaching 6,865 by the end of the century.

Part of this growth may be accounted for by increased employment opportunities in the textile industry - for example, the opening of Brook Mill by Reade and Wall and the expansion of the Shruggs bleachworks under the Stannings - but of increasing importance was the development of the rubber industry.

The Leyland Rubber Company

A trade directory of 1851 records 'William Smith, Manufacturer of waterproof cloths, piping and washers, Golden Hill Works', and in 1861 'James Quin, India Rubber Manufacturer, Golden Hill Lane'. By 1873 this firm was recorded as 'James Quin and Co. Ltd. (India Rubber, hose pipes, gutta percha etc.) Golden Hill Lane'. It is tempting to see the early attempts to weave waterproof cloth and hosepipe as a local outgrowth from the failing handloom weaving industry which had its last local stronghold along Golden Hill Lane.[1]

The increasing importance for local employment of the rubber industry, in which the town thus had an early lead, is clearly apparent from the census returns. Mr William Smith having recently died in 1861, his widow is listed as 'Hosepipe Manufacturer, Golden Hill Lane' with Robert Banister listed as works manager. Ralph Higham gave his occupation as 'hose-pipe weaver', and by 1871 many people in

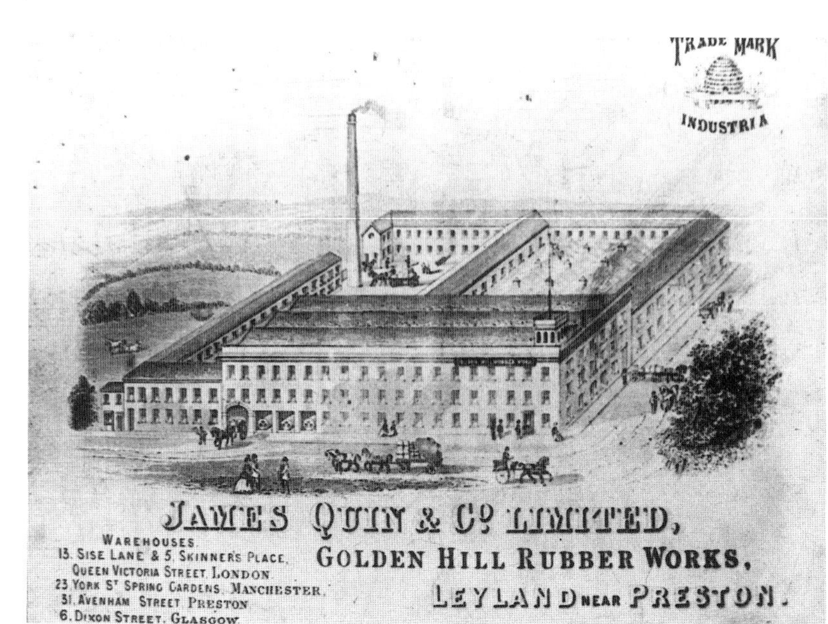

Advertisement: James Quinn's Rubber Works.
By 1890 Leyland had emerged as an important centre of the rubber industry. (Leyland Library).

the area were employed in the industry. James Quin (then aged forty-two) lived at Laburnum Cottage, and gave his occupation as 'India Rubber Manufacturer employing eighty-two men, five boys, twenty-six women', whilst in Peel Terrace, Cowling Lane, Mary Keeling and her four brothers and sisters are all listed as 'India Rubber Makers.' An early visitor to their factory was a certain Mr Mackintosh.

A part of the Leyland Workhouse c1950.
The Rubber Company used premises formerly belonging to the workhouse. (Leyland Museum).

In 1898 the Leyland Rubber Co. amalgamated with Stanley Morrison and Co. of London and with the Birmingham Rubber Co. to form the Leyland and Birmingham Rubber Co. In 1906 the Palatine Heel Co. of Preston and James T. Gaudie and Co. of Glasgow were incorporated in the firm. In the 1930s two employees, John King (aged seventy-two) and Robert Cheetham (seventy-seven), were both still working for the company, and recalled the early pioneer days:[2]

> Their recollections go back to 1872, when the works was then under the name of James Quin and Co., and was composed only of an old workhouse building. Flax-woven hose pipes, a small quantity of packing, and the manufacture of stack and cart covers kept about fifty men occupied very busily during the summer, although during the winter-time work was not quite so plentiful . . . No water was laid on to the works and had to be brought to the works by means of a tub slung between the shafts of a cart, which tub was filled up from a nearby brook . . . In those days, rubber arrived only from Brazil and in balls. When these were cut open it was not a surprising thing to find stones and bits of old iron in the centre; the natives would put these in the centre of the balls before wrapping them in order to increase the weight. In many cases livestock was included in the cases of rubber, and upon one occasion one of the men was bitten

Scenes following the fire at the Rubber Works in January 1913. Although damage was extensive, the fire did not seriously affect the long-term development of the works. (Leyland Museum).

Heavy Industry: conveyor belts. With the drive towards rationalisation and greater productivity in the mining industry, conveyor belts formed an important area of the company's business, being in use virtually all over the world. The staff magazine in November 1930, for example, contained a report by Mr Fred Bolton of Leyland describing the successful use of belts in the nitrate mines of northern Chile. (Leyland Library).

so badly by a centipede as to necessitate the amputation of his arm. Snakes were also a common find . . . Work used to start at six o'clock in the morning and finish at six o'clock every night excepting Friday, when they finished at eight o'clock. At two o'clock on Saturday afternoon our works finished for the week.

Leyland in those days was quite a small place, and probably deserved its old title – The Garden of Lancashire. One or two small cotton factories only were in Leyland and the people were rather amazed at a rubber works starting in their midst. Rubber being quite unknown to them and quite an impossible sort of material with which to work. Hose makers came up from Tottenham . . . and these commenced the manufacture of rubber hose . . . When the Zulu War was on a great number of rubber pontoons of eighteen to twenty feet long were made for use of the army. During the Russo-Japanese War we made an immense quantity of rubber pipes 2½ feet and 3 feet diameter and 20 or 30 feet long. What these were used for neither John nor Bob can remember.

One of the buildings – the hose room – was built of very rough stone obtained from nearby quarries, and the roof was not entirely waterproof. In heavy rain the men had to be very careful and move themselves and their work across the room to places where water did not drip through. Later in the history of the firm they tell of the days when Mr James T. Goudie came to Leyland and of the meeting which was held in the hose-room, when all the employees attended and Mr Goudie said, 'I have invested £30,000 in this Company and I am determined to make it go'.

As John King said 'It has never looked back since then'.

James Quins' firm was the largest of a number of rubber companies in the town, which by 1922 included J. E. Baxter and Co. Ltd., the Victory Rubber Co. ('Manufacturers of rubber heels, soles and tips,

Three scenes in the Leyland Rubber Works, c1930.
The successful application of rubber to a great range of domestic products was the key to continued growth in the industry between the wars, in addition to its more traditional applications in heavy industry.
Left, top: *The Hot Water Bottle Department.*
Left, bottom: *The Bulb Department.*
Above: *The Cushion Department.*
(Leyland Library).

rubber tilings and erasers'.) and Wood-Milne Ltd. ('Manufacturers of rubber heels, soles and tips, pneumatic tyres and inner tubes for motor cars and motor cycles, solid band types for motor vehicles, belts for motor cycles, footpumps for motor tyres, golf balls and all classes of manufactured goods'), who claimed to have been first to apply rubber to footwear manufacture. By 1932 Baxters had opened a respirator assembly factory, and the British Goodrich Rubber Co. was also established, on Golden Hill Lane. In 1924 Wood Milne Ltd. was acquired by an American company, which in 1934 became the British Tyre and Rubber Co., becoming BTR Industries Ltd. in 1957.

The industry also acted as a spur to the local engineering industry. On his return from America in 1885 James Iddon was appointed chief engineer to the then Leyland Rubber Co., and established the firm of Iddon Bros. in 1888. In a directory of 1892 they are listed as 'Machine Makers and Engineers for rubber manufacturers'. Throughout the inter-war period L and B pioneered the application of rubber to a wide range of uses, from bathing caps and hot-water bottles to enormous conveyor belts used in mining industries all over the world. One important contribution to the popular culture of the 1930s was their extensive development of multi-coloured floorings for public buildings, theatres and cinemas and, most spectacularly of all, the great ocean liners of the day, becoming a fundamental feature of the art-deco style of the period.[3]

A recent computer-based analysis of the 1881 census returns has clearly identified the expansion of the rubber industry as a major process in the town's evolution at this time.[4] Yet the process of urbanisation was still restricted, for as late as 1912, when the second six-inch Ordnance Survey map of the district was published, the rubber industry, Brook Mill and Leyland Motors Ltd. occupied a rough rectangle formed by Hough Lane, School Lane, Golden Hill

Another conveyor belt is ready for despatch.

Lane and the railway. This industrial zone was thus quite separate from the traditional centre of the town around the cross, and the outlying mill communities of Earnshaw Bridge and Seven Stars.

The old village and the emerging industrial zone were linked by Water Street, which still ran between broad fields to the east and west. To the west of the village the bleachworks was surrounded by fields. These developments thus rather passed the old village by, enabling it to survive relatively unscathed into the later-twentieth century and the attention of the town planners.

The Garden of Lancashire

A colourful picture of life in Leyland in the 1870s was provided by Anthony Hewitson ('Atticus') in *Our Country Churches and Chapels* (1872). This series of articles, originally published in the press, took the form of descriptions and his impressions of visits to the local churches. He obviously liked Leyland, then regarded as the garden of the county, but was impressed by its rising industries as well as the antiquity and natural beauty of its setting:

> In these modern days the parish of Leyland, which has an area of 19,091 statute acres, seems to be the paradise of potato growers on work days, and the elysium of currant-cake eaters on Sundays. There is no place under God's blue sky, taking size into account, where so much currant-bread is destroyed on the Sabbath, or so many good potatoes cultivated on week days, as at Leyland. And hardly any place do we know – no place do we know – where there are so, so many cottage gardens. We dare back Leylanders for gardening against all the known tribes of the earth. We rather like Leyland for its dogged, persistent faith in currant-cakes,

> potatoes and gardening – there is a rich bucolic eccentricity about its passion for them, which superinduces special admiration: but apart from all these things, we like Leyland for its genial, rural appearance. It stands in a pleasant place, is surrounded on all hands by a unique picture of pastoral beauty – by flowers and fruitful flocks, by blooming orchards and smiling homesteads, by grand old trees and fertile lands. Rather straggling and incoherent is it, in a topographical sense, and yet, as a whole, it makes up a sweet and congenial part of creation. It is like one long, quietly-wandering street, there is no clustering, no architectural crushing to death in it, you can breathe freely in the place . . . Leyland is a busy village, and an additional impetus is given to its commercial life by sundry adjoining manufactories.

At the parish church Hewitson noted the fine trees, the ringing of the ancient curfew bell, the frequent references to ale in the parish registers and the gooseberry tree which grew for many years 'at the side of the steeple near one of the clock dials'. The vicar, the Rev. T. R. Baldwin was fifty years old:

> A burly, condensed, strong-lunged, outspoken gentleman, has been seventeen years vicar, is unmarried, believes much in riding on horseback, dresses in a very horsey fashion, looks often like a cross between a learned steeplechaser and a gentleman farmer, is spirited, talks with a fashionable accent, reads and preaches very sharply, venerates piety, good horses, magisterial position, substantial dinners, English candour, light tight breeches and vicarial privileges.

The service was similarly colourful.

> It was in the forenoon, the time being exactly 10.35. The church below was well filled with an orderly congregation, made up of all classes of rural people, and those at the sides seemed to have a weakness for jamming their hats into the window bottoms. Above, all around in the gallery region, there were people of various kinds, all respectable, but only numerically small, considering the capacity of the seats.
>
> We have seen many ecclesiastical curiosities in our time, but this three-decker [pulpit] at Leyland takes the palm for whimsicality and intricacy. There is many a worse oddity in a show, and if ever it is dispensed with it would constitute an eligible investment for some travelling curiosity exhibitor.
>
> On the other side of the pulpit . . . there is a select corner, containing eight stalls, in which there are two elderly ladies, who are fronted by seven blooming females, apparently servants, and four men, three being in livery, and one dressed up in a finely antique style, with stiff powdered hair. This we presumed to be the private chapel of the Farington family; and our speculation afterwards turned out to be correct.

Most remarkable of all he found a high sided pew, which he had to reach over to see in, and which contained a host of young ladies from a local ladies' school. This was Mr Parker's pew.

> There is a fireplace in the pew – when Mr Parker . . . attended he used to have a fire lighted in it in winter – at one end there is a convenience enough for a cupboard, or a sideboard, along with a small bed. How exquisite it would be to patronise a neat refreshment cupboard, and then nestle upon an easy couch, before a warm fire, in such a genteely secluded pew, during a dull sermon in winter.

At the Roman Catholic church in Worden Lane, Hewitson found

> The average attendance on a Sunday, taking the morning and afternoon, is between 200 and 300 – not a good attendance when it is remembered

> that Catholicism has much to struggle with in Leyland. All the great folks here have keen anti-Popery instincts: Catholicism and dissent are not particularly fashionable articles: and whilst many may have the wish, few have the courage, to follow their own genuine inclinations. They have to live in the district, and it is a hard thing to quarrel with one's bread and butter. The congregation at the Catholic chapel we are at is made up for the most part of poor people who manifest a striking devotedness to their mission . . . some of them enter rather late: and a few of them have by their side most enormous umbrellas – not sentimental, ivory-handled, gossamer-winged things: but genuine, full grown, old fashioned articles, nearly big enough, if fairly held up, to keep a tree dry in a thunderstorm.

The Methodist Chapel was located in the industrial district.

> The principal Dissenting place of worship in Leyland belongs to the Wesleyans. It is called 'Golden Hill Chapel' . . . Gas, cotton, steam, railway wagons, and drink, five of the most certain coinmaking articles known, in fair weather, enter into the business of the immediate locality. Golden Hill stands in a thriving part of Leyland, and if its virtue is as vigorous as its surrounding trade, it ought to be a moderately paradisaical spot . . . [the chapel] is a small, stiff, strong, stone-building, like a respectable barn with windows . . . Just within and between the entrances there are some small, deep, green-painted pews, in which we notice a few elderly people and two or three youngsters devouring toffy. Beyond there is a large stove getting red hot at the bottom, and roaring away very fiercely up an iron pipe which goes through the ceiling. Ahead of us are about half a dozen forms . . . youngsters and elderly people are sitting upon them, and in front of all these are seven lads, nearly all of a size, who employ their time in feet swinging, yawning, and pushing the form back with the view of either upsetting it or frightening each other. A young man upon a stage, in front of the pulpit, is quietly engaged in playing a harmonium, and looking round occasionally to see who is coming in.

Erected before the large scale development around Farington Mill became apparent, the church of St. Pauls at Farington was

> The most striking specimen of a church in the wrong place that we have yet seen . . . The interior of the church is plain and rather bold, and a great nailing business seems to have been carried on at some time in it. There are scores of nails in the walls, and hundreds of places out of which nails have been pulled. The pews are heavy, high, broad, and closed at the sides with doors. They run in parallel order up the church. In the aisle, running down the centre, there are sundry small forms, and a rather cyclopean stove. The children sit behind and they are about as lively a body as we can think of . . . the organ playing is accurate and somewhat tasteful; the singing is vigorous, rough and ready, and is rather spoiled by the melodious capering of the school lads below, who prick up their ears astonishingly when a tune is started, and wander off into all kinds of noisy unmusical byepaths when it has got really on the swing. They have a knack of making everyone around them smile.

Hewitson also visited St. James Church in Slater Lane, built in memory of James Nowell Farington:

> This district is known as Leyland Moss – a flat, pastoral, peaty, moderately-civilised part of the county . . . the people belong to a supremely deferential race. The congregation, very small when we entered, is getting very large; and appears to be made up mostly of persons engaged in agricultural pursuits, and children. There are many young people of both sexes, and whilst the females with their clean bright faces and florid bonnets nip across the floor with a light hurried tread, to

various quarters, the lads and young men come tumbling in, and skelp across the floor with their heavy shoes, stroking their hair down as they go, and looking as if they were going to run against the first thing they met and knock it down.

Late-Victorian Leyland

MANNEX'S *Directory of Preston* for 1880 describes Leyland as, 'A large and respectable village. Numerous houses have been erected here within the last few years so that the place presents rather the appearance of a town than a village; and that important works are carried on will be seen on reference to the directory'. The large houses of the well-to-do at this date included Worden Hall, Golden Hill House, Wellington House, Broadfield, Beech Villa, the Vicarage, Lostock Grove, the Lodge, Moss House, Townfield House, The Grove, Crook Hey and St. James' Vicarage. In 1892 Barrett's *Directory* reported that 'numerous houses have been erected here in recent years . . . There are several important works carried on including cotton

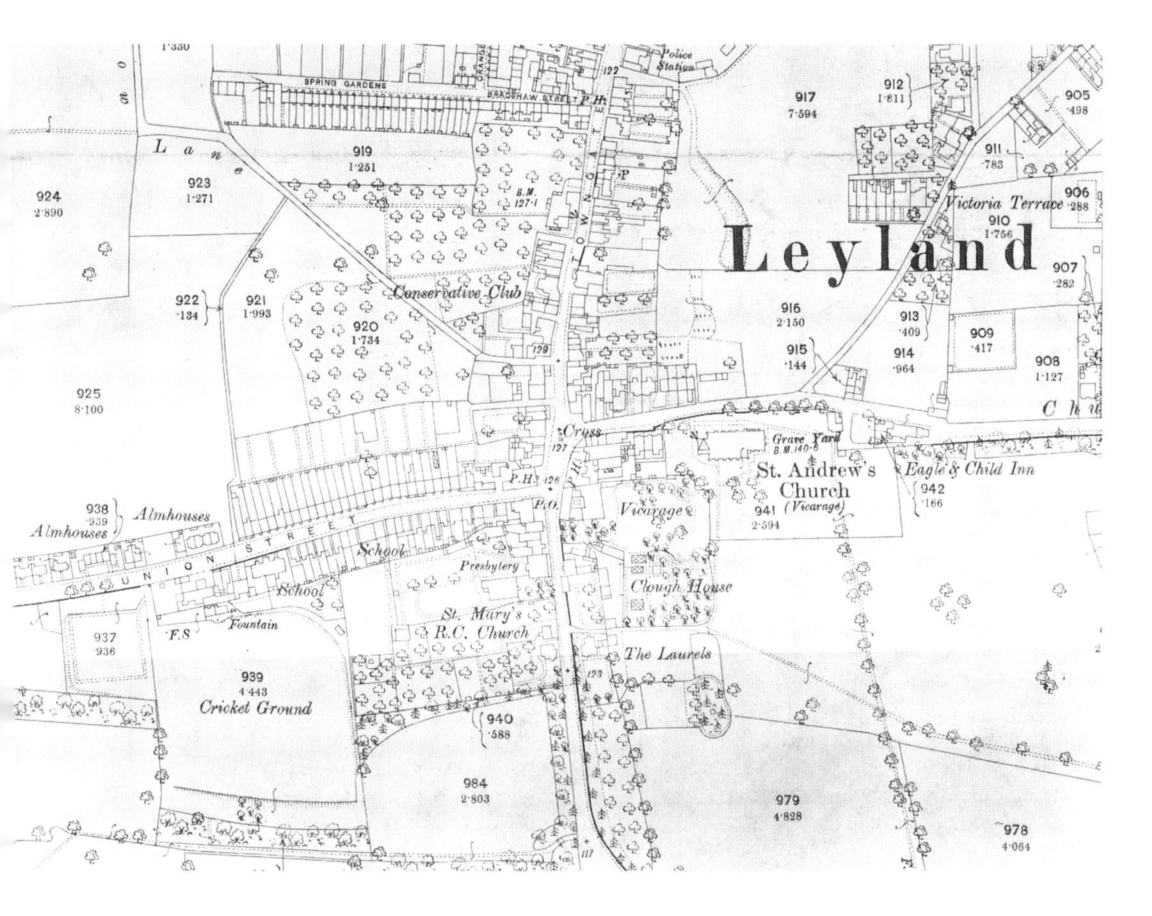

O.S. Map 1893. Central Leyland extract.
The town centre around the cross was to remain little changed until the extensive demolition and development schemes of the 1960s. The fragment which remains has been designated a 'conservation area' and forms part of a local history heritage trail devised by members of the Leyland Historical Society, leaflets for which may be obtained at the Museum.
Note the development of the cricket ground, the Catholic church on Worden Lane, and the gardens and trees which were still very much a feature of the townscape.

manufacturing and bleaching, rubber works, wire mill, machine works, etc. The bleaching works belong to the firm of John Stanning and Son, and rank amongst the finest bleaching works in the country.' This growth is further indicated by the town's rising rateable value – £23,600 in 1881, £31,246 in 1892 and £32,620 in 1901. The comparable figures for Farington are £12,236, £18,000 and £18,690.

In contrast to the trend towards a general levelling of incomes apparent for much of the present century, Leyland in the late-nineteenth century contained a number of conspicuously wealthy individuals, very rich by today's standards and able to employ considerable numbers of servants. The prevalence of 'old' and 'new' money is revealed in the census return of 1881. John Stanning, of Broadfield, Leyland, was recorded as 'Bleacher: Master employing 159 males and 61 females'. His household comprised:

John Stanning	(head)	Bleacher	aged40
Harriet	(wife)		30
Hannah Mary	(daughter)		5
John	(son)		3
Joseph	(son)		1
Mary E. Smith		Governess	26
Miriam Lewis		Servant, cook	37
Jane Smithson		Nurse	26
Mary Tippler		Housemaid	26
Edith Moxon		Kitchen Maid	18
Henry Sanderson		Day Waiter	67

In contrast to developments on Golden Hill, at Worden Hall the traditions of an eighteenth-century landed estate were continued by the two surviving sisters of James Nowell Farington:[5]

Susan Maria Farington	(head)	Landowner	aged 72
Mary Hannah Farington	(sister)	Landowner	62
Susan Barkett		Housekeeper	62
Sarah Williams		Ladies' Maid	59
Jane Nichils		Ladies' Maid	49
John Peckitt		Butler	33
Robert Pool		Footman	23
Jane Goodier		Laundry Maid	42
Jane Chamberlain		Dairy Maid	39
Alice Dickinson		House Maid	30
Jane Thomas		house Maid	30
Clara Ayses		Kitchen Maid	22
Lavinia Richards		Scullery Maid	12
Robert Chippett		Groom	21

The census returns of 1851-81 provide a glimpse of servant life at the hall. During this period there were never fewer than eleven servants, employed from widely separate parts of the north country. A majority of them were females, generally under thirty years of age. Only two were listed as having married, and only two of the servants recorded in 1881 appear on earlier censuses – so that it is perhaps fair to conclude that on marriage they left service. Beyond the house there was also a population of gardeners, gamekeepers and labourers and their families, housed in the various lodges and adjacent property.

Iddon and Baxters' Patent Tyre c1890.

In the late-nineteenth century Leyland was at the forefront of technological innovation, in contrast to the local mill towns whose economies remained largely dependent on textiles. (Leyland Museum).

Leyland Baldwin

THE Vicar of Leyland also continued to exert considerable influence in the developing town, and the Rev. Octavius de Leyland Baldwin (vicar 1891-1913: Leyland Baldwin, as he preferred to be known, 'Occy' Baldwin as he was popularly known) sought to harness these trends to the material advantage of the people of Leyland. The brother of W. C. Baldwin, the African Pioneer (the first European from the east coast to reach the Victoria Falls on the Zambia River on August 4th 1860)[6] he was a High-Church Anglican, Irish Home Ruler, social reformer, opponent of the Boer War, and educationalist. A man manifestly ahead of his time, he was frequently brought into conflict with the local council. In 1901 he opposed a scheme to remove Leyland Cross,

> It was told to me in sober earnest, by a man in authority, that as Leyland was a coming place, an improvement of which it stood in need, was the removal of the village cross, and the erection of an incandescent lamp in its stead, flanked on either side by a public urinal.

The Rev. Octavius de Leyland Baldwin, Vicar of Leyland (1891-1913).

The last of the line of Baldwin vicars, a progressive social reformer, Irish Home Ruler and High Church Anglican. (Leyland Library).

On another occasion he complained of the condition of the local roads, particularly Fox Lane, in wet weather. When these fell on deaf ears, the vicar began to deliberately riding his tricycle on the footpath each time he saw a policeman. Ultimately fined five shillings with costs, and duly given wide coverage in the local newspapers, money was found for the roads.

He offered land for the development of a public park, a children's playground, and swimming baths, facilities which the town would have had over fifty years before they were actually provided – all to no avail. He particularly clashed with a group styling themselves 'Leyland Ratepayers', whose principal object was cheap rates. He criticised the standard of the town's water, and the closing off to the public of traditional recreation grounds, such as the village greens, 'Where is Turpin Green? where are Clayton Green, Cuerden Green, Waterhouse

Green, Lucas Green, Flash Green, Shaw Green and many another? Gone! and if ever again public property, they will have to be bought from those who cribbed them.'

Perhaps his greatest battle concerned the offer by the millionaire, Mr Andrew Carnegie, of £1,800 for the construction of a free library. Amazingly, the local council was not enthusiastic about the offer, considering the expense of wages, lighting, heating etc, and after the opinion of the ratepayers had been consulted the offer was refused. Vicar Baldwin wrote

> Grateful to be saved the loss of a penny in the pound, it has been suggested that the portrait of the anonymous author of the 'Several Ratepayers' [an abusive letter denouncing Mr Carnegie and signed 'Several Ratepayers' was widely believed to have swayed the debate] should at once be hung in the council chamber, with the title 'The triumph of ignorance'. John Bull has in spite of pin-pricks and prods, rolled heavily round, and groaned in his sleep, 'Why don't you let me alone?'

Thus Leyland did not acquire the social facilities of a modern town. Their absence was to have profound implications, and was fundamental to the generally critical attitude to the existing town centre which is apparent in the various reports of the New Town planners and town-centre developers of the 1960s.

Leyland Baldwin began to sell off the traditional church lands in Leyland, which he saw as an anachronism in the modern age, including a large tract of land to the north of Hough Lane which was bought by James Sumner – the future North Works of Leyland Motors. In this respect the remarks of his curate E. G. Marshall are particularly significant, 'I believe he was ever thinking, not of himself, or indeed merely of the present, but of the future, and posterity. He wanted Leyland to be up-to-date, in sanitation, in education, in cleanliness and in all those things which promote the heath and happiness of the people at large'.[7] On his death in 1913 the 165 year old link between the parish and the Baldwin family came to an end. As on the death of Susan Maria Farington nineteen years earlier, another strand binding Leyland to its pre-industrial past was broken.

Leyland Festival

ONE of the more enduring innovations of this period was the establishment of the Leyland festival in 1889. Although based on the parish's flourishing Sunday Schools this popular event also drew on a long established tradition of Leyland Club walking days, and a not inconsiderable source of local amateur dramatic talent. In June 1889 the parish magazine reported the success of the event:

> The 29th of May proved to be a day of storm and sunshine, of hopes and fears. The weather was so uncertain, with gusts of wind and rain, that, until the time appointed for the procession to start, there seemed little probability of the festivities being carried out. Every preparation having

been made, the long line of children, dressed in every variety of character, took its way through the village and returned without experiencing any very great amount of inconvenience, although one heavy shower served to damp the joyous spirits, as well as the festal finery, of the processionists. A large number of people had gathered on the field, and the programme was gone through with as much care as possible under the circumstances. The plaiting of the May Pole and the other dances were admirably executed, and from the remarks of the company present it was easy to gather that the efforts of the children were appreciated, and that due credit was given

PROGRAMME

OF THE

LEYLAND MAY FESTIVITIES,

Wednesday, May 29, 1889.

The PROCESSION will be formed at 2-30 p.m. at the Schools, Union St., and proceed by way of Towngate, Hough Lane, Chapel Brow, as far as the Railway Station, returning by the same route to the Show Field.

The QUEEN will be CROWNED at 3-30 p.m., by Miss Master, of "Beechfield," when the National Anthem will be played by the Band and sung by the Assembly.

The Children will afterwards march in procession to the Schools for refreshments.

A Second Representation at 7 p.m., after which the Band will play for Dancing.

ADMISSION, 6d. Grand Stand, 1s. extra. Children half-price. Gates open at 2-45. Tickets may be obtained beforehand, which will entitle holders to admission by Sandy Lane entrance half-an-hour earlier. Special arrangements for admission for private carriages.

The Train arriving at Chorley at 2-13 will be extended to Leyland.

Proceedings in Ring.

1. As soon as the Queen, &c., are in order, March Round the Ring—Bands Playing.
2. Queen upon Throne—all in position.
3. Song "Now is the month of Maying."
4. Lubin Loo.
5. Infants' Exercise with Bells.
6. Song "Come, Lasses and Lads."
7. Royal May-pole Dance—Grand Plait.
8. Crowning Song "Hail, all hail!"
9. Coronation of Queen by Miss Master—National Anthem.
10. Presentation of Sceptre.
11. Scotch Reel.
12. Foot Guards Present Arms.
13. Presentation of Her Majesty's Loyal Subjects, with National Airs sung by Children—"Rule Britannia;" "Auld Lang Syne;" "The Minstrel Boy;" "Let the hills resound."
14. Royal May-pole Dance—Double Plait.
15. Song "Queen of fresh flowers.
16. Parasol Dance.
17. Tug of War—Sailors v. Niggers.
18. Royal May-pole Dance—Nursery Rhymes.

J. Threlfall, Printer, Caxton House, Leyland.

Programme of the first May Festival, May 1889. The festival has been held in most years since with only occasional lapses. In the years before the First World War it was particular popular, visitors attending from all parts of the country. The centenary was duly celebrated in 1989.

to those who had taken such pains with their training. The crowning of the Queen was entrusted to Miss Master, of Beechfield, who most graciously acceded to the request of the Committee, and performed the office with true courtesy and kindliness.

Placing the Crown of Flowers upon the head of the Queen (Elizabeth Marsden), Miss Masters said:-

"With fair flowers I crown thee Queen of May,
Let their beauty and fragrance be emblems of thy future, so that

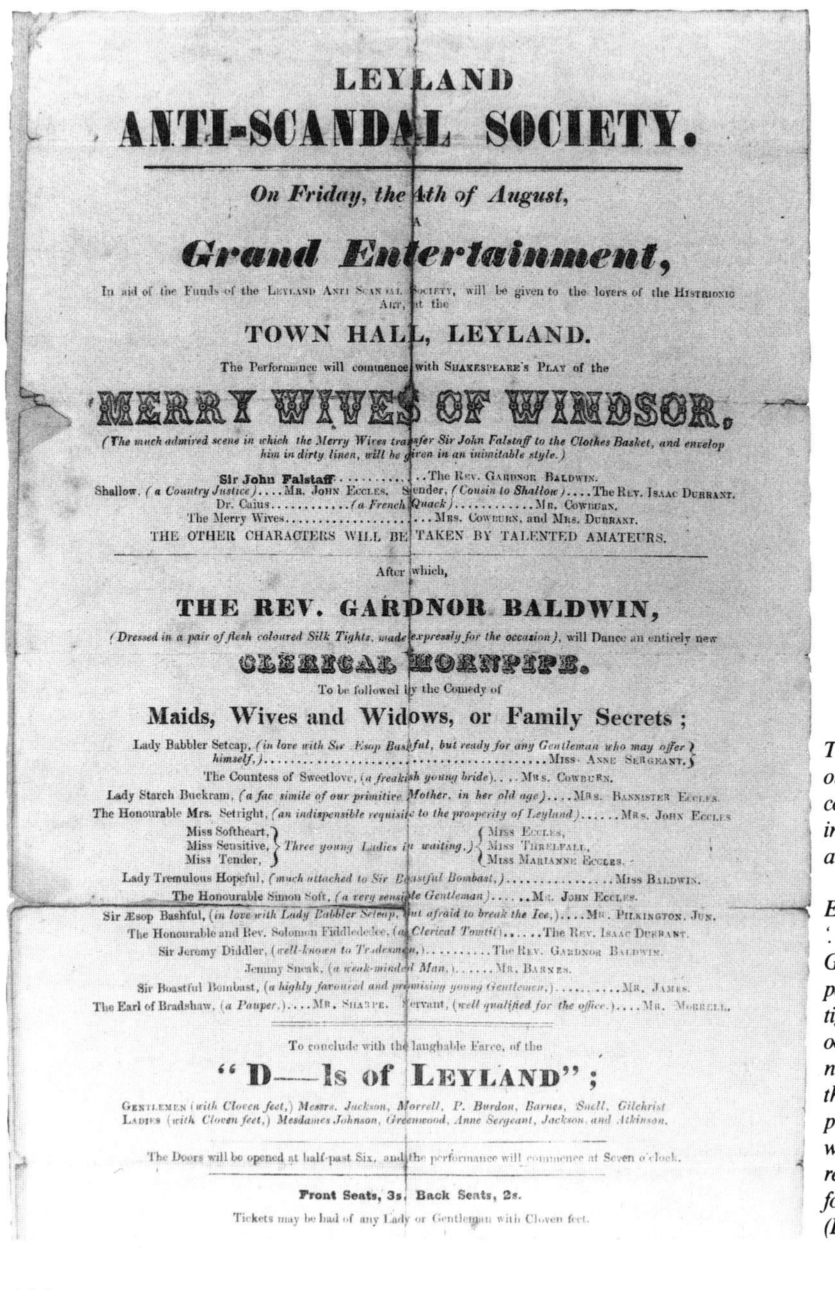

LEYLAND
ANTI-SCANDAL SOCIETY.

On Friday, the 4th of August,
A
Grand Entertainment,
In aid of the Funds of the LEYLAND ANTI SCANDAL SOCIETY, will be given to the lovers of the HISTRIONIC ART, at the

TOWN HALL, LEYLAND.

The Performance will commence with SHAKESPEARE'S PLAY of the

MERRY WIVES OF WINDSOR,
(The much admired scene in which the Merry Wives transfer Sir John Falstaff to the Clothes Basket, and envelop him in dirty linen, will be given in an inimitable style.)

Sir John Falstaff..............The REV. GARDNOR BALDWIN.
Shallow, *(a Country Justice)*....MR. JOHN ECCLES. Slender, *(Cousin to Shallow)*....The REV. ISAAC DURRANT.
Dr. Caius............*(a French Quack)*............MR. COWBURN.
The Merry Wives.........................MRS. COWBURN, and MRS. DURRANT.
THE OTHER CHARACTERS WILL BE TAKEN BY TALENTED AMATEURS.

After which,

THE REV. GARDNOR BALDWIN,
(Dressed in a pair of flesh coloured Silk Tights, made expressly for the occasion), will Dance an entirely new

CLERICAL HORNPIPE.

To be followed by the Comedy of

Maids, Wives and Widows, or Family Secrets;

Lady Babbler Setcap, *(in love with Sir Æsop Bashful, but ready for any Gentleman who may offer himself,)*..........MISS ANNE SERGEANT.
The Countess of Sweetlove, *(a freakish young bride)*...MRS. COWBURN.
Lady Starch Buckram, *(a fac simile of our primitive Mother, in her old age)*....MRS. BANNISTER ECCLES.
The Honourable Mrs. Setright, *(an indispensible requisite to the prosperity of Leyland)*......MRS. JOHN ECCLES
Miss Softheart, Miss Sensitive, Miss Tender, *(Three young Ladies in waiting.)* MISS ECCLES, MISS THRELFALL, MISS MARIANNE ECCLES.
Lady Tremulous Hopeful, *(much attached to Sir Boastful Bombast,)*................MISS BALDWIN.
The Honourable Simon Soft, *(a very sensible Gentleman)*......MR. JOHN ECCLES.
Sir Æsop Bashful, *(in love with Lady Babbler Setcap, but afraid to break the Ice,)*....MR. PILKINGTON, JUN.
The Honourable and Rev. Solomon Fiddlededee, *(a Clerical Tomtit)*......The REV. ISAAC DURRANT.
Sir Jeremy Diddler, *(well-known to Tradesmen,)*..........The REV. GARDNOR BALDWIN.
Jemmy Sneak, *(a weak-minded Man,)*......MR. BARNES.
Sir Boastful Bombast, *(a highly favoured and promising young Gentlemen,)*..........MR. JAMES.
The Earl of Bradshaw, *(a Pauper,)*....MR. SHARPE. Servant, *(well qualified for the office.)*....MR. MORRELL.

To conclude with the laughable Farce, of the

"D——ls of LEYLAND";

GENTLEMEN *(with Cloven feet,) Messrs. Jackson, Morrell, P. Burdon, Barnes, Snell, Gilchrist*
LADIES *(with Cloven feet,) Mesdames Johnson, Greenwood, Anne Sergeant, Jackson, and Atkinson.*

The Doors will be opened at half-past Six, and the performance will commence at Seven o'clock.

Front Seats, 3s, Back Seats, 2s.

Tickets may be had of any Lady or Gentleman with Cloven feet.

The Leyland May Festival grew out of a flourishing sense of community and a not inconsiderable reserve of amateur dramatic talent.
Notice of a Grand Entertainment c1852.
'. . . After which the Rev. Gardnor Baldwin dressed in a pair of flesh-coloured silk tights, made expressly for the occasion, will dance an entirely new Clerical Hornpipe'. Despite these shocking goings-on the price of 2/- for even a back sea would be sufficient to ensure a reasonably respectable audienc for the Vicar of Leyland. (Leyland Museum).

Coronation Arch 1902.
Located in Church Road, between the Eagle and Child and the Old Grammar School. Notice the barn which formerly stood by the end of Balcarres Road, almost blocking Church Road.
Festivals have continued to be popular throughout the twentieth century for royal and other national events. Perhaps the largest was the celebration of the Festival of Britain in 1951, which, coinciding with the heyday of Leyland Motors and the purchase of Worden Park by the local council for public recreation, marked a major milestone in the modern history of the town. (Leyland Museum).

kindly actions and gentle words may crown a life of sweet unselfishness;
Thus will Leyland rejoice in the career of its first May Queen.

The representatives of Scotland, Ireland, Wales, with John Bull and Britannia, then approached the throne to make their bow, while their advance was accompanied on each occasion by some national melody.

The uncertainty of the weather, and the risk of the children taking cold, rendered it necessary to slightly curtail the performance, and to postpone the repetition of the plaiting,&c., which had been announced for the evening, to the afternoon of the Saturday following. The young people were afterwards supplied with coffee and cake in the Union Street Schools.

Saturday, June 1st, turned out to be a brilliant day, and consequently everyone was in good spirits, and the anxieties of the twenty-ninth were forgotten. Many improvements were visible in the arrangements, which had been suggested by the experience of the previous occasion. Limitations of space prevent any detailed account in this place of the characters who took part in the procession, or of the subsequent diversions on the field itself, but a reference to the local newspapers of this date will give all that can be desired. The result was a success, financially as well as in other respects. The proceeds amounted to £142 6s. 5d., but the expenses were heavy, amounting to no less than £65 10s. 0d. The balance, after certain liabilities of the Sunday School had been met (owing to loss on the Chester Trip and deficiency of Subscriptions, &c., for the Whitsuntide Treats) amounted to £35 2s. 2d. This sum has been handed over to the managers of the Day and Sunday Schools (of which the Vicar is the Chairman), with an understanding as to the terms on which it is held."

The event has been held most years since, with occasional lapses due to epidemic, world wars and apathy. Its most significant disruption occurred during the incumbency of the Rev. G. H. Ensor from 1924 to 1933, when it became something of a focus for opposition to him, and for a few years there were two May Festivals. In the years up to the First World War the festival rapidly became a major 'event' for which the town was famous, and large numbers of surviving sepia photographs from these and later years attest to the imagination, planning, hard-work and expense which was invested in it. As one May Queen later remarked, 'It was the event of our young lives'.

Leyland Cricket Club

ANOTHER nineteenth-century institution which is still a source of local pride is the town's cricket club. Originally founded in 1848 and

Leyland has long had a considerable reputation in our national sports, football and cricket. The Leyland Cricket Club was long known as the 'nursery' of the Lancashire side and John Stanning, the local bleacher and the prominent figure in the town at the turn of the century, was a leading supporter of both.

(i) Leyland Cricket Club First Eleven, 1906.

Top Row: D. Brown, Janson, Turner, Tonge, Wilmot, Bennion, Cain, J. Hunt (scorer). Second Row: Messrs E. Stanning, J. Stanning (Jun), Walter Brearley, D. Stanning. (Leyland Museum).

(ii) Leyland Red Rose. Leyland has had a number of amateur football clubs, including Leyland Villa, and Leyland Red Rose here photographed c1910. Church records show that Preston North End rented thr Mayfield during the inter-war years for training purposes. (Leyland Museum).

re-formed by John Stanning in 1862 Leyland Cricket Club has long been an important nursery for the county. Of the many well known players who have been associated with the club, Allen Hill, the former Yorkshire bowler played in the first Test Match, taking the first wicket and first catch in test cricket. His son was to be one of the town's most accomplished artists. The club's first game was played on July 6th 1848 against a Chorley Eleven on the Vicar's fields. 'The towering canopies of the majestic beech trees which flank the vicarage grounds basked in ethereal splendour, and overshadowed the living current of spectators . . . A bank of musicians invoked at moot intervals the Spirit of sweet sounds . . . Leyland went in first . . .'

The match against Farington Mill appears to have been a popular fixture, and a number of games in the 1870s were played against North End of Preston at Deepdale Road – a happy hunting ground for visitors. On May 18th 1878 the latter made fifty-two runs, enabling Leyland to win by ten. On June 2nd 1880 'Twenty-two of Leyland' played a 'United South Eleven'. Mr James Grace taking fourteen wickets in the Leyland 1st innings and Mr James Lillywhite six in the second; 'As the game drew to a close the excitement became intense, the result being a win for the 11 by 4 runs . . . After the match dancing was engaged in on the field, music being supplied by the Clayton-le-Moors Brass Band'.[8]

Leyland Local Board and Council

NOTWITHSTANDING occasional altercations with the Rev. Baldwin and Miss S. M. Farington, the establishment of the Leyland Local Board in 1863 and the later Urban District Council mark important stages in the development of the town. The town's main employers, John Stanning and James Quin, were major figures on the Board and its sub-committees. From 1880 onwards attention was concentrated on the need to provide the town with a new water supply and sewers.[9] Prior to this water had come from wells cut through the sands on which the town stands. Wells at Seven Stars, Chapel Brow and Wellfield proving inadequate, it was decided in December 1880 to borrow £5,000 to provide a piped water supply, in addition to £7,000 for a sewage works. In May 1882 a revised estimate was produced:

New Well	£277–10– 0d
Cottage, engine and Boiler	£606– 9– 0d
Reservoir	£875
Iron pipes and 'specials'	£2,298– 9– 9d
Fittings, hydrants etc.	£168–19– 6d
Laying mains	£1,008– 0– 2d
Engines, pumps, condensor, boilers	£1,100
TOTAL	**£6334– 8– 5d**

By August this estimate had been raised to £8,500 to provide a well at Clayton, a reservoir and mains piping. The water was very hard, and Mr Stanning, who was opposed to 'doctoring with water', suggested

The Public Hall, Leyland c1920.
Formerly headquarters of the Leyland Urban District Council, this much-loved local landmark was demolished in 1988. (Leyland Museum).

The Eagle and Child Inn c1900. (Leyland Museum).

that Leylanders could soften it with collected rainwater when washing. At a later date the supply was switched over on Sunday evenings to water from Manchester's system, in order to cater for the Monday wash. By December 1883 works were sufficiently advanced for the Board to decide on the scale of charges for the water.

Contemporary with this scheme was the acquisition of 'Mr Wilding's field at Ulnes Walton . . . for the purpose of sewage disposal', and the post of 'Clerk of the Sewage Works' was duly advertised, the Board paying third-class railway fares for those selected for interview. Mr Brocklehurst was appointed at the salary of 45/- per week. Soon, great slits were appearing along the main thoroughfares of the town, and in October 1882 a Col. Cross's carriage crashed into the drain diggings in Hough Lane. His claim for damages having been

radley's Outfitters Shop, owngate, c1905.
The manager of this mporium obviously had a flair or advertising. Other photo- raphs appear to show a huge hirt blowing from a flagpole at he front of the shop, which tood almost opposite the ublic Hall.
n return for memorising a erse, children were awarded a Bradley's ruler':
ear not, fear not my darling wife,
or Bradley's shirt has saved my life.
t did not tear or let me down,
lthough it cost but half-a-crown.
The manager was later killed n the First World War. Leyland Museum).

ignored, he began legal proceedings against the Board, and though his convenient death some weeks later seemed to be the end of the matter, damages ultimately had to be paid. In December, Mr Swann complained vociferously that the energetic drain diggers, eager to link Mr Sumner's smithy and well to the system, had cut through his garden, and the gas company claimed that their mains had been damaged, and sought compensation. Week by week in 1882-3 the water pipes and drains spread across the town. Dr. Berry fought a long campaign to carry the sewers the length of Sandy Lane, and there was a rush on the part of property occupiers to have their premises linked up. The Board agreed to both the bleach and rubber works discharging waste into the sewer.

The Board fought long battles with recalcitrant landlords, particularly in Bradshaw Street. On April 15th 1880, 'The nuisance inspector drew the attention of the Board to a report he presented some time ago respecting the want of privy accommodation in Bradshaw Street: he said there were fifteen houses without either a back door, privy or drain'. In December the cellars flooded, but all efforts at persuasion having failed, in September 1882 'It was resolved that a legal opinion be taken with a view to bringing about a better state of things'. In November the owners were given six months notice to provide privies and ashpits, and in September 1883 the Board's clerk was accordingly empowered to prosecute.

The young authority sought to improve the environment in other ways. In 1880 it waged a campaign with the railway company to oblige more trains to halt at Leyland, and in September purchased twelve lamps to illuminate the town at the cost of 27/6d and 25/- each). Yet two years later it opposed the proposed introduction of electric lighting in the town.

The first gasworks in the town was set up in 1849 behind the Ship Inn on Towngate, an event duly recorded by the *Preston Guardian*:[10]

> The Oddfellow's Society of Leyland having some surplus money on hand, which was not required for the working of the society, have invested it in on gas works to light the village. The gas making apparatus and the pipes have been made and fixed up by Messrs John Ogle, Son and Co.,

> engineers of Preston. The village was lighted for the first time on Saturday evening last. The members of the lodge sat down to a good substantial dinner to celebrate the event, on New Year's Day, at Mr Gilchrists, the Roe Buck Inn, Leyland.

In 1863 the Leyland and Farington Gas Company was incorporated by a special act of Parliament. The development of the gasworks at the corner of Chapel Brow and Hough Lane was to emphasise further the industrial nature of the north part of the town, 'Even though the Gas Works only just intruded on Hough Lane in a physical sense, its presence through to the end of gas production in September 1956 was hard to ignore. A Fishwicks bus conductor during World War Two always referred to the Gas Works bus stop as "Leyland Perfumery".'[11]

In 1905 the Rev. E. G. Marshall in his *Story of Leyland: Past and Present* expressed the pride that the town took in its progress in the previous years, 'Leyland has the appearance of a town rather than a village, and building is still carried on to a large extent. The village is well off for manufactures, and work is, therefore plentiful, a sure sign of the prosperity of the place'. Among the list of manufacturers, he noted that 'Leyland has the proud distinction of having invented the first steam lawnmower; Mr James Sumner being the inventor. This gentleman is now a managing director and also a partner in the Lancashire Steam Motor Co. Ltd., whose extensive works are at Leyland'. In the next fifty years, the efforts of the 'Lawnmower Company' were to make the name of Leyland famous throughout the world.

Chapter Nine

The development of Leyland Motors

HERE has been a tendency on the part of chroniclers of the early days of Leyland Motors to depict the founder, James Sumner, at the outset of the venture, as little more than a village smith with a bent for mechanical innovations of the Heath-Robinson type, working at the forge in Water Street among the green fields of a rustic Leyland. Nothing could be further from the truth.

During the last quarter of the nineteenth century, economic trends in Leyland began to diverge markedly from those apparent in many of the Lancashire cotton towns, for alongside the old village a centre of 'modern' industries was beginning to emerge. An increasing range of trades was developing, with a firm base in light engineering, and a range of institutions able and prepared to advance capital to them. Large areas of flat farmland were available for development and the town was well located on the national railway system, a factor enhanced by the development of Preston as a port.

From earlier ages the village had been an important 'service centre' for the surrounding farms, providing smithy and basic metal-working facilities. Lancashire's early textile industry had been able to expand rapidly as demand for the wonder product cotton soared in the early-nineteenth century, and Leyland thus had the potential resources to develop in the 'new' markets for goods opening at the start of the twentieth century – not least in the rubber industry. Of course, this was true of many towns at the time: the further vital ingredient was an individual with the genius, foresight and sheer luck to capitalise on these factors, as John Horrocks had done in Preston a century before. James Sumner was to be such a man, and the new wonder product was to be motor vehicles.[1]

ext page:
p: James Sumner inherited a ll-established metalworking siness, and as early as 1884 had produced a steam gon. Significant expansion me when the Spurriers joined n.

ttom: Henry Spurrier the st, financier of the ncashire Steam Motor mpany, and by 1914 airman of Leyland Motors d., with an issued capital of 00,000.

Sumner's background was not that of just the rural smithy. The 1861 census records the family of Richard Sumner (aged thirty) living at No. 1 Water Street, his occupation was given as 'Blacksmith, fitter and turner'. His wife, Alice, who was two years younger than Richard, had recently given birth to a daughter Ann, a sister for infant James, and

the young family had a 'general servant', Elizabeth Prescot (aged just twelve), to help out. James's father was clearly much more than a simple smith and his premises probably more resembled a small engineering workshop. This certainly seems to have been the case when James Sumner took over running of the shop, which had lathes and a steam hammer, and was able to produce iron castings of up to half a ton in weight and brass castings up to half a hundredweight. When the firm moved to Herbert Street, the old premises became the successful base for another light-engineering firm, George Damp and Sons.

James Sumner was thus able to indulge his interest in motorised transport, a logical if tricky development following the success of the railway. He was clearly not alone in this, but was able to bring to bear considerable mechanical skill and ingenuity, sufficient at least to develop a small business in the town, based on his first successful product, the celebrated steam lawnmower. Simple, and by today's standards crude, it incorporated many of the features of much larger and more intricate self-powered units. From this base he was able to continue experiments of the trial-and-error variety, culminating in the successful development of his first steam lorry. In spite of these efforts, their modest success, and the progress of his business, it clearly required very considerable expertise to develop it into a major company and to compete in new markets. This skill was to be provided by the Spurrier family. James Sumner may have begun the firm, but it was the Spurriers who established Leyland Motors.

James Sumner, from his boyhood in the workshop, seems to have had a fascination for steam power, and produced a five-ton steam wagon as early as 1880 for Stannings Bleachworks. Using more coal than it could carry, however, it was not a success, and John Stanning was alleged to have lost a local election because of the damage it caused to the roads: he at least seems to have been convinced by the young inventor. More successful was a steam-powered twopenny-farthing tricycle built with his brother William. The engine was later used to power a lawnmower, and motor mowers soon became the main product of the workshop when James took over the business in 1892. Continued experimentation produced a successful three-wheel steam car built for Theodore Carr (of biscuit-making fame).

4 steam lawnmower.
The first successful motorised product, developed when James Sumner had sole control of the company, but after formation of the Steam Wagon Co., the company rapidly developed as a producer of much more sophisticated vehicles.

The second Henry, father of Sir Henry Spurrier.
With James Sumner he drove the early vehicles to the various agricultural shows. During his earlier stay in the U.S.A., he had worked as a cowboy. More important, however, was the experience he acquired as a railway draughtsman. By 1914 he was managing director of the firm.

The Leyland Steam Motor Co.

IN conjunction with T. Coulthard and Co. of Preston, a company called James Sumner Ltd. was formed, and when the former was taken over by a Manchester firm, their representative George Spurrier became closely involved in developments at Leyland. 1896 was a momentous year, George's brother Henry Spurrier II (among more relevant skills, a former cowboy) began working on development with the Sumners, and anti-motor vehicle legislation was eased. More importantly the Spurriers' father, Henry I, was persuaded to put up the capital for the establishment of the Leyland Steam Motor Co. The firm moved to new premises in Herbert Street and before the year was out had produced a thirty-hundredweight oil-fired steam van. The company grew steadily, acquiring a growing reputation for their 'traction engines' at trials and agricultural shows, prompting Henry I's somewhat indelicate, if instantly memorable, metaphor, 'If we don't make this firm a success now, we deserve to be kicked. We've got the world by the pants and a downhill pull!'

The company began to have a great effect on the development of the

The original Sumner 'Smithy' in Water Street.

In fact, a well equipped metalworking shop, subsequently occupied by George Damp and Sons, who were listed in Barrett's Director of 1932 as 'General smiths, oxy-acetylene welders, engineer and hardware dealers (lawn mowers a speciality)'. James Sumner moved to larger premises in Herbert Street in 1896.

First World War production.

The Company was reformed in 1914, and considerable expansion followed during the First World War when 6,000 vehicles were produced. Although this established 'Leyland's' as a major producer, the scale of expansio led to difficult problems of adaptation to the peacetime conditions of the 1920s.

town as early as the first year of the present century. In 1902 it began to build on land sold to it by the Rev. Leyland Baldwin to the north of Hough Lane (the future north works). Further expansion in the town followed in 1908, and in 1913 development at Farington began. In 1903 the firm was re-formed with a share capital of £50,000 and a workforce of 160. The first exports, three steam wagons, were sent to Ceylon in 1901, and in 1904 work began on developing petrol-driven vehicles and 'the Pig' was the outcome.

The first successful steam wagon (1896). Thirty hundredweight, oil fired, four gears, a vehicle well advanced for the time.

In 1907 the enterprise was renamed 'Leyland Motors'. In 1914, the company was again re-formed, Leyland Motors (1914) Ltd., with a share capital of £400,000, a workforce of 1,500, and had already built over 2,000 petrol-driven engines in addition to an array of steam-driven vehicles. The business had thus grown very rapidly in just twenty-two years, and was already by far the largest employer in Leyland. Yet greater expansion was to follow during the First World War, with the production in four years of six thousand petrol vehicles. James Sumner died in 1924, by which time the company, with Henry Spurrier II as Chairman and Managing Director, was emerging as a

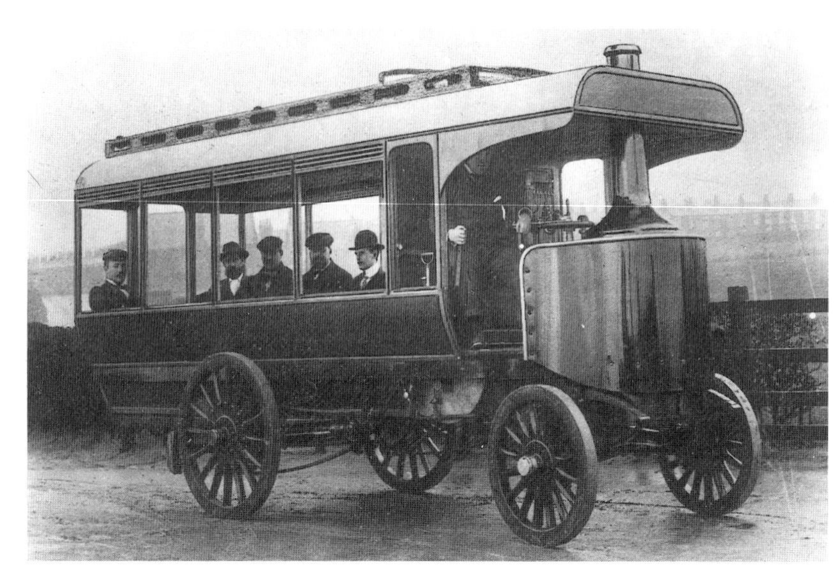

The first motorised bus (steam-powered).
Though the company began to produce petrol-driven vehicl in 1904, 'steamers' continued tc be produced and many were subsequently found to be operating efficiently well into the twentieth century.

The first petrol-driven vehicle the 'Pig' (1904).
The prototype of the company's subsequently worl famous and reliable range of vehicles, the model was never put into production.

Previous page:
James Sumner (left), Henry Spurrier (right) and the staff the Herbert Street works (189
Work began at 6.15 a.m. and finished at 5.45 p.m., bu average wages of twenty-eight shillings a week for engineers compared well with those in textiles. The firm had a good name for continuity of employment and many of its subsequently leading personalities rose through the ranks. Stanley Markland, lat a director of the Leyland Mo Corporation, was an apprent scholar at Wellington House the 1920s.

leader in the world market for commercial vehicles.

Between the wars, Leyland Motors continued to expand rapidly. An innovative product range was developed, and Lion and Titan buses and Hippo trucks, among many other types, went into service throughout Britain and the world. In this respect the inter-war history of Leyland contrasts markedly with the experience of the other Lancashire towns where the late 1920s and early 1930s are remembered for the slump of 1929, the depression of 1931, and wasted years of unemployment. Yet the 'thirties was a period of marked economic growth for the 'new' sectors of the economy, particularly electrical *'he first 3-ton wagon (1898). Purchased by a woollens' rm, Fox Bros. of Somerset. 'he vehicles proved much 'heaper to operate, and capable f moving much larger loads an horse transport. By 1903 irty-nine steam wagons had een sold, including the ompany's first export order – ree Royal Mail vans sent to 'eylon.*

'he production line in the 920s.

London's first petrol-engined Leyland bus 1905.

Only a year after the development of the hapless 'Pig', the London and Suburban Omnibus Co. ordered the capital's first 'Leyland bus', and repeat orders soon followed. The pac of successful innovation and development was very rapid a this time, and long after the First World War many of thes vehicles were still in service.

An early steam lorry in use near Blackburn.

goods and motor vehicles. Apart from a period in the early 'twenties, employment continued to be available in Leyland, whose works acted as a magnet to people, particularly from the hard-hit mill towns of eastern Lancashire. In addition, large numbers of people travelled in

The Lions bodyshop (South Works).

A Lion under construction.

daily from surrounding towns. Indeed in 1929, on the edge of the economic abyss, the company announced that orders for 1,400 Lions and Titans had been received.

The scale and complexity of the works at this time was phenomenal, grouped around three works in Leyland and Farington, and a factory at Chorley.[2]

> The main works are concentrated around the original site in Leyland, the steel foundry being situated a mile away at Farington . . . The North Works is devoted to the manufacture of chassis and their component

The Leyland 'Lion'.
By 1928 2,500 'Lions' had been sold, and were in use all over the world. In the early 1920s the firm also produced cars, including the Parry Thomas inspired 'Straight 8' and the solid-tyred 'Trojan'.

parts. It consists of machine shops, erecting shops, finished and rough stores, case hardening departments, smithy, tool room, etc. etc. The plant in this portion of the works comprises upwards of 650 machines. including examples of many of the modern British types of general-purpose machine tools as well as certain tools specially designed and built for the company. Five large machine shops are engaged day and night in the production of component parts, the machines in most cases being grouped according to the class of work which they perform . . . The erection of the chassis is carried out in two long bays, one being set aside for goods vehicles, the other for passenger chassis. Frames, stored adjacent to the department, are brought in at one end, axles and wheels are fitted and the chassis is then moved down the track to the various assembly stages until it is finally completed, inspected and proceeds on test . . .

The South Works buildings are principally set aside for coachwork and consist of timber-drying kilns, storage shed, sawmill, sheet-metal department, upholstery department, body-erection shops, paint, varnishing and cellulose rooms and finishing shops . . . There are two main body assembly shops, one devoted to the manufacturers of single-decked [bus] bodies, the other to the building of double-deckers. In each, the practice of line assembly is adopted, the bodies being moved on bogies to each stage of assembly until completed . . . The steel foundry has a total area of 7,000 square yards, having three bays, 350 feet long by 60 feet wide. It has a capacity for dealing with 130 tons of electric steel per week, large quantities of which are supplied to the Admiralty and leading shipbuilding and engineering firms throughout the British Isles. Two electric furnaces are used, current for which is supplied by the company's own 4,500 kilowatt generating plant. Extensive use is made of machine-moulding and of oil-sand cores.

. . . Bodies for goods vehicles are made at the Chorley works, a few miles from Leyland, as are fire engines and certain components of the heavy goods chassis. A large proportion of these branch works also concentrate on the manufacture of spare parts for the older models and acts as the company's main repair depot.

Beyond this lay a worldwide organisation: 'The company has

constantly pursued the policy of direct representation both at home and abroad, with no little success. It has ten branches in the United Kingdom and its own direct depots with their substations in Australia, Canada, India, New Zealand, South Africa and the Far East. In fact there are few parts of the world where Leyland is not represented either directly or by accredited agents'.

In so large an organisation, the company's staff magazine provided an important source of information, and the *Leyland Torque* of the early 1920s provides an insight into company affairs. Much attention was given to the economic climate, the affairs of the sports club, the Housing Society, and the apprentices' school, and general news. Staff changes were often complex . . . 'Mr Lockwood remains as head foreman of the erecting shops, including the axle and gear departments. He is directly responsible to Mr Lowe and will be provided with an assistant. Mr Buckley, foreman of the engine shop is now directly responsible to Mr Lowe'.

During widespread strikes in 1919 the *Torque* reported, 'Whatever the rights and wrongs of the last railway strike, it must be a source of satisfaction to all of us to know that the possible disastrous effect upon the supply of our principal foodstuffs . . . was averted by the use of motor lorries. Leylands were exclusively organized in very large fleets'. Company successes were also recorded. In 1920 1,400 people attended the Works Ball, and 'Mr Henry Spurrier, our Managing Director, has personally received King George V's new Royal Appointment for the Company as manufacturers of motor lorries to His Majesty'.

Leyland between the wars

THE development of Leyland Motors was mirrored by the growth of the town which, since most of its economic base had emerged after 1870, was not based on grimy heavy industry. Leyland began to develop in the 1920s and 30s some of the characteristics of a garden city. Indeed, it was this process of urbanisation – rather than the growth of a single industry – which was to be the main theme in the history of twentieth-century Leyland.

In the immediate years after the Great War housing was an important issue in 'A land fit for heroes to live in'. In 1919 Leyland Motors took the initiative, with the formation of the Leyland Motors Housing Society Ltd., to function in conjunction with Leyland UDC. Taking advantage of available government grants the society was to provide houses to sell, and the council houses to rent. The society was to build large numbers of steel and concrete houses in Church Road and Sandy Lane. An ambitious 'New Leyland' was planned, extending between Church Road and Turpin Green Lane and including extensive recreation and sports grounds (Leyland Motors Sports and Athletics Club), shops, school and a cinema – all very much in keeping with the most advanced concepts of town-planning of the day.[3] Although the financial crisis which the firm passed through in the

Company housing under construction (1920).

The Company's ambitious plans for a modern company town had to be curtailed following the firm's financial crisis of 1922-3: Leyland £1 shares could be bought for two shillings and threepence. Yet much was achieved in the housing sphere, and extensive welfare schemes were established for the workforce, including the Leyland Motors Social and Athletic Club.

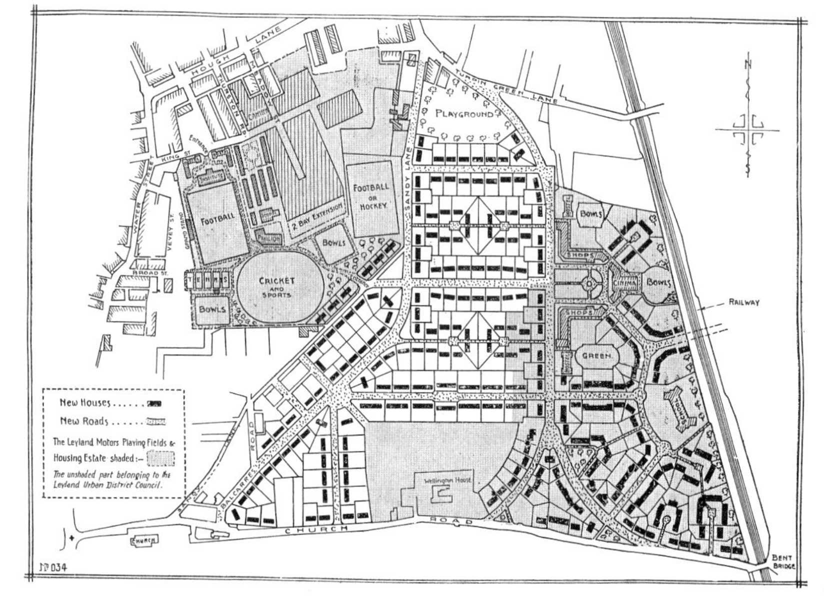

A plan of the proposed Garden City of Leyland, showing some of the facilities that were to be built, including ample provision for sports of all kinds.

early 1920s dealt the scheme a blow, the area did develop broadly along the envisaged lines. Thus, the semi-detached house became as much the symbol of inter-war Leyland as the double-decker bus was for the company. The standard of housing was high and local employment consistently fairly full. All this was in marked contrast to the situation in the older established steel, coal, cotton and heavy engineering centres, and much of the town still enjoyed an open rural aspect.

These trends are revealed on the 1931 Ordnance Survey map. Development was concentrated east of Towngate, whereas much of Leyland Lane, Moss-side, Fox Lane and Golden Hill Lane west of School Lane had changed relatively little from the previous map of

1912. To the north of Golden Hill Lane extended the rubber works, new housing on Northgate, the Farington Steel Foundry, and the Leyland Paint Works. Hough Lane, formerly a quiet district, Ralph Leyland's 'Sufficient cartway to his tenement in Leyland' (1685) was now dominated by the North and South Works.[4] From the map it appears that Balcarres Road and Canberra Road had been staked out, houses had been built in Nelson and Lindsay Avenues, about half of Broadway and Mead Avenue had been built, and Crawford Avenue was partially built. Some houses had been built along Church Road, formerly an ancient sunken track, Winsor and Denford Avenues had been partly constructed, as had the east side of Beech Avenue. But much of Towngate was little altered, and the Shruggs Bleach Works still stood in splendid isolation in the block of fields formed by Towngate, Fox Lane, Leyland Lane and Golden Hill Lane.

The material progress of the town during the period up to 1939 is again clearly revealed in the trade directories. By 1932 Leyland had acquired many of its modern characteristics, including P. E. Grundy, its first dental surgeon, a branch of E. H. Booths, and:

> J. Fishwick and Sons, Motor Haulage Contractors and Motor Omnibus Proprietors, daily service Preston, Leyland and Eccleston: Chorley (Tuesday and Sunday); Ormskirk (Thursday); Golden Hill Garage.
>
> John Heaton and Son, furnishing and general ironmongers, sheet metal workers and complete house furnishers; 53-4 Towngate.
>
> The Leyland and Farington Co-operative Society Ltd., grocers, drapers, boot and shoe dealers, bakers and confectioners, butchers, house furnishers, ladies and gents outfitters, and coal merchants. Central Stores, Chapel Brow: branches, Leyland Lane, Towngate, Hough Lane and Farington Road: Head Office, Chapel Brow, Warehouse and Bakery, East Street. W. Fann, General Manager.
>
> Leyland Garage Co.: Automobile agents and engineers, taxis and private hire cars and carriers to Chorley and Wigan: Forge Street. F. and R. Marsden, proprietors.[5]

In addition to the vast motor and rubber works the town had a good number of smaller engineering firms. In 1922 Mr Fred Jones, then aged fifty-four, founded what was to become the Leyland Paint and Varnish Co., Ltd., with a factory employing twenty-four people. With an innovating product range and rising demand from the housing sector, the firm expanded rapidly, and by 1939 had a considerable market and distribution network.[6] With its large factory, familiar to travellers on the west-coast railway line, the firm thus completed the triumvirate of local industry: Leyland Motors, Leyland and Birmingham Rubber Company and Leyland Paints.

Chapter Ten

'We continually progress'

INCE the Second World War, two inter-related themes have dominated the town's affairs - the changing fortunes of Leyland Motors and the implications of Leyland's urban growth and development. In the 1960s both became elements of much larger designs - the British Leyland Motor Corporation and the Central Lancashire New Town, but in the event things were to turn out rather differently than everyone had anticipated.

Leyland's war effort was prodigious, and by the end of 1945 the town's industrial base (including after 1938 the Royal Ordnance factory at Euxton) was greater than ever. Expansion at Leyland Motors was enormous. By 1944 the male workforce had risen from 6,500 to 9,000, and the female staff had increased 6 times, reaching 3,000, whilst the number of machine tools and consumption of electricity had doubled. A wide range of products was produced in huge numbers, including 3,000 medium and heavy tanks, 10,000 tank engines, almost 10,000 wheeled vehicles, eleven million incendiary bombs, five million twenty-millimetre shells, and over 10,000 tons of alloy castings, mainly for aircraft. Enemy efforts to bomb the factories had little effect, although there was serious loss of life during the bombing of Ward Street in nearby Lostock Hall. As a result of the Korean crisis a large tank factory was later developed in Farington, which in 1956 became the Spurrier Works of Leyland Motors.[1]

This apart, the company switched back to civilian production and the 1950s were years of successful development and expansion: in 1951 the firm acquired Albion Motors, in 1955 Scammell Lorries Ltd., and in 1962 their biggest British rivals the A.E.C. Group. Of profound significance for the future was the acquisition of the motor car manufacturer Standard-Triumph in 1961. In 1963 the Leyland Motor Corporation was established, making the company a major force in the British motor industry, with Donald Stokes as Managing Director becoming Chairman in 1967. Sir Henry Spurrier (III), who had done so much to develop the huge corporation, died in 1964.

The very successful export drive for Leyland vehicles at this time is perhaps best remembered through the Cuban bus order of July 1964. Production of the bus and truck plants at Leyland was healthy, and in

Griffith's Chemists, Towngate c1930.
Before the development schemes of the 1960s and subsequent wider scale demolition, Towngate was dominated by many small shops which catered for a wide range of local demand. Most occupiers 'lived over the shop'.

Palace Theatre, Leyland c1920.
From 1890 onwards the town began to acquire many essentially modern features, and particularly after the First World War new forms of leisure activity began to develop.

Leyland and District Home Guard: Officers of 'B' Company, 12th East Lancashire Battalion, Home Guard.
Back row, left to right: Lts. Collard, Boyle, Lewis, Goode, Samuels, Nicholson, Waterhouse, Beardsworth, Castle and Sallon.
Middle row, left to right: Lts. Bolton, Jones, Postlethwaite, Barrend, Morris, Hirstle, Sandham and Price.
Front row, left to right: Lt. Mills, Capt. Cank (Medical Officer), Capt. Bishop, Mjr. Waring, Capt. Melling, Capt. Birtill, Lt. Norris.

1966 a £60 million investment plan was announced for the facilities at Leyland. Early in 1968 the merger was announced with British Motor Holdings to form the British Leyland Motor Corporation, the fifth largest vehicle producer in the world, the second largest in Europe, employing 200,000 people, with worldwide sales in 1970 of £1 billion, making the name of a small Lancashire town famous throughout the world.

In this ill-fated attempt to save the British car industry the plants at Leyland were to form the Bus and Truck Division. Notwithstanding the almost endemic crisis in the car industry the bus and truck division (after 1978 'Leyland Vehicles') continued to do fairly well until the recession of the late 1970s. In 1976 British Leyland made a profit of £70 million, of which £40 million was contributed by the commercial

Luftwaffe air photograph (1940).

One of the best photographs ever taken of Leyland. An obvious target for enemy action, the North and South works are clearly marked on this map and a number of air raids actually took place. Most tragic was the bombing of Ward Street, Lostock Hall, apparently in a mistaken attempt to hit the motor works. The Second World War, like the first, saw an enormous increase of output. Notice the pattern of regular pieces enclosed on the moss to the west of Leyland Lane, and the town's location on the edge of these former mosslands.

vehicle operation, and the following year large-scale investment was announced in Leyland: there was to be a huge vehicle assembly hall built at Farington costing £33 million, research and development facilities at Moss-side (£22 million) and a £17 million investment programme at Chorley. In March 1978 the *Leyland Guardian* reported, 'The Farington skyline is undergoing a dramatic change, as construction goes ahead in Leyland Truck and Bus' £32.5 million truck assembly hall'.[2] The hall was to cover 120,000 square metres, allowing the company to build four hundred heavy trucks per week.

As early as 1974, however, company shares worth 45p in 1971 had fallen to 6¼p, valuing the entire company at a mere £47 million. From the late 1970s onwards there was widespread talk of splitting the corporation up, and particularly from 1978 onwards there were fears of serious job losses at Leyland. In 1979 British Leyland announced a plan to shed 25,000 jobs, 4,000 of them at Leyland Vehicles, and job losses at Leyland became a regular feature in the press.

By 1982 truck sales in Britain had fallen by thirty-two per cent and buses twenty-four per cent on the previous year, and losses made by Leyland Vehicles totalled £100 million. The situation had worsened greatly by 1985. Bus sales had fallen by over a half from 1984, and plans to run the Farington factory on half time were announced. 1986 was dominated by talk of takeovers: General Motors were apparently willing to take Leyland Trucks, whilst the bus division was 'bought-out' by its management and became a subsidiary of the Swedish company Volvo in 1988. Further redundancies were announced early in 1990. Leyland Trucks went to the Dutch firm DAF, amid plans to close the Farington engine plant and foundry and shed 1,400 jobs. Thus both arms of the mighty Leyland Motors, prime mover in the Leyland Motor Corporation had by 1989 become subsidiaries of foreign companies. As such, and with well-equipped local plants and a highly skilled workforce they may yet be set fair for the future. What Sir Henry Spurrier would have thought about this state of affairs is, of course, another matter.

Post-war Leyland

THESE changes in the fortunes of the town's largest employer obviously had profound effects on Leyland itself. With production shifted to the new plants at Farington and Moss-side the North and South works on Hough Lane (virtually in the centre of town) had closed by 1980, and a part of the latter was subsequently redeveloped as the highly successful British Commercial Vehicle Museum. The closure of the BTR factory adjacent to the North Works and the Hough Lane gasworks released considerable land for development, and industry was effectively moved out from the centre of the town.

In the early post-war years it was clear that housing was going to be a major issue in Leyland, as it had been at the end of the First World War. The great industrial capacity centred in the town and the employment if offered contrasted sharply with overcrowding and economic decay in other parts of the North West. Since a large proportion of the township remained as farmland, Leyland was clearly a major candidate for housing development.

A major programme of housebuilding by the Urban District Council lasted until 1967, with the development of good-quality housing on large open estates at Broadfield and Wade Hall from the late 1940s. The scale of this development is revealed by the six-inch O.S. map of 1967. Building to the east of Towngate and north of Church Road along Canberra Road and Balcarres Road was virtually complete; to the south of Fox Lane the Wade Hall estate had been built, and the Broadfield estate including the ancient site at Northbrook had been constructed to the north of the Shruggs Bleachworks. Subsequently, the closure and demolition of the Bleachworks released much of the remaining open land in the rectangle formed by Fox Lane, Leyland Lane, Golden Hill and Towngate for development, and the Lancastergate and West Paddock roads were constructed through it.

Development also began between Church Road and the ancient Back Lane (renamed Langdale Road), to be completed in the late 1980s when land formerly owned by British Leyland was sold for development: the M6 motorway became in effect the eastern boundary of the town. With the exception of land to the south of Shaw Brook adjoining Ulnes Walton and to the west of the Lostock at Moss-side, the ancient township was rapidly becoming one urban area, and the pre-war growth of the town's population continued; 1931 - 10,571; 1951 - 14,700; 1961 - 19,400; 1971 - 23,370 and 1981 - 26,507.

Much attention was given, from the early 1950s onwards, to the need to redevelop the town centre which historically and geographically lay around Leyland Cross in Towngate, but which had increasingly become centred on the congested North and South Works area in Hough Lane. It was felt that the town should have a centre with the facilities to reflect its economic importance and its growing size. It should have a civic centre, library, a police and fire station and recreation facilities.

By 1963, as the town appeared to be on the verge of further sustained growth and housing expansion, a bold, new town centre stretching along Towngate from the Cross was envisaged. A series of ambitious schemes was put forward, but little was accomplished, and the scheme was dealt a body blow by the proposal from the mid-1960s onwards that an alternative centre should be built in Runshaw as part of the Central Lancashire New Town. In 1974 the town's swimming pool was opened, and the foundation stone of the 'Mainstop' shopping centre was laid in 1979. By this time, many of the buildings on the southern end of Towngate had become dilapidated and the whole area was becoming increasingly run down. In 1988 demolition of the remaining buildings began. The following year the former Public Hall, once the pride and the political and social hub of Leyland with its sprung dance floor, was demolished, and a considerable length of Towngate was cleared for development. By the end of the 1980s it was possible for the first time in centuries to gaze across the top of the ancient lower Townfield from Leyland Cross, and the scheme still seemed a long way from completion.

Yet, more than any other issue, the proposed development of the Central Lancashire New Town came to dominate the town's affairs, with profound implications for its future.

Central Lancashire New Town

IN February 1965 Anthony Crossland announced to the House of Commons, 'That the Government has been considering as a matter of urgency how they can help Manchester to deal with its housing problems in a way that would contribute positively to the general prosperity and growth of the North West . . . [they] have decided to designate a site in the Leyland/Chorley area for a large new town.'[3]

In February 1966 consultants were commissioned and in 1967 produced *Central Lancashire: Study for a City.* The new town was to knit together Leyland and Chorley and most of Preston into a 'socially and economically cohesive whole', with new homes and employment for an extra 150,000 people in twenty years, and to be able 'To provide for every newcomer, as soon as he or she arrives, not just a house in a muddy field, but a balanced provision of all the necessities of life combined in rapidly established communities'. The population of Leyland was to expand from 20,000 to over 70,000, as the town expanded rapidly to the south and west. The proposals were implicitly critical of Leyland:

> Leyland has greatly increased in size over the last twenty years. The setting of the town on the eastern fringe of the Ormskirk plain is flat and uninteresting. Because of this, and because of its size in relation to the rest of the town, the vast industrial area around Leyland Motors dominates the place. Even the present shopping centre is severely constrained by the nearby industrial buildings.
>
> The development of new public buildings, and additional shopping provision to replace the existing outworn and constricted development, has started at a new site at Towngate about half a mile south of the present centre. New residential estates consisting almost entirely of one- and two-storey low-density housing have been built, mainly to the south of the old core and have done little to integrate new and old development or to create a sense of urbanity. The town at present gives an overwhelming impression of formlessness and lack of identity.[4]

In March 1970 the scheme was given the official go-ahead amid much enthusiasm as to what the new city would be called – Redrose, Ribblesdale, Pres-ley and so on. The *Leyland Guardian* reported, 'Leyland has welcomed the green light for the new super city. Council officials and trades-people spoke enthusiastically this week about the increased advantages and amenities which they feel the new development will bring'.[5]

In 1971 Peter Walker, Secretary for the Environment in the Heath Government, confirmed the go-ahead. A Development Corporation was to be headed by Sir Frank Pearson, holding its first meeting in August 1971 and the Corporation became operational in March 1972.

A city of 430,000 was to be completed by 1990, and in November 1971 the *Leyland Guardian* reported, 'Building work on the planned neighbourhood unit in the Slater Lane - Dunkirk Lane - Longmeanygate area of Leyland seems likely to begin within the next 18 months to two years. When finished it will be almost a 'duplication' of the actual existing town'.[6] Local people began a campaign to oppose the construction of a western primary road into the new town from the M6 at Euxton, which they feared would cut them off from Leyland. The new town was to cost £900 million at 1973 prices:[7]

Housing	£535 million
Industry	£63 million
Commerce	£54 million
Education	£29 million
Roads (non-estate)	£69 million
Health, social, community services	£88 million
Public utilities (sewers etc.)	£59 million
	Total £897 million

The cuts began almost at the outset: in December 1973 the Government announced cuts of twenty per cent in the Corporation's spending plans for 1974/5, and more significantly the *Strategic Plan for the North-West'* (1973) revealed a major shift in emphasis. The new town was now to be 'A major long term growth area, with a slower build-up than originally anticipated but making a major contribution in the late 1980s and 1990s'. Preference for jobs creation was to go the north-east Lancashire and the Mersey–Manchester belts, leading to claims in the press that the original new town plan had in fact been abandoned.[8]

In May 1974 the Development Corporation's own 'Outline Plan', was published, and like the report of 1967 was rather critical of Leyland. 'Overall townscape in Leyland is generally poor'. Over half of the town had been built in the previous thirty-five years in response to the rapid growth of industry and social facilities had not kept pace with the increase of population. The area around Towngate was to become the dominant service centre, with swimming pool, sports hall and library, and 'will make a great difference to Leyland and make the community much more self-sufficient'.

The existing stock of houses, many of them built as part of the council's own scheme, was very good, and large areas of land for future development were available in the south and west. The 'Outline Plan' proposed almost to double the population, to 51,000 by 1986, rising to 73,000 in 2001. Most of this development was to be at Runshaw, to the south of Worden Park, and a 'small village centre' was to be developed at Moss-side. By 1986 industrial traffic was to be reduced by the western primary road, the area around Leyland Cross was to be traffic free, and Towngate was to be developed with shops, market, library and swimming pool.[9]

During 1974 as the full implications of the plan became apparent, opposition to the new town grew appreciably, and on November 5th 1974 the public inquiry into the plan began at Preston. At the inquiry a former chairman of Leyland Urban District Council, 'Attacked the proposed closure of the local motorway junction; continuing blight on Leyland town-centre development, and detrimental effect to this which could come from the New Town's plan for a 20,000 township, at Runshaw, 2 miles south . . . I beg you', Mr Kelly told the Inspector, 'not to promote the development of Runshaw this century. This area has a high amenity value and should be left undisturbed'.[10]

Environmental Secretary Peter Shore's report on the inquiry was delayed, and in the interim it became clear that the scheme would be modified, as the *Lancashire Evening Post* reported in September 1976, 'The future of Central Lancashire's £900 million new town hung in the balance after Peter Shore disclosed a new shift in government policy. Dwindling resources are to be switched to rejuvenating decaying, inner-city areas, he revealed in Manchester'.[11] The Corporation had built up a land 'bank' of 8,000 acres, spent over £50 million in capital investment, was building on five sites with two thousand houses and thirty-nine factories under construction. In April 1977 the delayed report reduced the town's proposed population expansion from 100,000 to 23,000 – an eighty per cent cut. The land bank of about 10,000 acres was not to be used for building, and development in Ulnes Walton, Runshaw, Haighton and Grimsargh was to be cut from the plan.[12]

The existing housing programme continued and by March 1978, 1,000 houses for rent had been built and by August 1979 it was claimed that 10,000 people were living in New Town homes. Further changes came after 1979, with further cuts in the housing programme ordered by the Environment Secretary, Michael Heseltine, and by the end of 1980 £10 million of property had been sold off at government instructions. In February 1981 Heseltine announced that the Central Lancashire Development Corporation would close at the end of 1985. In July of that year New Town houses were handed over to housing associations, and in 1986 work began on the conversion of the former Corporation H.Q. – Cuerden Hall – for use as a Sue Ryder Home.

Life beyond the New Town

THE Central Lancashire New Town came to mark just another interlude in the long history of Leyland but it was a very important one in two ways. With the development of Moss-side, it brought to a conclusion the processes of landscape evolution initiated by the early clearance of woodland in prehistoric times, with the emergence of an extensive urban environment. Yet, by the curtailment of the plan short of what had been envisaged, it preserved the town for a generation, and perhaps longer, from engulfment in a much larger urban conglomeration. In particular, the open aspect to the south was preserved. The improvement of the economic infrastructure and the development of new industrial estates, combined with Leyland's increasingly important location in relation to the North West's motorway network, also bode well for future employment prospects.

In the midst of the New Town turmoil, as Leyland appeared about to be engulfed by urban development, the town suffered a further blow to its sense of identity, with the abolition of its Urban District Council. Henceforth Leyland was to be a part of the much larger South Ribble Borough, though it was to be its administrative centre. Extensive urban development, economic change, gradiose schemes of the 1960s, all with a resultant loss of the sense of local pride and identity, the experiences of Leylanders in the latter part of the twentieth century accurately mirrored those of their countrymen elsewhere, as they have been seen to have done throughout history, and it was perhaps difficult to remember that all who had gone before would envy their greater prosperity, better health and housing, ease of transport and longevity.

Back in 1842, agricultural depression and distress in the manufacturing districts, troubles abroad, the decline of the local handloom weaving industry and, in particular, the departure of the ancient colonies of rooks from Worden and Leyland Vicarage led the Leylanders of the day to fear for the worst in much the same way, and to recall the words of the Leyland prophecy:[13]

When in our ladie's lappe our Lord shall lie,
When to the balle the griffine fierce shall flie,
When Leyland church at Astelle take refuge,
To Lancashire shall happene a deluge such has not beene seen since old Noe's floode,
And Englande's men shall soake their feete in bloode,
A famine sore shall happene Britain's lande, and dismalle sorrows shall be nigh at hand,
Let warie wightes unto these words attende,
Brittania's glorie is almost at ende.

Notes on the text

Chapter One

1. W. T. Watkin, *Roman Lancashire* (1883, reprinted 1969), 229, 236-7; see also D. A. Hunt, *The Bronze Age in Lancashire* (Dissertation, 1978, copy in Harris Ref. Library); D. C. A. Shotter, *Roman North-West England* (1984).
2. E. Crompton, *Soils of the Preston District of Lancashire,* (1966). F. Walker, *The Historical Geography of South-West Lancashire before the Industrial Revolution* (1939). P. F. Barrow, 'Road, Place and Field Names of Leyland and the Neighbourhood', *Lailand Chronicle* xviii, 25-29; xx, 18-23.
3. E. Ekwall, *The Place-names of Lancashire* (1922, reprinted 1972), 133.
4. T. C. Porteus, *The Hundred of Leyland in Lancashire* (1931). G. L. Bolton, 'Domesday Revisited', *Lancashire Local Historian* (1984), 9-13. The transcript of Domesday is taken from vol. i of the *Victoria County History of Lancashire* (V.C.H.).
5. V.C.H. vi, 4-10. W. J. Sawle, *Leyland Parish Church* (1970).
6. W. J. Sawle, op. cit., 11.
7. V.C.H., vi, 4.
8. S. M. Ffarington, 'The History of the Ffaringtons of Worden', reprinted from the *Chorley Guardian* (1936), 23. This was produced as a booklet in 1936, but was first written in 1876. Hereafter S. M. Ffarington (1876).
9. V.C.H., vi, 4.
10. E. Iddon, 'Excerpts from the memoirs of the late Rev. Canon Jacques: Leyland 1861', *Lailand Chronicle,* xxiii, 38-41.
11. Quoted in H. Taylor, *The Ancient Crosses and Holy Wells of Lancashire* (1906), 50.
12. D. A. Hunt, 'An exploration of Leyland Cross', *Lailand Chronicle,* xxxiv, 7-8. G. L. Bolton, 'Cross Questions', *Lailand Chronicle,* xxxii, 20-2.

Chapter Two

1. Lancashire Record Office (LRO): DDF 2214.
2. LRO: DDF 2215.
3. LRO: DDX 102/4.
4. LRO: DDX 102/6.
5. LRO: DDX 102/13.
6. LRO: DDF 1548. G. L. Bolton, 'Leyland Mill or What Happened to Mr Crawshaw', *Lailand Chronicle,* xxx, 26-30.
7. H. S. Bennett, *Life on the English Manor 1150-1400* (1948).
8. G. Youd, 'The Common Fields of Lancashire', *Trans. Hist. Soc. Lancs. and Cheshire,* cxiii, 1-41. F. J. Singleton, 'The Influence of Geographical Factors on the Development of the Common Fields of Lancashire', *Trans. Hist. Soc. Lancs. and Cheshire,* cxv, 31-40.
9. LRO: DDF 1649.
10. LRO: DDF 168, Quoted by Youd, art. cit., 15.
11. LRO: DDX 102/11.
12. LRO: DDX 102/12.
13. LRO: DDF 1861.
14. LRO: DDF 1678.
15. LRO: DDF 52.
16. LRO: DDF 1932.
17. LRO: DDF 1594.
18. LRO: DDF 1627, 1631.
19. LRO: DDF 1942.
20. Crompton, op. cit.
21. LRO: DDF 1946, 1955, 1996.
22. LRO: DDF 1978.
23. LRO: DDF 1955, 1983-1984, 1991-1992, PR 2908/5/2 respectively.
24. LRO: DDF 1991.
25. LRO: DDF 2104, 1995.
26. LRO: AE 3/5, AE 3/6.
27. LRO: AE 3/3.
28. D. A. Hunt, 'The Industrial Revolution in South Ribble: Pt 1. Agriculture, *Lailand Chronicle,* xxxii, 5-10.

Chapter Three

1. G. L. Bolton, 'Leyland and the Feuds of 1315-23', *Lailand Chronicle,* i, 10-12; S. M. Ffarington, op. cit., 1-10; V.C.H, vi, 10-11.
2. S. M. Ffarington, op. cit., 12.
3. F. R. Raines, 'The Derby Household Books', *Chetham Society*, xxxi, iii.
4. 'Pleadings and Depositions in the Duchy Court of Lancaster', *Record Society of Lancashire and Cheshire*, xxxii, Pt1, 16-21.
5. S. M. Ffarington, op. cit., 13-15.
6. For an alternative interpretation see

V.C.H., vi, 63. Robert Farington left the rectorship of North Meols which his father had purchased for him, 'As he is said to have been in holy orders, this marriage could not have been valid by any law, Sir Henry appears to have been so offended that he settled lands on his grand-daughter Joan . . . whilst the estate of Worden . . . passed to William his youngest son.'
7. LRO: DDF 2300; S. M. Ffarington (1876), 15-17.
8. F. R. Raines, op. cit., 19.
9. Ibid, 24.
10. V.C.H., vi, 12.
11. Ibid, vi, 13.
12. S. M. Ffarington (1876), 16.
13. S. M. Ffarington (1876), 18-19. S. M. Ffarington, 'The Farington Papers', *Chetham Society*, xxxix (1856), 12-17. Hereafter S. M. Ffarington (1856).
14. Ibid, 5.
15. Ibid, 23-7.
16. Ibid, 44.
17. Quoted in G. Miller, *Hoghton Tower* (1948).
18. S. M. Ffarington (1856), 107.
19. Ibid, 93-5.
20. Ibid, 104.
21. Ibid, vi.
22. Ibid, 108-11.

Chapter Four

1. *The Lancashire Parish Record Society* has published the following local registers: Eccleston 1603-94, xv; Brindle 1658-1714, xi; Croston 1543-1727, vi, xx; Walton-le-Dale 1609-1812, xxxvii; Penwortham 1608-1753, lii; Preston 1611-35, xxxxviii; Chorley 1548-1653, xxxviii. See also W. S. White, 'Leyland 1653-1710' *The Record Society of Lancashire and Cheshire,* xxi; For an important note on the dating used in these documents see W. E. Waring, 'Give us back our eleven days!', *Lailand Chronicle*, xxxiv, 36-7. Basic statistical studies of the local parish registers and census analyses for Leyland (1851, 1881), Walton (1851, 1881) and Longton (1851), undertaken by members of the writer's adult education classes (1984-9) are available in the file 'Materials for a Demographic History of South Ribble' at Leyland Library.
2. W. S. White, op. cit., 170, 119-24.
3. LRO, 'Protestation Return, 1642' (Leyland); LRO, 'Hearth Tax 1664' (Leyland).
4. LRO. 'Wills at Chester, Listed by Name and Year'. This discussion of sources is largely based on research undertaken by W. E. Waring, who has kindly allowed me to use extracts.
5. LRO, 'Protestation Return 1642' (Leyland).
6. W. S. White, op. cit., 210-3.
7. S. M. Ffarington (1856), 101-3.
8 G. L. Bolton, 'Leyland's First Local Historian', *Lailand Chronicle,* xvi, 8-12.
9 This account is largely based on P. N. Cash, 'A History of Leyland Free Grammar School', (1967 Dissertation, copy in Leyland Library).
10. G. L. Bolton, 'The Grammar School at Leyland in 1674'. *Lailand Chronicle,* v, 7-9.
11. Quoted by Nash (1967) and in 'A Look at Leyland Free Grammar School' (Lancashire Library Service, South Ribble District).
12. This item was found by Mr W. Rigby on Worden Park in 1983.
13. LRO: DDF 1861; D. A. Hunt, 'William Ffarington's Alms Houses and Early Poor Relief in Leyland', *Lailand Chronicle,* xxxi, 2-5; W. Markland 'Samuel Crook', *Lailand Chronicle*, ii, 5-9; F. M. Eagle, 'Private Charities in Leyland, (Ffarington, Osbaldeston)', *Lailand Chronicle,* v, 31-5; 'Private Charities in Leyland (Samuel Crook, Ann Bentham), *Lailand Chronicle,* vi, 9-14.

Chapter Five

1. S. M. Ffarington (1876), 21. Family details in this chapter are based on her account.
2. F. Coupe, *Walton-le-Dale: A History of the Village* (1954), 141-9.
3. S. M. Ffarington (1876), 21.
4. Ibid, 23.
5. LRO: DDF 81.
6. The study of land measure in early documents is highly complicated. Locally three units of land measure were used: (A) The Leyland Traditional Acre = 9,000 square yards; (B) The Lancashire Acre = 7,840 square yards; (C) The Cheshire Acre = 10,240 square yards. The modern or statute acre contains 4,840 square yards. To convert the ancient units of measure into statute it is necessary to multiply the Leyland acre by 1.8, Lancashire acre by 1.6 and Cheshire acre by 2.1. To really complicate matters the 1725 summary (LRO: DDF 81) records Leyland in 'Leyland Acres', and the remaining estate in Cheshire acres. Except where stated all measures in this section have been converted to statute acres for comparative purposes with the 1838 tithe map.
7. LRO: DDF 92 (1746), Leyland Acres; LRO: DDF 101 (1800).
8. LRO: DDF 81.
9. LRO: DDF 85.
10. LRO: DDF 92.
11. LRO: DDF 92, Leyland Acres.
12. LRO: DDF 101.
13. S. M. Ffarington (1876), 25.
14. LRO: DDF 33.
15. LRO: DDF 32.
16. S. M. Ffarington (1876), 27.
17. LRO: 'Leyland Tithe Award 1838'; a copy is also available at Leyland

Library.
18. LRO: 'Farington Scrapbook', (a copy is also available at Leyland Library). *Preston Chronicle,* 24 June 1837, Obituary W. Farington.
19. 'Farington Scrapbook', *Preston Pilot,* 15 September, 1847.
20. 'Farington Scrapbook', Account of Leyland Agricultural Show, 1857.
21. 'Farington Scrapbook', Report of the Royal Agricultural Society, 1849.
22. 'Farington Scrapbook', *Preston Pilot,* 15 September, 1847.
23. 'Farington Scrapbook', *Leyland Agricultural Society* 1855, 1858.
24. 'Farington Scrapbook', Obituary J. N. Farington, 1848.
25. E. Shorrock, 'Shaw Hall becomes Worden', *Lailand Chronicle*, xxxiv, 9-16.
26. 'Farington Scrapbook', copy of a letter from Mr Morrell to Mr Farington 3 October 1847.
27. S. M. Ffarington (1876, Postscript 1913).
28. LRO: DDX 3/58: 1948 Catalogue.

Chapter Six

1. LRO: 'Wills at Chester'.
2. LRO: 'Leyland Parish Register'.
3. J. Holt, *A General View of the County of Lancaster* (1795 reprinted 1969).
4. R. W. Dickson, *A General View of the Agriculture of Lancashire* (1815).
5. L. Rawstorne, *Lancashire Farming* (1843).
6. D. A. Hunt, 'The Industrial Revolution in South Ribble: Part 2: Textiles', *Lailand Chronicle*, xxxiii, 20-4; Quoted from E. Baines, *History of the Cotton Manufacture* (1835).
7. LRO: DDHs 55/1; S. Birtles, *Horrockses: The Development of a Cotton Enterprise* (Dissertation, 1980).
8. LRO: 'Leyland Tithe Award' (1838); LRO: 1819 Survey PR 2797; E. Baines, *County Directory of Lancashire* (1825), 112; 1851 Trade Directory; 1841 Census, Leyland Library.
9. LRO: DDH 994a.
10. Union St. deeds: I am grateful to Mrs Baxendale, Mrs Rutter and Mr & Mrs Greenhalgh for this information.
11. Bradshaw St. Deeds: Transcript in Leyland Museum.
12. W. Rigby, 'Shruggs in Retrospect', *Lailand Chronicle*, v, 14-15.
13. *Preston Pilot,* 3 August 1835.
14. Quoted in E. Baines, *History of the Cotton Manufacture* (1835), 222.
15. Quoted in ibid, 434-5.
16. *Preston Chronicle,* 2 June 1838.
17. Census Extracts 1841, 1851, 1861, 1871, 1881: Leyland Library. The 1841 census required people to give their ages only to the nearest five years.

Chapter 7

1. LRO: DDX 472/3.
2. *Preston Pilot,* 24 December 1836.
3. Ekwall, op. cit., 135; V.C.H., vi, 61-5.
4. C. Townson, *The History of Farington* (1893).
5. Mannex: *Directory of Preston and District* (1851).
6. *Preston Chronicle,* 15 January 1825.
7. LRO: DDX 819/24.
8. Townson op. cit.
9. LRO: DDX 819/24.
10. LRO: DDX 819/6.
11. LRO: DDX 819/29.
12. This account is based on D. A. Hunt, '1838: The Year of the Railway', *Lailand Chronicle*, xxxiv, 26-32.
13. *Preston Chronicle,* 2 June 1838.
14. LRO: DDX 472/3.
15. *Preston Chronicle,* 14 April 1838.
16. *Preston Chronicle,* 3 November 1838.
17. *Preston Chronicle,* 3 November 1838.
18. Townson op. cit.
19. *Preston Chronicle,* 6 August 1842.
20. *Preston Chronicle,* 20 August 1842.
21. H. I. Dutton and J. E. King, *Ten per cent and no surrender: The Preston strike 1853-4* (1981); D. A. Hunt, 'Bamber Bridge Weavers and Farington Knobsticks', *Lailand Chronicle*, xxx, 19-23.
22. Townson (1893); LRO: PR 3153/12/1; Farington is considered in detail in D. A. Hunt, *Hard times in Preston: The story of the Lancashire Cotton Famine* (forthcoming).
23. *Preston Chronicle,* 6 December 1862.
24. *Preston Chronicle.* 24 January 1863.
25. Townson, op. cit.
26. *Preston Chronicle,* 14 January 1865.
27. *Preston Chronicle,* 27 September, 4 October, 11 October, 1862; statistics based on reports of monthly meetings of Chorley Board of Guardians 1862-5, in the *Preston Chronicle.*
28. *Preston Chronicle,* 29 November 1862.
29. *Preston Chronicle,* 4 June 1864.
30. *Preston Chronicle,* 20 August 1864.
31. *Preston Chronicle,* 20 August 1866.
32. *The Lancashire Textile Industry*, 55th Edition (1939).

Chapter Eight

1. Mannex, *Preston Directory* (1851, 1861 and 1873).
2. Leyland Rubber Relay, Vol. 1, No. 1, January 1930.
3. Barretts, *Preston Directory* (1892, 1922, 1932).
4. M. Hourigan. 'Residential Segregation in Leyland, 1881', (dissertation, Lancashire Polytechnic 1986).
5. I am much indebted to the late Noel Evans for use of his studies of the Worden Census returns 18,51-81.
6. Tablet in Leyland Church.
7. For this and previous extracts see: E.G. Marshall; 'Je n'oublierai pas: The Rev. Leyland Baldwin', (1913)
8. T. Kirby, *A Record of matches played by Leyland Cricket Club from the year 1877*

to 1897 (1898).
9. LRO: UDLI 1/3. Leyland Local Board Minute Book 1880-3.
10. W. E. Waring, 'When the lights went on in Leyland', *Lailand Chronicle*, xxxiii, 30-32; *Preston Guardian*, 5 January 1850.
11. W. E. Waring, 'Hough Lane in Leyland' (1987); *Lailand Chronicle*, xxxiii, 2-7. For other topographical histories of the town, see also W. E. Waring, 'Eagle and Child – Leyland's Oldest Inn?', *Lailand Chronicle*, xxxii, 17-19; G. Thomas, 'Further comments on Leyland Mill', *Lailand Chronicle*, xxxii, 24-6; W. E. Waring, 'Whittaker Lane, Leyland', *Lailand Chronicle*, xxx, 8-15.

Chapter Nine

1. G. Turner, *The Leyland Papers* (1971); Leyland Motors Ltd., *The first 50 years* (1946); Leyland Motors Ltd., *Seventy Years of Progress* (1966); Leyland Motors Ltd., *Official History 1896-1986* (1986). I have also had the opportunity to discuss various aspects of the company's development with former employees, including the late Mr Newton Iddon, Mr W. Preston and Miss G. Buckley.
2. Leyland Motors Ltd., *What Leyland Stands For*, 11-31.
3. *Leyland Torque*, December 1919.
4. W. E. Waring, 'Hough Lane in Leyland', *Lailand Chronicle*, xxxiii, 2-7.
5. Barretts, *Preston Directory* (1932).
6. 'The History of the Leyland Paint and Varnish Co. Ltd. (1972)', in *The Paint Journal (1972)*, Copy in Leyland Library.

Chapten Ten

1. Leyland Vehicles Ltd., *Official History 1896-1986* (1986).
2. *Leyland Guardian*, 2nd March 1978. I am grateful to Mr J. Moss for clarifying the recent developments in the history of the firm.
3. *Central Lancashire: A Study for a City* (1967), foreword.
4. Ibid, paragraph 6.7.
5. *Leyland Guardian*, 2nd April 1970.
6. *Leyland Guardian*, 7th November 1971.
7. *Lancashire Evening Post*, 8th November 1973.
8. *Strategic Plan for the North West*, Planning Team Report 1973; *Lancashire Evening Post*, 22nd March 1974.
9. *Central Lancashire Development Corporation: Outline Plan* (1974). Proposals for Leyland in 1974, 78; Leyland in 1986, 174.
10. *Lancashire Evening Post*, 12th December 1974.
11. *Lancashire Evening Post*, 19th September 1976.
12. *Lancashire Evening Post*, 4th April 1977.
13. W. Rigby, 'An Old Leyland Prophecy', *Lailand Chronicle*, xvii, 19.

Index

D

E

F

G

H

I

J

K

L

M

N

O

P

Y